797,885 Books
are available to read at

www.ForgottenBooks.com

Forgotten Books' App
Available for mobile, tablet & eReader

ISBN 978-1-333-86705-8
PIBN 10613297

This book is a reproduction of an important historical work. Forgotten Books uses
state-of-the-art technology to digitally reconstruct the work, preserving the original format
whilst repairing imperfections present in the aged copy. In rare cases, an imperfection in
the original, such as a blemish or missing page, may be replicated in our edition. We do,
however, repair the vast majority of imperfections successfully; any imperfections that
remain are intentionally left to preserve the state of such historical works.

Forgotten Books is a registered trademark of FB &c Ltd.
Copyright © 2017 FB &c Ltd.
FB &c Ltd, Dalton House, 60 Windsor Avenue, London, SW19 2RR.
Company number 08720141. Registered in England and Wales.

For support please visit www.forgottenbooks.com

1 MONTH OF FREE READING

at

www.ForgottenBooks.com

By purchasing this book you are eligible for one month membership to ForgottenBooks.com, giving you unlimited access to our entire collection of over 700,000 titles via our web site and mobile apps.

To claim your free month visit:
www.forgottenbooks.com/free613297

* Offer is valid for 45 days from date of purchase. Terms and conditions apply.

English
Français
Deutsche
Italiano
Español
Português

www.forgottenbooks.com

Mythology Photography **Fiction** Fishing Christianity **Art** Cooking Essays Buddhism Freemasonry Medicine **Biology** Music **Ancient Egypt** Evolution Carpentry Physics Dance Geology **Mathematics** Fitness Shakespeare **Folklore** Yoga Marketing **Confidence** Immortality Biographies Poetry **Psychology** Witchcraft Electronics Chemistry History **Law** Accounting **Philosophy** Anthropology Alchemy Drama Quantum Mechanics Atheism Sexual Health **Ancient History Entrepreneurship** Languages Sport Paleontology Needlework Islam **Metaphysics** Investment Archaeology Parenting Statistics Criminology **Motivational**

CAMDEN THIRD SERIES

VOL. XVIII

LONDON
OFFICES OF THE SOCIETY
6 & 7 SOUTH SQUARE
GRAY'S INN
1910

DA
20
R9.1
v. 18
cop

CONTENTS

	Page
TWO LONDON CHRONICLES, FROM THE COLLECTIONS OF JOHN STOW. EDITED BY C. L. KINGSFORD, M.A., F.S.A., F.R.HIST.S.	iij
LIFE OF SIR JOHN DIGBY (1605–1645). EDITED BY GEORGES BERNARD, L.ès-L.	61
ITER BELLICOSUM: ADAM WHEELER HIS ACCOUNT OF 1685. EDITED BY H. E. MALDEN, M.A., HON. FELLOW OF TRINITY HALL, CAMBRIDGE, V.-P. AND HON. SEC. R.HIST.S.	153
COMMON RIGHTS AT COTTENHAM AND STRETHAM IN CAMBRIDGESHIRE. EDITED BY W. CUNNINGHAM, D.D., F.B.A., PRESIDENT OF THE ROYAL HISTORICAL SOCIETY AND ARCHDEACON OF ELY	169

TWO LONDON CHRONICLES
FROM THE COLLECTIONS OF
JOHN STOW

CAMDEN MISCELLANY
VOL. XII

LONDON
FFICES OF THE SOCIETY
6 & 7 SOUTH SQUARE
GRAY'S INN
1910

The two short London Chronicles here printed are both preserved amongst the Collections of John Stow in the British Museum, and both illustrate (though in very different degrees) the manner in which he composed his History of England, beginning with his *Summary of English Chronicles* and ending with his better known *Annales*.

The first and much the more important is copied in *Harley* MS. 540 ff. 7-21, partly in Stow's own writing and partly by another hand. At the beginning it is stated to be 'copied out of Myster Lordynge's booke.' Who Mr Lordyng was I cannot say. But his book was probably a copy of one of the old Chronicles of London, as the four brief notes, with which the Chronicle in the *Harley* MS. begins, seem to indicate. It would be quite in accordance with custom for a later owner to have entered at the end of the original Chronicle from time to time a continuation of his own. This is the character of the main Chronicle here printed for the years 1523 to 1555. Really there are two separate Chronicles, entered no doubt in the original by two different owners. The first is for the years 1523 to 1540; the second for 1548 to 1555. For the intervening years 1540 to 1548 the names of the mayors and sheriffs, with a single bald note under 1543-44, had been entered, possibly by the writer of the second Chronicle. These two Chronicles of *Harley* MS. 540 are clearly of different authorship, having nothing in common save for certain indications that the writers of both were of anti-Protestant feelings.

The chief interest of the earlier Chronicle (1523-1540) consists in the fact that it formed the principal source for Stow's narrative in the first editions of his *Summary of English Chronicles* published in 1565 and 1566. It is somewhat amusing to find that Stow was, for matters almost within his own memory, copying so slavishly from a written Chronicle, at the very time when he was censuring Grafton for having made an unfair use of his own printed work.[1] It is true that Stow added for these years a little from Hall, but the early editions of the *Summary* are substantially a mere reproduction from the Chronicle here printed. In the subsequent editions of the *Summary* in 1570 and 1575, and still more in the final history as given in the *Annales*, Stow drew much more freely on other sources. A great deal of matter contained in this Chronicle was thus gradually dropped. Meantime something had been borrowed by Holinshed without any specific acknowledgement of his source. It is thus necessary to recognise that the successive editions of Stow's *Summary* are deserving of more attention than they have commonly received.

Though Stow for the most part followed the Chronicle very closely, his departures from his original in some places are noteworthy. The original contains certain matter, which, when Stow wrote thirty years later, it would not have been judicious to repeat. Under 1528-9 a reference to the " selling of Martin Luther's books" is omitted.[2] So also is that to the burning of Tyndal's books in Nov. 1530. More remarkable is the omission of the reference to Catherine of Aragon ' a blysyd lady and a good, '[4] and of the pathetic story of the two women, who ' fortified theyr saying still to die in the quarell for Queen Catherine's sake.'[5] On the other hand it is to be noted that the Chronicler had not recorded the proclamation of the king's supremacy in 1534, passed over Anne Boleyn's wedding and the birth of the princess Elizabeth, and even the birth of Edward VI ; the omission to mention the suppression of the monasteries under 1537-8 may also be due to anti-Protestant sympathies, which the writer feared to express. Through Stow the Chronicle is several times quoted by Holinshed;

[1] Dedication of *Summary Abridged* for 1567 ap. *Survey of London* i. lxxvii.
[2] p. 3   [3] p. 5
[4] p. 7   [5] p. 8

INTRODUCTION

as for the events of 1534-5, for the procession on 11 Nov. 1535, the jousting at Westminster on 29 June 1536, the penance of Thomas Newman on 12 Nov. 1536, and the execution of the Vicar of Wandsworth on 8 July 1539.[1]

For the most part the Chronicle consists of brief notes, probably written down immediately after the events to which they relate. Executions, penances for heresy, and incidents of civic history furnish the principal staple of the narrative. Passages of more moment, which may be mentioned, are the reference to Queen Catherine noted above, the description of the prosecution of the Maid of Kent,[2] the long account of the procession on 11th Nov. 1535,[3] and the curious notice of Thomas Cromwell's alleged parentage.[4]

The chronology of the Chronicle calls for some explanation. The note[5] that ' this boke doth accoumpte ye yere to begyn at Novembar,' was probably inserted by Stow, who did not recognise that the years were mayoral not regnal. But the numbers of the years as given in the text have been frequently altered, the original numbers having been a year earlier ('xvj.' for 'xvij.' etc.). The explanation probably is that the original writer put down the mayor, who held office in April 1509, as the mayor for the 'first year of Henry VIII.' Thus the mayor and sheriffs for 1509-10 would have been entered as those for 2 Henry VIII ; and Thomas Baldry would have appeared under 16 Henry VIII, though he really held office 1523-24 in the 15th and 16th regnal years. The dates as given in the text are the corrected ones ; they follow the most common custom of the London Chronicles and of Stow's *Summary*, in accordance with which the first mayoral year of Henry VIII was that of the mayor, who took office on 29th October 1509.

The second Chronicle for 1548-55 is distinguished from the first by its much greater fulness in matters which it describes, and by less attention to trivial incidents. Partly for these reasons, and

---

[1] Holinshed, iii. 793, 798, 803, 810 ; cf. pp. 10, 13, 15 below.
[2] pp. 8-9.　　　　　　[3] p. 11-12.
[4] p. 15.　　　　　　　[5] p. 1.

INTRODUCTION

partly because Stow, from whatever cause, made much less use of it, it is of far more interest. Stow had by this point reached a time well within his own recollection, and may consequently have depended less on written memorials. When he first wrote, moreover, events of such recent happening required discreet handling. When later on he expanded his history, he had at his disposal the manuscript *Chronicle of Queen Jane and Queen Marie*[1], and also as it would appear a copy of Charles Wriothesley's *Chronicle*. Thus he not only made less use of our Chronicle from 1548 to 1555 in his *Summary*, but also omitted more of what he had at first borrowed, when he came to write his *Annales*.

The Chronicle opens with a long account of the disturbances of 1549. The description of the rising at Exeter is followed fairly closely by Stow. The story of the disparking of Thame and Rycote, as here given, seems to be novel, and the account of Kett's rebellion differs from that given by Stow.[2] The first arrest of Somerset,[3] and the story of Captains Charles and Gambold,[4] are given without any particular additions to other accounts. Most of the history of 1550-52 appears in a very similar form to that adopted by Stow in his *Summary*.[5] Of the events which attended the accession of Queen Mary we get an independent and interesting account of which Stow made little use.[6] Wyatt's rebellion is described freshly, as by one who wrote from his own knowledge; the most notable new point being the story of how Wyatt managed to get into Fleet Street without being recognised.[7] There is a good deal of detail on the subsequent incidents of the spring of 1554, but with nothing that calls for comment till we reach the trial of Nicholas Throckmorton,[8] where the sufferings of the stalwart jurors, who would not find him guilty, are told at more length than elsewhere. The arrival of Philip of Spain is described with

---

[1] Harley MS. 194: printed in Camden Society 1ˢᵗ Series No. 48.
[2] pp. 17-19
[3] p. 19
[4] p. 20
[5] pp. 22-26
[6] pp. 27-29
[7] pp. 31-33
[8] pp. 35 and 39

three words together.' Of this, the most interesting passage in the whole Chronicle, Stow made no use at all. So far as I can discover no other writer gives so minute an account of Gardiner's sermon. The Chronicle ends with the death of Gardiner in November, 1555. But the history of the last eleven months includes nothing of importance, which cannot be found elsewhere. The description of the flood in October, 1555,[3] shows how Stow used this Chronicle in his *Summary*, but discarded it in the *Annales*. The use of the Chronicle by Stow, and the points in which it differs from other contemporary records are illustrated sufficiently in the footnotes to the text. Except where otherwise noted the *Summary* is quoted from the edition of 1566 (which here differs little from that of 1565), and the *Annales* from the edition of 1605. (Stow's own final and anthoritative text).

The brief City Chronicle for 1547 to 1564 is of a different character to the previous one. *Harley* MS. 530 ff. 105-110, whence it comes, consists of short historical notes written early in the reign of Elizabeth. The first note is for the 54th year of Henry III taken from Fabyan. Other notes of fourteenth century history follow from Froissart. A notice of Wiclif is borrowed from John Bale. On f. 107 comes a note, which is worth quoting as a characteristic specimen :—

" Mr. Hall writeth the batayle of Egyncorte to be in the 4 yere, & I do think it gode to referr the redar to m^{tr} hall, who writeth of it at large takyn owt of the frenche cronicle made by enguyron,[4] who did write ymmediatly after frosard. "

[1] pp. 37-38
[2] pp. 40, 41
[3] p. 43
[4] Enguerrant de Monstrelet.

INTRODUCTION

On f. 108ʳᵒ there are a few notes on the reign of Henry VIII. The last alone is of any interest :—

" In the 25 yere the statute was made for the selling of flessh by waight ; toke effect the first day of August. " [1]

There then begins the more regular and original Chronicle here printed. [2] The writer, unlike the authors of the previous Chronicle, seems from his notices on religious matters to have been a Protestant. There are a few entries of political matters. But the more interesting part of the Chronicle consist of notes, which would appear to have been made by a London merchant trading abroad. They relate chiefly to incidents and disasters at sea : to captures of French and Spanish ships : to the pirate Strangwysh ; and to the naval warfare off Newhaven, or Havre, in 1563-64. The reference to an exploit of John Hawkins in the autumn of 1563 seems to be novel. Other entries on the rate of exchange with Antwerp, and on prices, also indicate that the writer was interested in commerce. Two amusing notes are of the rainy season of 1563, which caused such a dearth of hops that beer was brewed with broom and bay-berries, and of the abundance of fruit in the following summer. The statement as to the causes which led to the English intervention at Havre in 1563, appears to have been borrowed by Stow for his own narrative in the *Annales*.

Apart from its contents this Chronicle has a certain interest as illustrating how long the practice of keeping written records in the form of civic Annals persisted with London citizens.

[1] Cf. Stow, *Survey of London*, i. 187.
[2] pp. 47-49.

1523-1555

The notes folowynge wer copied out of Myst'. Lordynges boke.

Richard yᵉ seconde

The iij^{de} yere of his reygne yᵉ galyottis of Spayne wᵗ othar small shipps cam a land at Gravesende, & robbyd & brent yᵉ moaste parte [of yᵉ] towne.

The xviij. yere of Richard yᵉ second yᵉ heresies of John Wykclyffe began to spryng in England.

Henry yᵉ fourthe

Yᵉ xj. yere of his reygne began yᵉ alaye of goulde : & yᵉ kyngs sons betyn in yᵉ Chepe.

Henry yᵉ vij

The first yere of his reyne yᵉ crosse in Chepe was new buylded, Hughe Bryce beyng mayre.

The xiij of his reygne yᵉ wedercoke of Powlls was new made.

Henrie yᵉ viij

This boke dothe accowmpte yᵉ yere to begyn at November, but yt dothe not begyn tyll Aprill next foloynge, which is to be noted.[1]

---

[1] This is a note made by Stow, who did not then realise that these London Chronicles were dated by mayoral years beginning on 29ᵗʰ Oct. The regnal years of Henry viii began on 22ⁿᵈ April. See *Introduction*, p. iii. above.

2 TWO LONDON CHRONICLES

Y^e xv. yere of Henrie ye viij, Tomas Baldry beyng mayre, was ye lady Hungarford and hir man hangyd at Tyburne.[1]

The xvj. yere of his reyne ye castell of Grenewyche was buyldyd. Y^e same yere, ye xviij daye of June, was creatyd at Brydewell Henrie, ye kyngis bastard, duke of Richemont & Somersete, & earle of Nothyngham, highe steward of Englande, warden of all ye marches agaynst Scotlande, hyghe admyrall of ye sea, highe Justice of all ye kyngs parkes, chaces, mayrynes, & forestis from Trent to Scotland, & hyghe steward to ye byshope of Yorke & Doram.[2]

The xvij. yere of his reygne, ye xj. day of februarie, beynge shroffe sondaye, v. men of ye Stilaard dyd penaunce, iij. of them bare fagotes at Powles, & ij. of them bare taperes. And an awsten fryar callyd doctor Barns of Cambryge bare a fagot at Powles ye same daye. The same yere ye vj. day of September was proclamyd of goulde ye frenche crowne iiij.s. vj.d., ye halffe noble iij.s. ix.d., ye angell noble vij.s. vj.d., and ye riall xj.s. iij.d., & so every pese affter y^t valewe.[3]

The xviij. yere, Thomas Seamar mayre, of his reygne, ye iij. day of Julii, ye lorde cardenall rode thorowe Chepe, & so toward Fraunce[4]; & ye xv. day of ye same monythe was one Harman drawyn from Newgate to Tyburn, & there hangyd for qwynynge of falce golde.[5] And in ye same yere in Julii & in August was ye slewcys made in Fynsbery fylde to convaye ye yll watars ovar ye towne dyche by pypes of lede in to ye Temes.[6] In ye same yere was great skarsnes of breade at London, & all England, y^t many dyed for defaut therof : & ye bread cartes y^t came from Stratford to London were mett by ye way at Myll ende by ye citisens of London,

---

[1] The notice for this year is added in the margin.
[2] *Summary* omits.
[3] This forms the whole notice for the year in the *Summary*, save for an addition as to the sermon preached by bishop Fisher at St Paul's on 11th Feb.
[4] At more length in *Summary*.
[5] *Summary*, but reading : 'coynynge'.
[6] Abbreviated in *Summary*, and in *Survey*, ii. 77.

y^t ye mayr and shrivis were fayne to goo & reskew them, & se them browght to ye markytis apoyntyd.[1]

The xix. yere, of his reygne, James Spencer mayre, ye first day of Novembar, my lord cardinall w^t ye Ambasadours of Fraunce wer at Powles, & ther was proclaymyd a generall peace betwene kyng Henrie of England & Francys ye frenche kynge durynge theyr lyves, & a xij. monythe & a day afftar.[2]

The viij. day of Novembar iij. scolers of Cambryge, & one Fostar a gentyllman of ye cowrte bare ffagotts at Powlis for heresy.[3]

This yere was no watche at mydsomer. ye vij. of October cam to London a legat from Rome.

The v. day of January ye cardynall, & many byshopes, & abbotis, & priours, went a prossecion at Powles, & sange te deum for ye eskapynge of ye pope from ye emperour.

The xiij. day of January was a great fyar at Andrewe Moreys key in Tems strete, & anothar key by it, wher was myche hurte done. The vij. day of Aprell ye lord master of ye Rodes cam to London, & lay at sent Johns in Smythfyld. The xvij day of June ye terem was aiournyd to myhellmas aftar, becaws of ye swetynge sykenes y^t reygnyd at y^t tym in London & in othar placis.[5]

The xx. yere of his reygne, J. Rudstone mayre, ye xxix. of November ye parysshe prist of Hony lane & a yonge man, y^t some tyme was vsshar of seynt Anthonys scole, bare fagottis at Powlis. And ij. othar men, one a duche man, ye othar an englyshe man, bare tapers of wax for sellyng of Martyn Leuthars bokes.[6]

The viij. daye of Maye a powche maker bare a fagote at Powles

---

[1] *Summary* with additions from Hall.

[2] *Summary.*

[3] *Summary.*

[4] Because of the sweating sickness. This and the following note are transferred in the *Summary* to their proper chronological position at the end of the year.

[5] The whole of this paragraph appears in the *Summary*, with the addition of a note as to how two French and Flemish vessels chased one another from Margate to Tower wharf.

[6] *Summary*, but omitting, 'for sellyng etc.' A note on the sessions of the Cardinals at Blackfriars is then inserted from Hall.

for heresye. The vj. day of September one John Skotte, wodmonger, dyd penaunce in Chepe and othar placis of ye citie, goynge in his shurte, bare leggyd & bare fottyd, and a proclamacion made at ye Standard, at Ledyn hall, & at Grace churche vpon misdemeanor agaynst ye mayre & ye aldermen wt ye shrives.[1]

The xviij. day of October was ye cardynall dyschargyd of his chauncelourshype, & ye kynge seasyd all his goods & his place at Westmystar : & ye xxv. day of ye same monythe he went from Yorke place to Ashehere[2] wt xxx. persones & no more, & ther to abyde tyll he knew furdar of ye kyngs pleasure. And the xxvj. day of Octobre was sir Thomas More made chauncelour of England, & sworne, & kepte his rome all one day.[3]

The xxj. yere of his reygne, Rauffe Dodmer mayre, ye viij. day of Decembre was one sir Thomas Bolyn, callyd lord of Rocheforde, was made earle of Ormonde & of Wylshere, & ye lorde ffughe Watars[4] was made earle of Sussex, & my lorde Hastynges was made earle of Huntyngton.[5] The xiij day of Janewarie was a great fyar in ye Vyntry, & myche hurte done. The xxiij. day of Janewarie was iij. men, one a Gaskone, & ij. eryche[6] men, drawne from Newgat to ye Towerhyll, and ther hangyd & quarteryd for countarfeytynge ye kyngs coyne. The xvj. day of Maye was a gebyt set vp in Fynsbery filde, & a man hangyd in chaynes for kyllynge of doctour Myles, vykar of sent Brydes. The v. day of Julii was one hangyd in chayns in Fynsbery fyld for kyllynge mastres knevytt's mayd in sente Auntolyns paryshe.[7]

The xxij. yere of his reygne, Thomas Pargetour mayre, ye xix.

[1] *Summary*, but reading : ' his demeanor '.
[2] Esher.
[3] *Summary*. Three notes are then added on William Tyndale, the peace, and the parliament at Blackfriars.
[4] Fitz Walter.
[5] The notice of these creations is omitted in the *Summary*.
[6] Irish.
[7] The whole of the latter part of this paragraph appears in the *Summary*, together with two notes on Tyndal's translation of the New Testament, and on the proclamation prohibiting communication with Rome.

watche. The xiiij. day of Julii maystre Lacis servant was hangyd in Fynsbery fylde for ye morderynge of a mayde, & for ye robynge of this sayd mistar Lacie.

The xix. day of August ye byshope of Norwyche brynt a master of Arte callyd Thomas Bylneye. The xxij. day of October Paytmer, a merchant & a glayssyar, bare fagotis at Powles.[4]

The xxiij. yere of his reygne, Nicholas Lambarde, mayre, ye v. day of November ij. men bare fagotis at Powles, one of them was Parnylls servant, a drapar. The xj. day of Novembar Haric Thomson was commyttyd to perpetuall pryson for eresye: the same Harie cam owt agayn by ye kyngs chartar: ye same day on Pattmer, a pryst, was commyttyd to pepetuall pryson for heresye.[5] The xxvij. day of November was a monke of Bery[6] burnt in Smythefylde for heresie.[7] The iiij. day of December was one Risse[8] Gryffyn, a gentylman of Wales, behedyd at ye Towre hyll, & his man hanged, drawne, & quarteryd at Tybourne for treason. The xx. day of Decembar was a pouchemaker brent in Smythefyld for heresie.[9] The xxvij. day of Janewarie, a douche man bare a

---

[1] Omitted in *Summary*.

[2] *Summary*, but reading: 'poysonynge dyuers persons at the byshop of Rochesters place'; and giving the cook's name 'one Richarde Rose'.

[3] These two notes are omitted in the *Summary*.

[4] *Summary*; but Bilney is called 'a bacheler of law', and 'Paules crosse' is substituted for 'Powles'

[5] These notes are omitted in the *Summary*.

[6] Bury.

[7] *Summary* omits 'for beresie'

[8] Ryce, *Summary*.

[9] *Summary* omits this note.

fagot at Powles crosse for beresie. Yᵉ xj. day of February one bare a fagot at Polls crosse. The xxj. day of August one bare a fagot at Powlys for heresye.[1] The laste day of Apryll was one Baynam brent in Smythefylde for herisye. The xxv. day of Maye was takyn between Grenewyche & London ij. greate fyshis callid herlpoles, both a male & a female. The iiij. day of June was dyscharged syr Thomas More of his chauncelourshipe, & for him was chosyn mistar Audleye, sergant of yᵉ coyffe, & was made cheffe justice in yᵉ chancerie, & cald by his offyce lorde brode seale.[2] The xv. day of June was v. men drawne from Newgate to yᵉ Towr hyll, & then hangyd & quarteryd for qwynynge of sylvar & clypynge of gowld.[3] The xxviij. day of June was one othar man hangyd in chaynes in Fynsbery fylde for yᵉ kylynge of mystris Lacis mayd.[4] The v. day of Julii was a pryst dwellynge at S. Andrews by syd yᵉ wardrope drawne from Newgate to yᵉ Towr hyll, & ther hangid & quarteryd for clypynge of gowlde.[5] Allso in Julii yᵉ kynge put downe yᵉ priour of Christchurche in London, all yᵉ chanons of yᵉ same place yᵉ kyng sent to othar placis of yᵉ same relygyon, for be caws yᵉ same priour lyvyd vnthriftely & wt his vngracious rewle brought yᵉ same house in debt, yᵗ he was not able to kepe his housse and mayntayne it.[6] The xvij. day of Auguste ij. prestis of Allhallows in Bredstrete fell at variance, yᵗ yᵉ one prist drew blode on yᵉ othar, wherfore yᵉ same churche was supendyd & and no servys sayd nor songe in one monythe.[7] This yere in August & Septembar yᵉ kynge repayryd Yᵉ Towr of London, & mad ther myche buyldynge. The fyrst of Septembar

[1] *Summary* omits the last two notes.
[2] Stow records this in his own words, and adds notes on the king's supremacy, and on Cromwell's promotion.
[3] *Summary*, but reading : ' coynyng '.
[4] *Summary* omits.
[5] *Summary*.
[6] *Summary*, but omitting from ' for be caws ' to ' mayntayne it.' Compare Stow's story of the prior's hospitality ap. *Survey* i. 141 and ii. 291, and Hall, *Chronicle*.
[7] Given with the subsequent note of their penance by Stow in *Survey*, i. 347.

bokes in theyr hands, & so dyd theyr penaunce.

The xxiiij. yere of his reygne, Stephen Pekoke, mayre, ye xv. day of Decembar was a great fyar at ye byshop of Lyncolnes place in Holbourne, & myche hurt done.[2]

The xvij. day of Marche was chosyn Edward Hall, gentylman, of Greys In, to be comon sargaunte of ye citie of London.[3] The x. day of Aprill was a dole at sent Mary Overies in Sothewarke, & at ye same dole was so great preace of pore people y^t ther was smoulderyd in ye strete iiij. men, ij. wemen, & a boye, starke deade.[4] The xij. day of Aprill was ye countes of Penbroke, lady Anne Bolyne, dowghter of syr Thomas Bolen, bacheylar knyght, but ye kynge made hym lorde of Rocheforde, & earl of Wylshire & Ormonde, on Estar eve ye xij. day of Aprill she was proclaymyd quen of England; & quene Katheryn was put downe, & hir dowghtar Mary, pryncis, was lykewyse put downe, beyng his owne dowghtar gotyn on quene Katheryn, whiche was xxiiij. yere his wyffe & quene of England, a blysyd lady & a good.[5] Y^e xij. day of May Pavyar, ye towne clarke, honge hym selffe. The iiij. day of Julii was brent in Smythefyld John Frythe, a scolar of Oxforde, & a taylours servante, bothe together for heresye.[6] The vj. day of Julye was quen Katheryn proclaymyd princis Arthours

---

[1] The last three notes in *Summary*, with an addition on the king's marriage to Anne Boleyn.

[2] *Summary*.

[3] *Summary* adding: 'Whiche Edward Halle made the notable boke of Chronicles'.

[4] *Summary* but reading, 'Audries' for 'Overies', and omitting 'in ye strete'.

[5] For the proclamation of Queen Anne the *Summary* follows Hall's *Chronicle*, and omits the reference to Queen Katharine altogether.

[6] Wriothesley's *Chron.* 1. 22. The second was Andrew Hewit.

Wydowe.[1] The xvij. day of Julii were ij. marchauntis slayne on yᵉ watar toward Westmynstar by one Wolffe & his wyffe. The xxiij. day of August wear ij. women betton abowght the Chepe nakyd from yᵉ waste vpwarde, wt roddes, & theyr eris naylyd to yᵉ Standard for bycause they sayd queue Katheryn was yᵉ treu quen of England, & not quene Ane: and one of yᵉ wemen was byge wt childe: & whan thes ij. wemen had thus bene punyshed, they forteffyed theyr sayenge styll, to dy in yᵉ quarell for quene Katheryns sake.[2] The v. day of Octobar was a great fyar at Baynards castell, & great hurt don.

The xxv. yere of his reygne, Christopher Askewe, mayre, yᵉ xxiiij. day of Octobar was ther a skafolde set up at Powles crosse, & ther on stode a none namyd Anne[3] Barton, callyd yᵉ holy mayd of Courtopstrete[4] bysyde Cauntourbury in Kent, & ij. monkes of Cauntourbery, yᵉ one was doctor Boccynge, a devyn, & ij. obsarvant fryars, one was yᵉ father of yᵉ house of Richemount & yᵉ othar was of Cauntourbery, & yᵉ parson of Aldermary in London callyd Mst. Gowlde, & anothar priste confessor to yᵉ same none, & ij. lay men, & at yᵉ same crosse was a sermond made by yᵉ byshope of Bangowre, callyd yᵉ Abbot of Hyde, wher was shewyd all theyr offencis, & so they wer from thence removyd to yᵉ Towr.[5]

[1] The *Summary* omits the last two notes. It gives the enactment for butchers, which reappears in the *Survey*, i. 187.

[2] This pathetic story is omitted in the *Summary*. It is remarkable that the Chronicle has no notice of the birth of Elizabeth on 7 Sept, which Stow duly inserts before the note on the fire at Baynard's Castle.

[3] Should be 'Elizabeth'

[4] Court-up-street, or Court-at-street.

[5] In the *Summary* Stow transfers this verbatim to the 24ᵗʰ mayoral year, to which it properly belongs. The true date was 23ʳᵈ Oct. see *Letters and Papers* vi. 1433, 1460 and vii. 72, p. 29, and Gairdner, *Lollardy and the Reformation*, i. 455. Wriothesley *Chron.* i. 23 gives the date as 23ʳᵈ Nov. The monks were Edward Bockyng and Richard Deryng, the friars Hugh Rich and Richard Risby, the priest Richard Masters, parson of Aldington, and the laymen Edward Thwaytes and Thomas Gold.

of ye northe araynyd of treason, and acqwyted of ye same.[2]

The xj. day of August was all ye placis of ye obsarvant fryars, as Grenewyche, Cantorburie, Rychemonte, & Newarke, & Newcastell, put downe, & Austyn fryars put in ye same places, & ye same obsarvantis wer put in placys of graye fryars &c. The xiij. day of August was a great fyar at ye Temple barr, & myche hurt don & certayne persons byrnt. The xv. day of August ye kyngs place at Charynge crosse, callyd ye Mewse, was a fyre.[3] The xxj. day of Septembar doctor Taylor, mastar of ye Rolls was dyschargyd, & for hym Mst. Thomas Cromwell was made maystar of ye Rolls, & sworne ye ix. day of Octobar.[4]

[1] *Summary* adds : 'and theyr bodies buried'.

[2] *Summary* has 'treason, where he so wittily and directly confuted hys accusers, that to theyr great shame, he was founde by his peres not gyltie'. Stow then inserts from Hall a notice (misplaced, see above under 1532-33) of the martyrdom of John Frith and Andrew Hewet.

[3] This is differently described in the *Summary*.

[4] *Summary* adds : 'who afterwarde bare great rule.'

TWO LONDON CHRONICLES

The xxvj. yere of his reygne, John Champneys mayre,[1] y^e xxix. day of Apryll y^e prior of y^e Charterhouse of London, the 'prior of Beuall,[2] the prior of Exsam,[3] & a brodar of ye same callyd mistar Raynolds, & a pryste callyd Mast. John Hayle, vicar of Thystylworthe[4] were all condemnyd of treason & judgyde at Westmystar to be drawne, hangyd, & quarteryd at Tybourne, who wer executyd at Tyborne ye iiij. day of May, & ther heds & quarters set at every gate of London, & at ye Chartarhous in London one quartar. The viij. day of May the kynge comaundyd all about his court to powl theyr bedes, & to gyve them ensample he dyd cawse his owne hed to be powllyd lykewyse. The xxv. day of May was a great examynacion of erytykes borne in Holand beyond ye see; ther was examynyd xix. men & vj. wemen of ye same country borne.[5] The ij. day of June mistar Hall was chosyn vndar shrive by ye mayre & comon counsell, who was before ye comon sargante of London.[6] The iiij. day of June a man & his wyffe borne in Bothe in Holand[7] wer byrnt in Smythefyld for heresye.[8] The xviij. day of June wer thre monkes of ye Chartarhouse, Exmew, Mydlemor, & Nydygate, drawn to Tyborne, & ther hangyd & quarteryd. The xxij. day of June was doctor Fyshar, byshope of Rochestar, behedyd at ye Towre hyll,[9] [his body buryed at Barkynge[10]]. The xvj. day of Julii syr Thomas More was behedyd at Tour hyll[11] [then ye body of byshope of Rochestar was taken vp,

---

[1] In the *Summary* Stow inserts a note on the Parliament of November, 1534.
[2] Beauvale.
[3] *Summary* reads 'Hexham'. It should be 'Axholme'
[4] Isleworth.
[5] *Summary* then adds "their opinions".
[6] *Summary* adds : 'as is aforesaid.'
[7] *Summary* : 'borne in Holland '.
[8] *Summary*: 'for the Arrianes beresie '.
[9] *Summary* inserts: ' his head was set on London-bridge, and '.
[10] Allhallows Barking.
[11] *Summary* inserts: 'for denyall of the Kynges supremacy ', and omits the following clause. The words bracketed above are an insertion, and perhaps did not appear in the original. In the *Annales*, 963. Stow follows the Chronicle, as

& abbayes all theyr relikes & jewells [2]

Syr John Allyn, mayre, ye xxvij. [3] yere of ye kynge, ye xj. day of Novembar, beyng styll in ye xxvij. yere of Henrie ye viij., was a great procession at London by ye kyngis commandement : fyrst went ye wayts of ye citie all vj., [4] & nexte folowynge ye children of ye gramer scoll of sente Thomas of Acres w^t ye schollmayster afftar them ; [5] next aftar them came sent Anthonys scole & ye mastar & vshar aftar them : nexte came ye scholars of Powles schole wt theyr mastar & vshar aftar them : next came all ye mynstrells of London in theyr best apayrell, & ye mastar of ye sayd mynstrells wt his gyrdyll abought hem as he doth were on myd lent sondaye : [6] nexte aftar them com ye crwchyd fryers, & every fryer had a coppe and theyr crosse : nexte aftar them com ye fryars Austyns w^t theyr crosse & every fryar a cope : next came ye white friars wt theyr crosse & every friar a cope : next came ye graye fryars & theyr crosse & every fryar a cope : next came ye blake fryars w^t theyr crosse & every fryar a cope, syngynge ye letany w^t faburdyn : [7]

---

above, except that in each case he states that the execution was for denial of the king's supremacy.

[1] *Summary* inserts a note on the Earl of Kildare and his son.

[2] *Summary*.

[3] Originally this was ' xxviij.' See *Introduction* p. iii.

[4] *Summary :* ' citie goynge formoste.'.

[5] *Summary :* ' schole of the mercers chapell with theyr mastar.'

[6] *Summary :* ' mynstrels, with his collar.'

[7] *Summary* gives simply a list of the Friars, and ends: ' all in copes, with theyr crosses and candelsticks.'

next cam yᵉ chanons of sent Marie Overyes,¹ yᵉ chanons of sent Barthelmewis, wt yᵉ chanons of Esynge² spityll, & yᵉ chanons of sent Mary spitill, wt yᵉ priours of yᵉ same howsys wt theyr crosses & candelstykes and theyr vergirers before them, & every chanon & priour in a cope : next aftar them came yᵉ clarkes of London, & every one of them a cope : aftar them yᵉ prystis of London, & everie one in a cope : aftar them cam yᵉ monkes of Newe abbeye, & yᵉ monkes of Barmondsey, wᵗ yᵉ monkes of Westmystar, syngynge, wt theyr crossys & vergerers & sensars, wᵗ candylstyks, & every monke a cope, yᵉ Abotis of thes placis in copes, myteryd.³ Aftar them cam Powles quere, every priste & clerke had a cope wt all theyr residentaris in copes, syngynge the letany wt faburden ; aftar them cam yᵉ Abotes & priors, yᵗ was myteryd men, in theyr pontefycallibus : than cam ij. mynstrells before yᵉ byshope of London, who come vndar a canypie wᵗ a cope on his bake, berynge betwen his hands a crosse wᵗ yᵉ ost therin, & othar relykes, & abowghte hym was borne by yᵉ byshopis servantis xij. torch prikes of wax brenynge lyght : ⁴ aftar them come yᵉ bachilars of yᵉ company of my lorde mayr in theyr aparell ⁵ wt theyr hoods as they dyd whan yᵉ mayr toke his othe. Aftar them come my lorde mayre in a gowne of blake velvyt wᵗ a hode of velvyt of yᵉ same. Aftar hym com xix.⁶ aldarmen in theyr gownes of skarlet : & aftar them yᵉ craftis of London in theyr degres. Yᵉ nombar of copys that ware worne in this prossessyon was vij. hundred & xviij.⁷

The last day of Decembar my lord mayre gave comaundement

---

¹ *Summary*, 'Auderies'.

² Elsing.

³ *Summary*: 'all syngynge the Letany wyth Faburden, theyr crosses, candelstyckes, and Vergerers beefore them'.

⁴ *Summary*: "Powles quyer, with theyr Resydensaries: The byshop of London, and the Abbottes mytered in theyr Pontificalibus."

⁵ *Summary*, 'best apparell'; and omits " wᵗ theyr... othe ".

⁶ *Summary*, " and the "

⁷ *Summary* adds: " This procession was for the recoueryng of the french kyng to hys helth ". See also Wriothesley *Chron.* i. 32, a short account with date 12ᵗʰ Nov. Stow has only a bare note in the *Summary* for 1575, p. 436, & in the *Annales*.

ij. of yᵉ marynars.³

Sir Rauffe Warryn, mayre. The xij. day of Novembar sir Thomas Newman bare a fagot at Powles crosse, for yᵗ he song mas wt good alle. The xiij. day of Novembar Mst. Packenton was slayne wᵗ a gone in Chepe as he went to S. Thomas of Acres to here masse.⁴ The xix. day of Novembar Myryll, a tylar, dwellynge in sent Pulkers⁵ paryshe, bare a fagot at Poles crosse for heresye. The x. day of Decembar yᵉ parson of Sansted bysyd Hoddon⁶ bare a fagot at Poles crosse for heresye.⁷

The xxix. day of Marche, beynge maundy Thursdaye, wer xij. men of Lyncolne drawne from Newgate to Tyborne, & ther hangyd & quarteryd: v. wer prystis, & vij. wer laye men, one was doctor Makeryll⁸, a whit canon, another was yᵉ vycar of Lowthe⁹ in Lyncolnshire.

¹ *Summary*, " who badde the gyfte of the same ". Stow then adds nearly two pages from Hall's *Chronicle*.

² Called ' one Gates gentleman ' in *Annales*, 965.

³ *Summary* then inserts an account of the insurrection in Yorkshire.

⁴ In the *Summary* Stow gives the account of Packenton's murder in his own words, adding " the murderer was never openly knowen ". In the *Summary* for 1575, p. 439, as in the *Survey*, i. 261, he says: "the murderer was neuer discouered, but by his owne confession made when he came to the gallowes at Banbury, to be hanged for fellony. " See Hall, *Chronicle* ; Holinshed, iii. 883; and Gairdner, *Lollardy and the Reformation*, ii. 382.

⁵ St Sepulchre's.

⁶ Stanstead near Hoddesdon, Herts.

⁷ *Summary* omits the last two notes, but adds notices of the rising in Yorkshire, and other matters.

⁸ Matthew Makkarell, prior of Barlings, Lincolnshire. D.N.B. xxxv. 391.

⁹ Thomas Kendall. They were executed for their share in the Lincoln rebellion. See *Letters and Papers*, xii. I. 70, 734 (3), 760.

14 TWO LONDON CHRONICLES

Y^e xxviij. yere of his reygne, ye xv. day of Maye, my lord, Darcie & my lorde Hussaye wer had from ye Towr of London vnto West-mystar, & thar condemnyd.[1] The xviij. day of Septembar was a grete fyar at sent Antholyns, & myche hurt done.[2]

Richard Greshame, mayre, ye xxix. yere of ye kings reygne.[3] The xviij. day of Januarie a saltar of London was set on ye pilorie in Chepe for pakynge & sellynge of rotton herrynge, & vsynge of fals waytes. The xxv. day of Januarie one stond on ye pelory in Chepe, & his eres cut of & nayllyd to ye pyllorye for raylynge on ye kyngs councell.[4] The xviij. day of Februarie a sarvant of my lady Pargiters'[5] was drawne, hangyd, & quarteryd for clypping of golde. The xxv. day of February sir Allyn, a pryst, & a gentyllman[6] were bothe drawne to Tyborne, & ther hangyd, & quarteryd for treson. The xxj. day of Marche Hary Harssam, customar of Plomouthe,[7] was drawne from Newgate to Tyborne, & ther hangyd, & quarteryd for treson : & one Thomas Ewell[8] lykewyse hangyd & quarteryd.[9] Y^e xxvij. of May was ye fyar in Rode lane. Y^e first day of Septembar ye hangman was hongyd at ye wrestlyng place.[10]

Wylyam Ferman,[11] mayre, ye 30 yer of ye kynges reygne.[12] Y^e xvj. day of Novembar was ye blake fryars in London put downe, &

[1] *Summary* adds a notice of their execution.
[2] *Summary* omits, but adds notes on Cromwell's creation as K. G., and on the birth of Edward vi.
[3] *Summary* inserts notices of the burial of Queen Jane, and of the Christmas court.
[4] *Summary* omits.
[5] Wife of Sir Thomas Pargitor, mayor, 1530-31. See Wriothesley. *Chron.* i. 73.
[6] 'Sir John Allen... and an Irish Gentleman of the Garrets'. *Annales*, 969.
[7] Thomas Harford of Plymouth. *Letters and Papers*, xiii. I. 580, with date 22nd March. So also Wriothesley, *Chron.*, i. 77.
[8] Wriothesley calls him Yewer; and *Greyfriars Chron.* p. 201, Hever.
[9] *Summary* adds a note on Friar Forest.
[10] *Summary* gives these two notes at more length, and between them inserts a note of the treason of Edmond Conyngsbie. The year closes with notes on the removal of images, and suppression of abbeys from Hall.
[11] Or Forman.
[12] *Summary* inserts a long note on Nicholas Gibson's charities.

Nycholas Carrow, knyght & mastar of yᵉ horsse, was hedyd at yᵉ Towr hyll.⁶ The viij. day of Maye was yᵉ great mustar in London.⁷

Yᵉ viij. day of Julii yᵉ vycar of Wandworthe,⁸ his chapleyne, & his servante, & fryar Wayre wer all four drawne frome yᵉ Marshalcy vnto sent Thomas Wateryng, & ther hangyd & quarteryd for treson.⁹

Yᵉ xxxj. yere of yᵉ kynge, Mastar Holyes, mayre. The x. day of June yᵉ lorde Cromewell was sent to yᵉ Towre of London. This Cromwell his fathar was an Irysheman borne, & a smythe by his occupacion, & aftar that he kepte a brewe howse at Wandworthe, & ther was this Cromwell borne, & at yᵉ last comynge in favour wt yᵉ kynge Henry yᵉ eyght, he made hym knyght, & lorde privy seale,

---

¹ *Summary* adds: 'and so al the other immediatly after.'

² *Summary*: 'John Nicholson otherwyse Lambert, a priest,' from Hall. Wriothesley *Chron.* i. 88 calls him William Nicholson.

³ *Summary* omits these two notes, but inserts one on the arrest of the Marquis of Exeter and Sir Henry Pole.

⁴ His real name was John Harridaunce: he used to preach in his garden at Whitechapel. See Gairdner, *Lollardy and the Reformation*, i. 208, Wriothesley, *Chron.* i. 82, 93, and *Letters and Papers*, xiv. ii. 42 (1, 2).

⁵ *Summary* inserts a note on the execution of John Johns and others for murder of Roger Cholmeley.

⁶ *Summary* is somewhat fuller, and then inserts notes on the promotion of Paulet & Russell, the fortification of havens, & attainders in Parliament.

⁷ *Summary* has a full notice similar to that in *Survey*, i. 103.

⁸ Griffith Clarke, *Annales*, 972. Wriothesley, *Chron.* i. 101 calls him 'chaplaine to the Marques of Exceter.

⁹ *Summary* adds notes on O'Neill's rebellion in Ireland, and the negotiation of Henry's marriage to Anne of Cleves.

16 TWO LONDON CHRONICLES

& then vycegerent, & aftar lord chamberleyne, & then yearle of Essyxe, & thus he browght hym vp of noghte. The xxviij. day of Julii was the lord Cromewell,[1] & ye lorde Hongarforde behedyd at ye Towr hyll for treson.

The iiij. day of August wer drawne from ye Towre to Tyborne vj. persons, & one led betwen ij. sargantis, & ther hangyd & quarteryd: one of them was ye prior of Dancastor, a monke of ye Chartarhouse of London, Gyles Herne a monke of Westmystar, one Fylpot, & one Carrow, & a fryar: all were put to death for treason.[2] This yere ye dychys abowt London wer new cast.

Syr Wylyam Roche, mayre, in ye 32 yere ye kyngs reygne.

The xxxiij. yere of his reygne.

Michaell Dormer, mayre, in ye 33 of Henrie ye vilj.

The xxxiiij. yere of ye kyngs reygne.

John Cotes, mayre. The xxiij. day of Novembar wer ij. men hangyd in Holborne fylde for kyllynge a woman[3]

The xxxv. yere of his reygne.

Sir Wyllyam Boyere, mayre, in ye 35 yere of Henrie ye viij.

The xxxvj. yere of his reygne.

Syr Wylyam Laxton, mayre, in ye 36 yere of Henrie ye viij.

The xxij. of Aprill ye xxxvij. of his reygne.

[1] The whole of this curious note is omitted in the *Summary*. Though clearly a contemporary story it is in point of fact inaccurate. Thomas Cromwell's father, Walter Cromwell or Smythe, was it is true a blacksmith and brewhouse keeper at Putney: but the family had been settled there since 1452, and came from Norwell in Nottinghamshire. See *D.N.B.* xiii. 192. The *Summary* has a long and independent account for this year, borrowing only the next paragraph from the *Chronicle*.

[2] See *Annales*, 977; Laurence Cooke, prior of Doncaster, William Horne, laybrother of the Charterhouse, Giles Horne, gentleman, Clement Philip, gentleman, Edward Bromholme, priest, Darby Gening and Robert Bird executed for denying the king's supremacy. Wriothesley, *Chron.* i. 121 has 'Clement Philpott,' and says Charles Carow, gentleman was 'hanged for robbing of my Ladie Carow'.

[3] *Summary* omits. Wriothesley *Chron.* i. 137: 'In November were hanged on the backsyde of Lincolnes Inne two persons for murtheringe one Thomas Chesshers mayde in the same place'.

Mst. Hamcotis,[2] fishemongar, mayr, y{e} 2 yere of Ed. 6.

The xx. day of Marche sir Thomas Seymar, knyght, lord admyrall, was behedyd at Towre hyll. This yere y{e} comons in all y{e} parties of England made sondry insurreccions & commocions about whitsontyde, & so forthe vntyll September: amongs whome dyvers of comons of Cornwall & Devonshire[3] in sondry campes besegyd Excester, whiche manfully was defendyd[4] by y{e} inhabytauntes & dyver gentylmen which were flede into it. And agaynst thes rebells were sent y{e} lorde Russell, lorde privy seale, who lay longe ther at Hontyngton,[5] vntyll y{e} lord Graye w{t} certayne strayngars horsmen in redd cottes came thether, & syr Wyllyam Herbart w{t} dyvers Welchemen, & at a towne callyd Byshopps Clyffte[6] they assaltyd one campe furnyshed w{t} a greate number of y{e} sayd rebelles & them vanquished. And y{e} othar Rebells lying before Exceter, herynge of y{e} ovarthrow of theyr companyons at Bysshoppis Clyfte, beynge in feare of y{e} kynges Army, fled frome y{e} sege beyonde Excester into Cornwall,[7] so that the lordes aforesayd entred into Exceter w{t}out any further troble, yet y{ey} left not y{e} sayd rebells but chasd them into Cornewall, & take one Humfrey Arundell, one of y{e} capitaynes,

---

[1] *Sic.* Perhaps an error for 28{th} Sept.; Wriothesley (i. 175) says Hubberthorne was the first mayor chosen on that date.

[2] Sir Henry Amcotes.

[3] *Summary* inserts: " rose agaynst the nobles and gentelmen: and."

[4] *Summary*, 'whyche was valyauntly defended.' Stow then continues more briefly in his own words.

[5] Honiton.

[6] Bishop Clist.

[7] Another handwriting begins.

& one [1] Pomery, wt dyuerse other, & slewe very many : the contry was very sore wasted not only by reason of thar long lyenge ther in sondry campes, but also for that all the company of yᵉ lordes yᵉ strange had leave to spoyle.

[2] Also durynge this seege yᵉ comons of Oxfordshire, Northamptonshire, & Bedfordshire,wt dyvars of Somersettshire & others, arose in great numbers, & wt great angre towards sir John Wyllyams disparkyd his parke called Thame parke, & kyllyd all yᵉ dere : from thens they went vuto Rycote, & ther dysparked yᵉ parke called Rycote parke, & kyllyd all his dere, entered into yᵉ place, & dranke theyr fyll of wyne, ale & bere, slew many shepe, & ete them, wt dyvers other myscheves : from thens they went vnto Woodstocke, & then herynge yᵗ my lorde Gray wt yᵉ kyngs powre was comynge towards them, many of thern forsoke theyr companye, & thos whiche remaynyd went vnto a towne callyd Chyppynge Norton, where they encampyd themselves, whithar my lorde Graye folowyd them, & ther ovarcame them, & toke one Thomas Bowldrey, who aftar was hangyd & quarteryd, & one Bowlar, whiche aftarwards had his pardon : those ij. were capitayns at the brakynge vp yᵉ parks.[3]

And also duryng yᵉ sege at Exetar yᵉ comons of Norfolke & Suffolke arose in great nombar, & came vnto Norwytche, & nere there vuto in a wode callyd S. Nicholas wood they encampyd themselves, & aganst them was sent yᵉ Erle of Essex, whyche was made markes Northampton, wt dyvers straungers & englyshe men, all horssemen,[4] whome these rebelles suffred to enter into Norwiche peceably ; but after yᵗ he had entered yᵉ towne they neuer left of from molestynge & assaultynge yᵉ towne, so yᵗ in yᵉ conclusion he was fayne to forsake yᵉ towne & leave behynde many of his companye wt moch mony, stuff, horses, & other caryage : after yᵗ those rebelles wt ther capyteyn, called Keet [5] yᵉ tanner,

---

[1] Blank in MS. He was Sir Thomas Pomeroy.
[2] Stow resumes writing.
[3] Stow makes no use of this. In future I shall note only his quotations.
[4] The other hand resumes.
[5] Robert Kett.

hys also, wh. were both broughte vnto ye Tower.

ffor ye which offence ye sayd Keet ye tanner was hanged vppon ye toppe of ye castell of Norwytche, and his brother also.[2]

xxix° September, a° iij. Regis E. vj^{ti}.

Sir Rowland Hyll, mercer, mayour, ye 3 yere of Edward 6.

This yere ye iiijth of October ye lord protector & ye erle of Warwyke fill at controversye aboute ye reasonynge of certeyn things, & so ye erle of Warwyke wt other lordes of ye counsell assembled, & y^t herynge the lord protector wt all spede departed from Hampton courte, & tooke ye kynge w^t hym to ye castell of Wyndsore vppon ye sixte day of October at nyghte late, & gathered thyther moche people, & w^t hym went ye archbishope of Caunterberye, sir Thomas Patchett,[3] & secretary Smythe:[4] wherfore ye lordes cam together vpp to London, as the lord chauncellor,[5] ye lord St John, lord grete master, wt dyuerse other of ye kynges counsayll, & satt at ye mercers hall in Chepesyde ye vijth daye of October: & ye viijth day of October ye said lord protector wt all hys complices was proclaymed a traytor in London for dyuerse causes then declared in ye proclamacion: & ye tenthe

---

[1] On 26th August.

[2] The copyist first wrote: 'but his brother had his pardon.' His brother William was hanged at Wymondham. Two other brothers were pardoned.

[3] Probably Sir William Paget.

[4] Sir Thomas Smith.

[5] Richard, lord Rich.

daye ye lord protector was comytted to ward in ye castell of Wyndsor, & after y^t vppon Mondaye, beinge ye xiiij^th of October, ye same lord protector was brought from Wyndsore vnto ye Tower throughe ye citye, & w^t hym ye same tyme was broughte M. Stanhope,[1] grome of ye stole, & secretarye Smythe w^t other : & after y^t, vppon Thursdaye, beinge saynte Lukes eve, viz. ye xvij. day of October, ye kynges M^tie Edward ye sixte, accompanyed w^t all ye nobilite came from Hampton corte vnto Suffolke place in Sothewerke, wher he dyned, & after dyner rode throughe ye citie vnto Westmester in moste goodly order.

Also be it remembred[2] y^t vppon Sondaye, beynge ye xix^th day of January, A° R. E. vj.^ti tertio, in ye evenynge after super betwene Newgate & Smythe filde one called commonly captayn Gambold,[3] & an other captayne w^t hym called   [4] were both slayne by one called captayne Charles,[5] whoo of very malyce & dispyte slewe ye same Gambold, & for ye same offence ye sayd captayne Charles had hys hand stryken off vpon ye carte whelle, wher in he w^t iij. others[6] w^t hym were caryed from Newgate, & vpon ye waye before ye kynges hedd taverne[7] lost hys hand, & so were they all iiij. hanged in Smythfeld ye Frydaye, next folowynge, which was ye xxv.^th [8] of Januarye.

Also ye xxvj.^th day of January, a.° iij.° E. vj.^ti, foure westerne men, viz. one called Humfrey Arundell, a gentellman borne, one Berrys,[9]

---

[1] Michael Stanhope.

[2] Stow *Summary*, and *Annales*, 1017, describes this rather more fully. See also Wriothesley, *Chron.* ii. 31, 32.

[3] 'Sir Peter Gambo,' Stow and Wriothesley; 'Gambolde' in *Greyfriars Chron.*

[4] 'Filicirga', Stow.

[5] 'Charles Gauaro', Stow; Degavaro, Wriothesley.

[6] Kynges head dore before Smithfield, where the Murther was committed. *Summary*.

[7] Balthasar Gauaro, Nicholas Disalueton, and Francis Deualesco, *Annales*; Michael Desaluaron, and Frauncis Desalvasto, Wriothesley.

[8] So *Summary*; 24th, *Annales*, and Wriothesley.

[9] Bery, Stow.

same nyghte supped w^t y^e erle of Warwyke at y^e shreffes called mr. Yorke.[2]

Also vppon Mondaye, beinge y^e tenth daye of ffebruary afforesayde, one _____ Bell, a Suffolkeman was drawen from y^e Tower vnto y^e Tyburne, & ther hanged & quartred, which as they sayd was for a newe insurreccion, wh. he w^t certayne other of his complyces moved in Suffolke & in Essexe.[2]

Also vpon Mondaye, beinge y^e last daye of Marche, a.º R. E. vj.^{ti} iiij^{to}, a generall peace was proclaymed throughe London betwene ye kynge our M., & ye ffrench kynge, & in ye same peace were included themperor & ye scotes :[3] ye condicions of ye wh. peace as some sayd were thes y^t followe.[4]

Be it remembred y^t ye xxvj.th of Aprill, anno R. E. vj.^{ti} quarto, ye towne of Bulloyne was yelden vp vnto ye french kynge, & hys capitaynes tooke ye possession, which was so greate comforte & joye to ye ffrench men, y^t as some sayd at ye entrye in to ye towne many of them kneled downe & kyssed ye stones of ye stretes.[5]

Be it also remembred y^t vppon ffryday, beynge ye seconde daye of Maye, one Joan of Kent, otherwyse called Joan Bocher, was borned in Smythfild for heresy, whose pryncrypall article was our saviour Chryst tooke nether flesh nor blood of ye vyrgyn Mary.[6]

The xxix of October a.º iiij^{to} E. vj.^{ti}

M. Andrew Jude, skynner, mayor, 1550, a.º 4. E. vj.^{ti}

---

[1] Thomas Holmes, Stow.
[2] Quoted with slight variation in *Summary*.
[3] *Summary*.
[4] Not given in MS., nor by Stow.
[5] *Summary*.
[6] *Summary* with some variations.

This yere vppon a Thursdaye, beynge ye xvijth of Decembar, ye Temes beneth ye brydge dyd ebbe & flow thre tymes wt in ix. howres, & ye very same daye ye bishope of Winchester, who had lyen in ye Tower from ye mowow after saynt Peters daye a.° primo E. vj.^{ti}, was broughte vnto Lambethe before ye bishope of Caunterbery & certeyne of ye kynges comyssyoners ther vnto appoynted, where were obiected vnto hym certeyne articles on ye kynges behalfe, & daye assigned vnto his answere,[1] at wh. daye he exhibyted a matter Justificatory wt certayne Interrogatoryes, vppon ye wh. articles, mattier justifycatory, & interrogatoryes were very many nobell men & other witnesses examined, & dyuerse dayes ye sayd L. of Wynchester hadd accordynge to ye order of ye lawe.

A.° v^{to} E. vj.^{ti}

Also be it remembred y^t vppon Satterdaye ye vj. off ffebruary ye same L. of Winchester was before ye sayde comyssyoners, & was deprived from his bisshoprik.

Be it remembred y^t vppon ffrydaye, beynge ye 13 of Marche, one Thomas Morysbye & his syster were both hanged in Smythfild for murderyng of a gentyllman dwellynge in ffeuersham, called Arden, who was murdred by his owne wyffe, & thother ij. abouenamed: for ye wh. murder as ye saynge was his wyffe was also barned at Canterbury aboute ye xiij.th daye of Marche, & twoo other also suffred at Feuersham ye same daye.[2]

Be it also remembred y^t this yere were clene put downe all ye alters wh. were left stondynge in London; for in dyuerse places in England, & in sondry parishes of London ye had been pulled downe longe affore, excepte S^t. Nicholas Willows, & tables of waynscott set in ye myddest of ye quere; & in ye begynnynge of ye moneth of Aprill[3] ye yron gates of ye quere of Paules were mured vpp wt bryke bycause many people cam thyther dayly & worshipe ye sacrament.

---

[1] Thus far in *Summary*. Gardiner was remitted from time to time till 14th Feb. 1551.

[2] *Summary* gives this at more length from another source.

[3] "Against Easter", Wriothesley, *Chron.* ii. 47.

wares or victualles as they occupyed, dyd dayly inhaunse & encrease ye prises both of wares & victualles, most miserably oppressynge ye poore.³

Nota. Y^t vppon Mondaye, beynge ye xxvth. of Maye, betwene ye howres of xj. & one of ye clocke at none was an erthequake of halfe a quarter of an hower longe at Blechyngelye, at Godstone, at Croydon, at Albery, & dyuerse other places ther aboutes : ye cause therof is onely knowen vnto God, who be merciful vnto vs.⁴

Also be it remembred y^t vppon Thursdaye, beinge ye ixth. of July, ye forsayd proclamacion, wh. was appoynted to take effecte ye last day of August next comynge, by reason of ye insatyabell covetous of ye people oppressynge ye pore in ouerprysing, especially of vytayll & generally all other kyndes of warres, was shortened vnto this presente daye, & tooke effecte ymedyatly vppon ye publyshynge of ye same, wh. was doon betwene ix. & x. of ye clocke beforenone of ye same ix. daye, so y^t ymedyatly a shyllynge went for ix.d. & a grote for iij.d., & no word spoken of ye small money as pence & halfe grotes, by reason whereof ther was no small money to be gotten to geve ye poore people.⁵

---

¹ *Summary* ending: 'who helde the detestable opinion of the Arrians'. His name was George of Paris, *Annales*, 1021.

² Read 'dearth' as in *Summary*.

³ *Summary* with slight variations.

⁴ *Summary* ending: 'places in Southery and Myddlesexe.' See Wriothesley, *Chron.* ii. 49.

⁵ *Summary*.

Be it also remembred y^t vppon ffrydaye, ye x^th. of July, ye swetinge sycknes was very vehemente in London. But specially Watlyngstret, so y^t in ye same daye dyed many.¹

Bee it remembred y^t at St. Nicholas wyllows ye altars stood yet styll, as y^t ye precher M. Horne was very ernest agaynst them in ye afternoon y^t he made.

Be it remembred y^t vpon a Monday, beinge ye xvij^th. of August a°. R. E. vj^ti Quinto, ye proclaymacion cam forth for a shyllyng to be currant for vj.d., a grote for ij.d., a peny of ij.d. for a peny, a peny for a ob., & a ob. for a qr.²

Be it remembred y^t vppon Sondaye ye xj^th. of October ye lorde marques Dorset was created duke of Suffolke, ye lord erlle of Warwyke was created duke of Northumberland, & ye erle of Wyltesh. was created marques of Wynchester, & sir Willyam Harbert ye master of ye horse was created erle of Penbroke, & dyuerse men made knyghtes.³

Be it further remembred y^t vppon ffrydaye ye 16 of October ye duke of Somerset was brought vnto ye Tower, & in ye next mornynge beynge Satterdaye ye duchesse his wyfe was broughte thyther also, & ther wente also w^t ye duke the lord Grey of Wylton, sir Raffe Vane, & sir Thomas Pallmer,⁴ & sondrye other men bothe of ye dukes seruauntes & of others.

29 Octobers 1551.

M. Richard Dobbes, skynner, Mayor, ye 5 yere of Ed. 6.

No^m.⁵ that vppon ffrydaye, beynge ye 30 of October, a newe proclamacion cum forth for sondrye newe peces of money both sylver & golde of dyuerse valewes, viz. souereignes of fyne gould at xxx. s., angelles of fyne golde at x., & dyuerse other peces of gold

---

¹ *Summary* much longer.
² *Summary* with some variation.
³ *Summary*.
⁴ *Summary* inserts: " Syr Mylles Petrydge, syr Michell Stonhope, syr Thomas Arundell.
⁵ *sc.* Notandum.

of Somerset was areyned at Westmynster hall, & was then & ther acquyted of treason, but he was condempned of felonye by vertue of acte of parlyamente made agaynst conventicles & vnlawfull assemblies.[3]

Also vppon ye Mondaye after, beynge ye vijth. daye of December was a generall muster of ye horsemen, wh. were in ye wages of ye nobles of this realme, & for ye wh. ye kynges majesty allowed yerely for each man xx.li., the wh. muster was made vppon ye brod cawsey ouer agaynste ye brode causaye ouer agaynst ye kinges place[4] at saynte James : & as y^t was reported ye nomber of ye horsemen was a thousande.

Note y^t vppon ffrydaye, beynge ye xxijth. day of January, ye duke of Somerset was broughte vnto ye skaffold vppon ye Tower hyll, & ther was beheaded.

And vppon Satterdaye ye xxiijth. daye of Januarye ye parlyament began wh. ye lordes assembled.

Also about this tyme ye flud of ye ocean & flemyshe sea of ye Temes swelled so hyghe y^t yt dyde greate hurte vpon all ye cost of Flaunders, & ouerflowed Lesynge[5] mershe besydes Wolwytche, & ye mershes beyond saynte Kateryns.

Also aboute this tyme ther was found dead in ye mouth of ye Humber in ye north a greate whale of vij. or viij. cubites.

---

[1] *Summary.*

[2] *Summary:* ' The old Quene of Scottes. '

[3] *Summary.*

[4] So in MS. *Summary:* ' made vpon the caussey ouer against the kynges palace.'

[5] Lesnes. A somewhat different account in the *Summary.*

Note, y^t vppon Fryday, beinge ye xxvj^th. of ffebruary, one sir Raffe a Vane, & on sir Myles Partryge were both hanged [at] ye Tower hyll vppon ye gallowes, & sir Mihell Stanhope & sir Thomas Arundell were beheaded vppon ye skaffold ther : all wh. foure were condempned by vertue of ye acte of vnlawfull assembles as accessaryes to ye duke of Somerset.[1]

Note, y^t vppon good Frydaye ye xv^th. of Aprell ye parlyament was cleane dyssolued & broken vpp, wherin were many goodly lawes & statutes ordeyned & stablyshed.

[2] The third day of August in a towne called Myddelton Stony in Oxford, there was borne a double child, whiche was two children from ye brest vpwarde, in all partis perfyte w^t one body, one navle, & one ishew where out passyd both ordure & water, havynge ij. legges growynge out of ye one syde of ye belye, & one ye other, one lege havynge ij. bones in one skyne, ix. toes, & ij soles of ye foote, callyd & christenyd by ye mydwyfe Johan Joane : thone always slepynge whiles ye othar was wakynge, in August anno 1552.[3]

Also in ye same monythe of August began to gooe forwarde ye great provysyon for ye poore, towards ye whiche every man was tributorie & gave a certayn wykelye, & also somewhat to begyne ye same on hande : ye first hous which was begon was ye graye fryers in Newgate market, wh. wente forwarde w^t all spede. [4]

Mihelmas daye, 1552.

George Barnes, habardashar, mayre, ye 6 yere of Ed. 6.

Be yt remembryd y^t at this mychelmas ye lorde Wyllyam Hawarde was apoynted to be deputie of Calice, & ye lorde Willoghby was commaundyd home, & ye lorde Gray of Wylton was made leftenaunte of Gwynes.

Vpon ye Sondaye, beynge ye xvj. daye of Julii, Nycholas Rydley,

---

[1] *Summary*: "Scaffold, which fowre wer condemned as accessary in that whyche the Duke was condemned for."

[2] Stow resumes copying.

[3] In the *Summary* this monster is described somewhat differently; it lived eighteen days.

[4] *Summary*.

xix.[th] of Jully, at v. of y[e] clocke in y[e] afternone y[e] hole body of y[e] counsel, wh. were lefte behynd in y[e] Tower, assembled at Baynardes castell, & ther communed w[t] y[e] erle of Penbroke, & ymedyatly came into Chepesyde w[t] y[e] kynge of heraudes, wher they proclaymed y[e] vertuous lady Mary, doughter of quene Kateryn, quene of England, ffraunce &c.,[2] in earth ẏ[e] supreme heade : y[e] Joye wherof wonderfull, for some caste money abrod, & some made bonfyars thorowe y[e] whole cyte : y[e] prayses were geuen to God in y[e] churches wt te deum & orgaynes, belles ryngynge & euery wher y[e] tables spredd in y[e] stretes, meate & drynke plentye, wyne geuen ffrely of many men, and a greate peale of ordynaunce was shote of at y[e] Tower.

After thes thinges thus done, euen y[e] sellfe same xix.[th] daye of July at ix. of y[e] clocke in y[e] nyghte, y[e] erle of Arundell w[t] y[e] lord Patchet rode to y[e] quenes grace to fframyngham,[3] & as y[e] was sayd caryed wt them y[e] greate sealle of England, & then also ye counsell sent letters vnto ye duke of Northumberland wt his adherentes to retyre, & proclayme ye quene in his campe : ye wh. thynge done he returned homeward, & at Cambrydge was taken & commytted to warde. Y[e] 21 of July, beynge ffrydaye, ye byshope of London, who befòre prechyd so abhomynabillye, ye xvj.[th] of July, rode erly ye same 21 day in ye morninge towardes her grace, to submyte hym vnto her gracious mercy.

[1] The other hand resumes.

[2] Stow in the *Summary* quotes thus far from 'assembled', but ends: ' and Irelande, defendour of the faythe etc'. In the *Annales*, 1033, he substitutes an account closely resembling that in Wriothesley, *Chron.* ii. 88. Wriothesley says that the style of the proclamation could not be heard for the cheering.

[3] Framlingham.

And vpon Thursdaye, beinge ye 21 of Julii, ye duke of Northumberland havynge receyved ye sayd proclamacion from ye lordes, he returned ye same nyghte to Cambridge, & ther proclamed her grace queue of England ; & ye same nyghte after he was layed in his bede ye garde came & seased vppon his weapons & his body & tooke hym in charge : & ye next day ye lord erle of Huntyngton, ye lorde Graye, & dyuers other, & ye capeteyne of ye gar[de][1] also were arested by ye quenes commaundement.

And vppon Sonday, beinge ye 22 daye of Julye, as it was sayd, dyuerse of ye lordes of ye counsell here rode towardes her grace. Vppon Tewesdaye, beinge ye xxvth. day of July in ye feast of sainte James thapostell, aboute iiij. of ye clocke at afternone thes persons followynge were broughte as prysoners into ye Tower of London, y^t is to saye ye duke of Northumberland, ye erle of Warwyke his sonne, sir Ambrose Dudleye his sonne, & Harry Dudley his sonne, therle of Huntyngton, & ye lorde Hastinges his sonne, one [   ] Sandes[2] a prest of Cambrydge, who had preched in Cambrydge in all condycions & rather worse than ye bishope of London, Sir John Gaates capteyne of ye garde, & Harry Gaates his brother, Sir Androwe Dudley, & sir Thomas Pallmer.

And ye morrow after, beynge Wednysdaye ye 26 of July,[3] ther were broughte into ye Towre the prisoners folowynge, The lord marques Northeampton, The byshope of London, Rydleye, sir Richard Corbyt knyt of Suffolke, & a serchar of Gravesende called Harmonde. Thes came in at Allgate. And ye same nyght ye two cheff Judgys of England, ye lord Mountagwe, cheff judge of ye comon place, & syr Rogar Cholmley, cheffe justice of ye kyngs benche were bothe comytted to ye Towre. And neverthelesse they were sone delyveryd, beyng fynyd at serten somes of money.

Vpon Fryday ye xxviij. day of Julii the duke of Suff., Mster. Cheeke, whiche was ye kynges schole-mastar, wt divers othar, were commytted to ye Tower.

---

[1] MS., 'game.'
[2] Dr Edwin Sandys, the Vice-Chancellor of Cambridge. The MS. is damaged.
[3] Stow resumes copying.

of Somersett, & myster Courtneye, sonn to ye marquess of Exceter had theyr pardon grauntyd vnto them by hyr graces owne mouthe.

Vppon Sattarday, beynge ye v. of August, ye byshope of London, doctour Bonar, who hadd lyen in ye Marchallse aboute v. yeres, was delyveryd & set at lybertie. And doctour Tunstall, byshope of Duresme, was also delyveryd out of ye Towre.

Vppon Twesdaye, ye viij. of August, ye corps of kynge Edward ye vj. was buryed in ye churche of sent Petar at Westmyster. And ye nyght before ther was placebo & dyrige sayd in latyn before ye quene wt yn ye Towre : & this present Twesdaye ther was a messe of requyem songe in latin before ye quene by ye byshope of Wynchestar w^t in ye Towre.

On Twesdaye beynge ye xxij. daye of Auguste, The Duke of Northumberland, sir John Gaates, & buskynned Palmer were all thre behedyd vppon ye skaffolde at ye Towr hyll

The xxvij. of August, beynge Sondaye, ye bakesyde of ye highe altar of Powles churche beynge made up w^t brike some what above an altar but not clearly fynyshed, ther was hyghe masse songe in lattyn wt bothe mattyns & evensonge lykewyse in lattyn. And dyvers churches in London had ye lyke servyce.

Vppon Satterday, beynge ye laste daye of September, ye quenes highnes rode through ye citie in moaste goodly manere. The pageauntes in all places accustomyd beynge moste gorgyously trymmyd : amongest all ye thre pagauntes made by ye straungers wer ye myghtyest, wher of thone made by ye Gennayes[1] at Fanchurche, the othar at Grasechurche made by ye Stilliardes, & y^e

---

[1] Genoese.

third in yᵉ myddes of Gracious streate made by yᵉ Florentynes were all made wt gattes to passe throwghe, & yᵉ buyldynges wer very highe statlye. And so hir grace passyd forthe vnto Westmyster, & as she passyd by Pawles a certayne duche man stode vpon yᵉ wetharcoke wᵗ a flagge in his hande, & ondar hym vpon yᵉ crosse a skaffolde wt flaggs, & oudar yᵗ vpon yᵉ ball an othar skaffolde wt flaggs & streamers.[1]

Vpon Sonday, beynge yᵉ fyrste day of October, yᵉ quenes grace was crownyd at Westmystar, & before here went all yᵉ byshoppes wt myters & croysers, & yᵉ clerks syngynge yᵉ servyce all in lattyn.

Vpon Thursdaye, beynge yᵉ v. day of October, yᵉ barge of Gravesend by greate mysfortune of a catche comynge vpon hir was ovarthrowne and aboute fortye persons drownyd'[:] our lord be merciful to them.

On Monday, beynge yᵉ xxiij., on wednysday yᵉ xxv., & Fryday, beynge yᵉ xxvij. day of October were certayne dysputacions in yᵉ longe[3] chapell at yᵉ northe doore of Paules concernynge yᵉ transubstanciacion, but no thyng throughely determynyd.[4]

Thomas Whit, marchaunt tayloure, mayie, yᵉ xxviij. of Octobar, 1553.

Vpon Fryday yᵉ iij. day of Novembar, 1553, yᵉ aforesaid doucheman, who stode vpon yᵉ wethercoke at yᵉ queens rydynge thrughe London, dyd set up yᵉ wetharcoke of Poules agayne vpon yᵉ crosse, whiche he had causyd to be amendyd wᵗ a brode rownde vane set vpon yᵉ tayle to thend yᵗ she myght turne wt every wynde, & even yᵉ same day he stroke downe both yᵉ skafoldes, whiche he before had made agaynst yᵉ queens comynge.

Vpon Wednysday yᵉ viij. of Novembar an obyt was kept in Poules

---

[1] Stow uses this paragraph, but omits 'amongest' to 'statlye,' and varies the last clause. In the *Annales* he follows *The Chronicle of Queen Jane and Queen Mary*, pp. 27-30.

[2] *Summary* but ending: "and xiiii. persones drowned, and xvj. saued by swymmyng."

[3] So Stow. The MS. has 'londe.'

[4] *Summary.*

Vpon Satterday, beynge y̆ᵉ xxv. of Novembar, & Y̆ᶜ yere of our lord 1553, Anno I. Regyne Marie, at vj. of yᵉ cloke at night S. Katheryns lyghts were cryed aboute yᵉ battylments of Paules steple, whiche had not ben many yeres before.[1]

Vpon Tewesdaye or Wednysdaye yᵉ v. of Decembar, yᵉ parlyament was dissolvyd, wherein was repeallyd ix. servall actes, viz. for mariage of priestes, yᵉ legitimacion of prestis children, yᵉ receyvynge of yᵉ sacrament in bothe kyndes, yᵉ makynge of deacons & pristes, the vniformytie of devyne prayer, the pluckynge downe of altars, Roods, & Images, the observacion of holydayes & fastynge dayes, wt ij. othar actes.

Vpon yᵉ 14 day of Januarye, 1553, yᵉ lord. chauncelour wt othar of yᵉ counsell declaryd openly vuto yᵉ queens Maiestie howseholde y̆ᵗ ther was a mariage concludyd betwene hir grace & yᵉ kynge of Spayne,[2] whiche was yᵉ fyrst tyme it was certaynly knowne abrode.

Aboute yᵉ xxv. day of Januarie, Anno 1553, anno primo Regine Marie, began yᵉ comocion in Kent, yᵉ cheffe captayns wherof was sir Thomas Wyat & one syr Henrie Illisleye[3] : but it was sayd y̆ᵗ lorde Cobham had taken parte wᵗ yᵉ queene : the cause of theyr

[1] *Summary* in Stow's own words.

[2] *Summary* reading: 'xx. day of January.' The emperor's ambassadors had public audience of the queen on 14ᵗʰ January, & the queen's decision was communicated to the lord mayor next day. In the *Annales* this is given correctly from *The Chronicle of Queen Jane and Queen Mary* pp. 34, 35.

[3] Isley, Stow.

comocion (as ye brute went) was because they woulde not be subiecte to ye kynge of Spayne: for thappesynge where of ther was a great nombar of men made out of ye citie of London, & all ye companyes chargyd ther wt

And vppon Candelmas day, beynge Frydaye & ye ij. day of Februarie, all ye aldarmen of London & ye inhabytauntes of every warde were ye whole day in harnes for feare of ye aforesayde Rebells, who as it was sayd approchid : & my lord mayre was at Ledyn hall w^t a great nomber of men in harnesse, whiche were apoyntyd forthe by ye companyes of ye citie, double so many as before, for wher ye marchaunt taylours at ye fyrst tyme armed xxx. at this tyme they armyd lx. &c.

Vppon Satterday, beynge ye iiij. day of February, ye morow after Candelmas day, s. Thomas Wyatt, who had lyen at Grenewitche by ye space of ij. nyghts & a daye, cam sodeynly aboute one of ye cloke at aftar none into Sothewarke wt his band of men, whose sodayne comynge drave ye citizens into great feare so that they were fayne to close vp ye gatte on ye brydge, & cutt downe ye draw brydge & let it fawll in to ye watar, & all men ran to harneys for ye deffence of ye citie. How be it sir Thomas Wyatt made to¹ proffer of entrie, but went streyght wayes to worke & his men w^t hym & trenchid Sothewarke at every end, and plantyd his ordenaunce for his deffence. The citizens in ye meane season preparynge great watche & warde. And thus lay syr Thomas Wyat from ye Satourday at noone vntyll shrove Tewesday in ye mornynge next folowynge. The queens maiestie durynge this tyme preparyd greate power to goo agaynst hyme. The aforesayd shrovetewesday, beynge ye vj. day of Februarie, early in ye mornynge ye sayd syr Thomas Wyate removyd all his people & theyr ordynaunce all save one pece, & went vnto Kyngston, & ther beyng sumwhat resysted at ye last he by entreatie passyd ye brydge, whiche brydge was by hyme & his foarcyd & made, for ye brydge y^t before was ther was cutt downe or he cam : & then he marchyd to London wardes a bowght xij. of

---

¹ So MS.; read 'no'.

myster, whithar it was sayd ye rebells purposyd to come : and aboute two of ye cloke they came : the queens ordynaunce was schott of, & ye horsemen marchyd fortheward, & set vpon them : & sir Thomas Wyate perseyvynge his dystruction at hand devysyd w^t hym selffe this pollicie : he w^t a certayne nombar slyppyd bye, & havynge theyr swerds drawne cam in at ye Temple barre cryenge, God save quene Marie : ye people, knowynge hym not to be Wyatt, sufferyd hym wt his companye to entre, thynkynge them to have bene some of theyr frynds : & ymediatly pursuite was made aftar hym by ye quenes armye, and in Fletstrete he was taken & dyvers othar wt hym, as two of ye Knayvatis,[1] & two of ye Cobhams, Captayne Brett,[2] whiche went away w^t ye Londoners at Rochestar. Thar was slayne aboute ye numbar of an hondred[3] of ye Rebells. And then ye quene of hir clemencie & pitie grauntyd pardon to all ye rest of theyr lyves : and aftar a day or two syr Henry Isley wt dyvers othar were brought vnto ye Towre.

Vpon Monday, beynge ye xij. day of Februarie, ye lorde Gylforde Dudley, forthe sonne to ye duke of Northumbarland, hosband to ye lady Jane, pretendyd quene, was behedyd at ye Towre hyll : and ye sayd day lady Jane, ye pretendyd queene, was behedyd ye same day wt in ye Towre. Abought two days afore ye duke of Suffolke wt one of his brythern, whiche before fledd to Lester, ther to rays

---

[1] Knyvet or Knevet. *The Chronicle of Queen Jane and Queen Mary* p. 50 mentions William Knevet and Thomas Cobham as taken prisoners here; other prisoners were Thomas Knevet, Anthony Knevet, George Cobham and Sir William Cobham.

[2] Alexander Brett; see *Chron. Q. Jane*, pp. 38, 51.

[3] 'hondred' was afterwards struck out, and 'xx' written above.

yᵉ people ther to ayd syr Thomas Wyat, was brought in to yᵉ Towre of London.

Vpon yᵉ sayd Monday, beynge yᵉ xij. of Februarie,[1] yᵉ lord Courtney, therle of Devonshire, who was delyveryd out of yᵉ Towre at yᵉ queens entrynge, as is afore sayde, was nowe agayne comytted vnto yᵉ Towre. The same Monday ther were gallowes to yᵉ nomber of xviij. payre sett vp in dyvers placis of London: as two in Chepesyde, wherof one was beyond yᵉ cross towarde Poules, & thothar almoast at yᵉ great conduyte: at dyuers of yᵉ gates othar.

Vpon Wednysday folowynge, beynge yᵉ xiiij. day of Februarie, ther were vj. persons hangyd in Chepe syde vpon yᵉ two payr of galowes. And vpon thothar gallowes in othar placis of yᵉ citie to yᵉ nombar of fifftye[2] persons, whiche wer of yᵉ Londoners yᵗ were set out by yᵉ citie and rane away from yᵉ duke of Northfolke vnto Wyatt, & wer taken in yᵉ fylde vpon ashewednesday.

Also yᵉ Sonday before,[3] Captayn Bret wᵗ xxv. more wer layd in a cart in Sothewarke by ser Robert Sothewell, shrive of Kent, yᵉ whiche wer asygnyd to be executyd in dyver placis in Kent, but many of them were aftarward pardonyd.

Vpon Thursday, beynge yᵉ xxj.[4] day of Februarie, yᵉ remaynante of yᵉ sayde rebells, whiche hadd bene emprisonyd, some in Newgate, some in the Countars, some in Sothewarke, & some in seynt Petars chirche at Westmystar in dyvers chapells ther, whiche wer to yᵉ number of xij. score persons or more, were brought to yᵉ crosse in Chepe, where yᵉ quenes mercifull pardon was declaryd vnto them to theyr great comfortes.[5]

---

[1] So also *Chron. Queen Jane and Queen Mary*, p. 59 and Stow, *Annales* 1052. But Stow. *Summary*, and Wriothesley, *Chron.* ii. 113 have 15ᵗʰ March.

[2] Machyn, *Diary*, p. 55 gives 46. Grafton (ii. 543) says 50. Other chronicles smaller numbers.

[3] Machyn and Wriothesley (ii. 112) give 18ᵗʰ February, which was the Sunday after.

[4] Should be 'xxij.'

[5] *Summary* somewhat differently, with date 23ʳᵈ February.

beynge appoyntyd to begyn vpon yᵉ Monday aftar lowe Sonday yᵉ iij.² day of Apryll; & yᵉ tearme also was apoynted to be kepte at Oxford lykewysse.

Vpon Saterday, beynge yᵉ xvij.³ of Marche, yᵉ lady Elisabeth, doughter of quene Anne Bulleyne, was comyttyd vnto yᵉ Towre.

Wheras yᵉ parlyament & tearme were bothe appoyntyd to have bene kepte at Oxenforde, it was now reiournyd vnto London by proclaymacion, and begand at Westmystar yᵉ second day of Apryll, beynge Monday.

Vpon Wednysday, beynge yᵉ xj. of Apryll, sir Thomas Wyat capitayne & ryngledar of yᵉ sayd Rebells, was behedyd at yᵉ Towr hyll.

Vpon yᵉ xxvij. day of Apryll one Nicholas Thokmorton,⁴ a gentylman, was arraygnyd at yᵉ Gyldhall as accessarye vnto Wyats conspiracie, & vpon his quest were chosen dyvers sytysyns, one was Whetstone,⁵ haberdashar, Emanuell Lucas,⁶ marchant taylor, Watur Yonge, Mst. Baskerfylde, Symon Lowe, Wyliam Bankes, Mstar. Poyntar, Mst. Martyn, and fowr othars, whiche dyd acquyt hym, and shortly aftar sent for before yᵉ counsell, & ij. of them sent to yᵉ Towre, yᵉ rest were sent to yᵉ Flete.

Vpon Fryday, beynge yᵉ xviij. day of May, one Wylyam Thomas, a gentylman who had bene clarke of yᵉ counsell, who had bene wt Wyat, and allso detarmynyd to have slayne yᵉ quene wt a dagar,

---

[1] Should be 'xxiij.'
[2] Should be 'ij.'
[3] Other authorities give Palm Sunday, 18ᵗʰ March.
[4] Throckmorton. He was arraigned on 17ᵗʰ April, and acquitted on the 25ᵗʰ.
[5] See Holinshed IV. 31, 64, 74 for the jurors, and 31-54 for the record of the trial.
[6] Lucare, Wriothesley.

was drawne from ye Towre of London to Tyborne, & ther hangyd & quarteryd.

Vpon Satarday, beynge ye xix. day of May, ye lady Elizabeth was brought out of ye Towr, & so convayed by watar vuto Rychemonde, & from thence ye next day she went to Wyndsore, & so by my lord Wyllyams to Rycote in Oxenfordeshire, & from thens to Wodstoke, where as it was sayd she shuld remayne.[1]

The fyrste[2] day of June ye gallowsys in London were commandyd to be takyn downe, whiche thynge was done accordyngly.

And aboute ye sayd fyrst[3] day of June ther was grauntyd by acte of comon counsell a fyvtyne & a halfe to be levyed of ye citezens for ye gyldynge of ye crosse in Chepe, & for makynge of pagauntes agaynst ye comynge of ye prynce of Spayne; & ther vpon skaffolds were made aboute ye crosse, & werkemen set a werke for makynge of ye pagauntis.

Vpon Sonday, beynge ye xv. day of Jully, 1554, & anno Regine Marie secondo, a yonge wenche[4] of ye age of xvj. or xvij. yeres dyd open penaunce at Poules crosse, standynge vpon a skaffolde all ye sermon tyme, & confessyd hir falte openly: that she beynge intysed by lewde counsell had[5] counterfetyd certayne speaches in an house in Aldarsgate strete, about ye whiche matar ye people were wondarfully molestyd, some saynge yt it was a sprite that spake in a wall, some one thynge, some an othar: on this manor she vsed hir selffe, she lay in hir bed, & whistelyd in a strange whystell made for ye nones, then was ther (as she confessyd) vj. falce knaves,[6] whos names she ther declaryd, confederyd wt hir, whiche toke vpon them

---

[1] *Summary.*

[2] *Summary*, 'fowerth'. Machyn, *Diary* p. 65. 4th June.

[3] Machyn says 4th June.

[4] *Summary*, 'Elizabeth a yonge wenche.' Wriothesley, ii. 117, calls her Elizabeth Crofte.

[5] *Summary*, 'had vpon the xiiij. day of Marche last passed. Wriothesley ' in Apryll.'

[6] *Summary*, 'iiij. or vj. companions.' Wriothesley and Machyn name one as John Drake, a servant of Anthony Nevill or Anthony Knevett.

maiestie.

Vpon Sonday, beynge ye xxix. day of Julii, one doctour Harpefeld[2] preachyd at Powles crosse, and after he had made his proposycion he exortyd all men to become newe men bothe in mynd & doyng, for so myche (sayd he) as I have newe thyngs to declare vuto you and therfore ye must become newe, for accordynge to Christis saynge no man puttythe newe wyne into olde vessyles etc.; and thervpon he declaryd vuto ye people ye style in maner folowynge: fyrst I command vnto.......[3] Philipp and Marye by ye grace of God kynge & quene of England, Faunce, Napyles, Jerusalem and Irlande, defender of ye faythe, pryncies of Hyspayne & Cicile, archedukes of Austrie, dukes of Mylayne, Burgoyne, & Brabant, countes of Ausborow,[4] Flaunders & Tiroll: & then procedyd forthe wt his prayer.[5]

Vpon Lamas day, beynge ye fyrst of August, ye proclamacion was made consernynge ye sayd style in ye forenone, and at aftar none ye same stylle pryntyd bothe in Englisshe & in lattyn, was set up in dyvers placis of the citie.

And vpon Satterdaye, beynge ye xviij. day of August,[6] ye kynge

---

[1] *Summary*, ' sedicious and opprobrious.'
[2] Nicolas Harpsfield.
[3] The edge of the leaf is worn.
[4] *sc.* Habsburg.
[5] Compare Machyn, pp. 66-7.
[6] So Stow in the *Summary*, but in the *Annales* he gives 12th August. Wriothesley (ii. 122) has 18th August, and so also *Chron. Queen Mary*, p. 78. Stow makes only slight use of the account above.

& yᵉ queue bothe togethar wᵗ ij. swerdes borne before them passed ovar London brydge from Suffolke place in Sothewarke, wheŕ they had lyene yᵉ nyght before, and so rode bothe togethar thrughe yᵉ citie. And at Gracious strete yᵉ house of yᵉ Stylyard at theyr cost made a sumptious & a large pagaunte fowr square wt stones of dyvars sortis. And at yᵉ Stokes[1] was a great pagaunte made at yᵉ cities cost declarynge yᵉ nobylytie of iiij. Philyppes,[2] whiche have excellyd in vertue,& praysynge ye kynge for yᵉ fyfthe. At Iremongare lane[3] ende was an othar greate pageante of Orpheus syttynge on yᵉ toppe, playenge on a harpe, and lytyll boyes dressyd lýke wylde beastis dawnsynge aboutes yᵉ mownt wheron he satt. The crosse beynge newly gyldyde shone very fayre. At yᵉ lytyll conduite was yᵉ whole genelogie of yᵉ quenes maiestie & yᵉ kyngs, brought from Edward yᵉ thyrde, fathar to John of Gaunte : and at yᵉ weste ende of Poules yᵉ kynge & yᵉ quene bothe alyghtyd and entryd into yᵉ churche, & so into yᵉ qwyre, wher they entryd into ij. traversys made for them. And afftar rode forthe. And round abowte yᵉ conduyte in Fletestrete was a large & a fayre greate pageaunte wᵗ turretts & dyvers other thyngs, And at yᵉ gatte at Temple barr was a longe declaracion of yᵉ prayse of yᵉ kynge, wᵗ a bryffe rehearsall of all yᵉ sayd pagauntis.

Not.,[4] yᵗ from yᵉ 10 day of Octobar vntyll yᵉ xvj. day a greate preparacion was made in Smythefylde for yᵉ spanyards to bayte yᵉ bull aftar yᵉ maner of Spayne, called Juga de Tauro, vpon sainte Lukes day, & a great frame for an house newe sett vp ther ; and vpon yᵉ even of saynt Luke, beynge yᵉ xvij. day of Octobar, it was knowen yᵗ yᵉ same pastyme shulde be put of, so Yᵗ all yᵉ preparacion for this tyme was voyde.

Vpon sent Lukes day, beyng Thursday yᵉ xviij. day of October,

---

[1] Stock Market.

[2] *Chron. Queen Mary*, p. 80, gives them as: ' Phillipus rex Macedoniae, Phillipus bonus, Phillipus imperator, and Phillipus audax.'

[3] Ironmongers Lane.

[4] *sc.* Notandum.

Wherstone, Emanuell Lucas, Walter Younge, Baskevyle, Wyllyam Bankes, Marten, Kyghlehe, & Calthrope, were broughte out of ye Flete before ye counsell in ye Starre chamber, wher as yt was sayd ye lordes, consydderynge the obstaclenes, detyrmyned y^t ye sayd [Wherstone]² because he was forman should paye for his fyne a thousande markes, & euery of ye other syxe hondreth poundes apece : but yet was not thes fynes ymedyatly sett vppon ther heades, but they were all viij. remytted to ye Flette : & as for ye othar fowre, N. Poynter, who neuer came in by reason y^t he was syke when thother was apprehended, Symon Lowe, merchuaunte tayllor, who had bene delyuered shortly after he was committed, one [ ] Oates, who lately vpon submyssyon was lett out, & one other, who [s] name I knowe not, were not appoynted to paye any fyne.

And vppon Satterdaye, beinge ye x.th of Nouember, 1554, ye shrefe of London enteryd into ye houses of ye said viij.³ men, & seased vppon all ye goodes in them for ye levyinge of a fyne of a thousand markes apece, sett vppon ther heades in thexcheqwyre, & processe directed vnto ye shreffes of London for ye levyinge of ye same.

Also vppon Mondaye, beinge ye 12 day of Nouember, cardynall Poole came vnto Lambeth by water & ther dyned.

⁴ Vpon Sonday, beinge ye xxv. day of November, the spanyards made a pastyme before y^e cowrte gate at Westmystar, callid Juga de Cane; for y^e preparacyon wherof ther was a wall, & posts pallyd

---

¹ The other hand resumes.
² Omitted in MS. at foot of f. 19ro
³ The MS. has 'xiij'
⁴ Stow resumes copying.

dyd enclose y̓ᵉ tourneyinge place ther, & y̓ᵉ way also was all pullyd vp before y̓ᵉ place.¹

Aboute iij. dayes past y̓ᵉ viij. quest men, whose housys were seasyd by y̓ᵉ shreves, (as is afore sayd) were asygned to pay y̓ᵉ thyrd parte of a M. markes, & so had ther houssys delyveryd agayn into thandis of theyr wyves, all whiche thynges was done (as it was sayd) by y̓ᵉ kynges meanes & procurement : but yet were not they delyveryd ont of pryson.

Vpon Sonday, beynge y̓ᵉ second day of Desembar, 1554, and in y̓ᵉ fyrste & second yeres of y̓ᵉ reygnes of our soverayne lorde & ladye Philipp & Marie, The lorde Chauncelour² made a sermon at Paules crosse, at the whiche sermon y̓ᵉ kynge & y̓ᵉ cardenall were present, stondynge above ovar the lorde mayres hedd : & in y̓ᵉ same sermon my lorde Chauncelor declaryd y̓ᵗ we had bene long in ignoraunce of derknesse, wherfore accordynge to y̓ᵉ wordes of saynt Paule in y̓ᵉ epystyll redd in y̓ᵉ chyrche y̓ᵉ sayd Sunday³ he exhorted all men wt *abiiciamus opera tenebrarum*,⁴ & there vpon shewyd y̓ᵗ we must nedes have y̓ᵉ pope to be our supreme heade, and y̓ᵗ y̓ᵉ lorde cardynall Poole was come from hym wt his blessynge vnto vs, who dyd persecute hym wt all maladyccion, and therin (sayd he) owr moaste holy fathar dothe fullfyll y̓ᵉ saynge of Christ, whiche is *benedicite maledicentibus vobis*,⁵ wyllynge y̓ᵉ people to put all vayne fantasyes & ymaginacions ont of theyr heades of any dyscorde to ensewe : for (quod he) *a domino factum est istud*,⁶ and therfore shall ther be *gloria in excelsis deo et in terra pax homynybus*,⁷ and for because *hec est dies quam fecit dominus, exultemus et letemus in ea*,⁸

---

¹ See Machyn p. 76. 'The kynges rydyng at Jube de Cane.'
² i.e. Gardiner.
³ The first Sunday in Advent: *Romans*, xiii. 8-14. Wriothesley (ii. 124) gives the text, 'Fratres, scientes quia hora est jam nos de somno surgere' from verse 11.
⁴ *Romans*, xiii. 12.
⁵ *Matthew*, v. 44.
⁶ *Matthew*, xxi, 42.
⁷ *Luke*, ii. 14.
⁸ *Psalm*, cxviii. 24.

And then comynge to his prayers he prayed for yᵉ spiritualtye, yᵉ temporalltye, & yᵉ sowles departyd, prayenge for yᵉ pope as yᵉ supreme heade. Aftar this yᵉ belles in Paules began to rynge, & in othar churchis, whiche made souche noyse that I coulde not vndarstond iij. wordes togethar, & by reason therof & allso yᵗ yᵉ day was furre spent (for it was past one of yᵉ clocke) he made a shorte ende.

Vpon Tewesday, yᵉ 11 of Decembar, 1554, Mst. Whetstone, Mst. Yonge, Mst. Bankes, Mst. Baskervyld, and Mst. Martyn were deliveryd ont of yᵉ prison of yᵉ. Flete by vertewe of yᵉ quenes leter; & thothar thre, Emanuell Lucas, Kyghtley, & Caltrop, were lefte styll behynd in pryson, bycaus they had not payde there parte of yᵉ fyne accordynge as thothar fyve had done.

The parlyament endyd aboute yᵉ xxij.[2] day of Januarie.

Vpon Fryday, beynge yᵉ xxv. day of Januarie, generall procession[3] was through Chepesyde downe yᵉ one and vp thothar, yᵉ byshope of London, wᵗ many othar bysshopes, beynge mytryd, & yᵉ byshope of London goynge vndar a canapie : and at nyght by yᵉ comaundement of yᵉ lord mayre & yᵉ aldarmen bonefyars were made thrwghe out yᵉ hole citie wᵗ bells ryngynge solomly ; all whiche thyngs wer done for Joye of yᵉ restorynge of yᵉ trewe & catholyke relygyon, and for yᵉ abolysshment of schismes and heresyes.

Vpon Monday, beynge yᵉ fowrthe of Februarie, one [John][4] Rodgers, vycar of sent Sepulchres, was burnyd in Smythefelde.

[1] This is clearly corrupt. 'One' and 'vnytie' have marks of abbreviation over them. Perhaps 'in omni unitate.'

[2] Wriothesley (ii. 125) says 16ᵗʰ January. *Summary*, xxii January.

[3] The procession of the buck: see Machyn, p. 80.

[4] Blank in MS.

Vpon Monday, beynge yͤ 18 of Februarie, yͤ byshope of Ely, callyd doctour Hethe,[1] wt yͤ vycounte Broune,[2] and dyvers othar well apparylyd rode forthe of yͤ citie towards Rome.[3]

Vpon Thursedaye in yͤ night, beynge yͤ xiiij. of Marche, yͤ Image of a byshope,[4] whiche was newly sett vp of late ovar yͤ dore of sent Thomas of Acars, was shamefully mangled, yͤ heade & yͤ ryght arme beynge cleane smyttyn of : yͤ whiche Image ones before this tyme had yͤ hede lykewyse stryken of, and was aftarwarde newly set vp, and nowe eft sones broken.

Vpon Saterday in yͤ mornynge, beynge yͤ xvj. day of Marche, a wevar whiche dwellyd in Shordyche was burned in Smythefylde for heresye.[5]

Vpon Eastarday, beynge yͤ xiiij. day of Aprill, 1555, a certayne desperate person wt a wood knyffe woundyd a priste, as he was mynestrynge the sacrament in sent Margaretes churche at Westmystar, vnto yͤ people : of whiche wounde yͤ pryest was in great daunger of deathe, the churche of sent Margaretis was imedyatly shut in, and no more servyce don.[6]

Vpon sent Marks even, beynge Wednysday & yͤ xxiiij. day of Aprell, yͤ sayd desperate persone, whiche hurte yͤ priest at Westmystar, was burnyd for heresy at Westmystar in sent Margaretes churche yarde.

Vpon Tewesdaye, beynge yͤ vij. day of Maye, a certayn lewd heretyke called Tolly,[7] a pultar, who aboute x. days past had bene hangyd for robberye, & had ben buryed betwen Charinge crosse &

---

[1] Nicholas Heath had been already translated to York; it should be Thomas Thirlby.

[2] Anthony Browne, viscount Montague.

[3] *Summary* but reading: 'byshop of Ely, with the lord Mountacute.'

[4] Thomas Becket. See Wriothesley, ii. 127.

[5] *Summary*, Wriothesley (ii. 127) gives his name Thomas Tompkins.

[6] *Summary*, but adding the miscreant's name (William Flower) and giving more particulars of his punishment.

[7] Wriothesley (ii. 128) calls him John Towley, and says he had been hanged on 26th April, for the robbery of a Spaniard at Shrovetide.

raygne y^t sent Gorgis² felde was coveryd wt watar, & betwen sente Gorgis and Newynton, that for ye space of vj. dayes whyres myght go ther : and it cam into Westmystar hawle halffe a yarde depe, & in to ye palace of Westmynstar, & in to Lambythe churche, that men mowght rowe aboute ye churche wt a whyrey.³

About ye ix.⁴ day of Nouember folowynge ye byshope of Wynchest. doctour Styvene Gardenar, departyd this mortall lyffe : and his body was buryed at Wynchestar.⁵

[1] The lower half of f. 20ro is left blank.
[2] St George's, Southwark.
[3] *Summary* with slight variations. In the *Annales*, 1061 Stow gives a somewhat fuller and different account from Wriothesley's *Chronicle*, ii. 130.
[4] On 12th November.
[5] The remainder of f. 21 is blank.

A BRIEF LONDON CHRONICLE

1547-1564

K. Edward the 6.   Hobilthor.[1] mayor

A° 2.

This yere the kynges ship named the menyon did take a grete spaynysh shyp in the naro sease mannyd weth scott & halff ladyn wth costly goods.

The 15 day of May doctor Smyth[2] of Oxforde, y^t did rede the dyvynite lector at Whitingdon colege, did recant at Poulis crosse.

Doctor Langriche,[3] archdeacon of Clefland in Yorkeshire, did willfully lepe out of the cloyster of saint Magnus into the Temse, willfully drownyd hymselff yn ye month of May.

A° 2° J. Gressam,[4] mayor.

In the latter end of Januarii was soche vehement windes that damaged sore the western barges, & ye lade barges from London to Grauysende to London : a grocer of this citie, his wyfe, his seruant all were drownyd in a whery, sauyng the seruant & one of ye whery men.

In the latter ende Februarii one of the kynges bregendynes did

---

[1] Henry Hubbarthorne.

[2] Richard Smith (d. 1563) see *D.N.B.* liii. 101.

[3] Richard Langriche, Langridge, or Langreth, Rector of Weldrake, Yorkshire, Archdeacon of Cleveland from 1534, and prebendary of South Muskham, Southwell, from 1538 (Le Neve, *Fasti*, iii. 148, 432).

[4] Sir John Gresham.

Ther were dyuerse rebellions yn sondry placis of ye realme : the mayor & citizens of Exciter manfully kept ye city from the rebelles of Deuonshire, till thei wt in were almost famyshed.

This yere was partyes put yn by the nobilite of this realme for the safegard of the kinges royall person, but praysed be God it was gentilly quieted.

500 souldiers of Arde [3] com nere to Guysnes purposyng to had a great boty of catell; but ther were resisted by the men of Guysnes, & of ye men were 50 prisoners takyn, and 103 of them slayne.

Hill, mayor.

A° 4° trynyte terme was reiournyd to myhelmas, ffor that the gentylmen shuld kepe the people quyete wt owt comosion. This mayor was a gode mynystrer of Justice, & a grete ponyssher of adultery.

[Jud [4]] mayor.

In a° 5 be reson that o^r mony was so base the exchaunge to Andwarp was vnder 17 s. the li.

In May there cam a hoye to London wt Holond chese, whiche was solde for 2 d the lb., and that after the rate of Essex chese vj. s. the way.

[1] Of Wriothesley *Chron.* ii. 2.
[2] Sir Henry Amcotes.
[3] Ardres.
[4] 'dobs' was written in MS., but afterwards crossed out.

Dobs, mayor.

A⁰ 6. the erle of Arundell & the lorde Paget were comytted prisoners to the Tower. The erle was afterward relesed, the lorde Paget by a chapter of yᵉ knyghtes of the gartar dymyssed from the same order.

Barns, mayor.
Quene Mary.

When the bisshop of Win., chaunceler, did mynyster the othe to Justices of this realme he wolde not mynyster to Justice Halis,[1] ffor he sayde he had to talke wᵗ him in maters of religion.

The ix. of September yᵉ archebyshop of Cauntorbery and Mʳ Latymer wer comytted prisoners to the Tower.

T. Whight, mayor.

A⁰ 1⁰. the 13 of Nouember the lady Jane, before proclaymyd qwene, & the archebyssop of Cauntorbery wer araigned at the gwylde hall ffor treson, & shortly after she was beheded at the Tower hill.

In Feuerer the archebysshop of Cauntorbery, doctor Ridleye, & Mʳ Latymer were remouyd from the Tower to Oxford.

Ironmonger.[2]

In Marche died Julius,[3] bisshop of Rome, for whom yᵉ qwene caused a solem funerall seruice to be done at Powlis.

In the iij. yere the qwen did remyt the first frute of Xᵗʰˢ

Garett,[4] mayor.

Doctor Gardynar, bisshop of Winchester & chaunceler died.

---

[1] Sir James Hales. See *D.N.B.* xxiv. 29. See also Grafton, *Chronicle*, ii. 537.

[2] This is inserted; 'ironmonger' had first been written after the next sentence. The mayor for 1554-55 was John Lion, grocer.

[3] Julius III died on 5ᵗʰ March, 1555; the service for him at St Paul's was on 17ᵗʰ April, see Wriothesley, *Chron.* ii. 127.

[4] Sir William Gerard.

men & women.

In the begynnyng of Julii iij. shipes of this citye comyng from Andwarp ladin w{t} riche marchandise were takyn by Scottes and Frenchemen, whiche were estemyd to be better worth than 20000 li.

Quene Elisabeth.   Leigh, mayor,

In a⁰ 1⁰ no thing to noate.

Hewet, mayor.

A⁰ 2⁰ the qwene did send ij. of her ships to the see to take a pirate namyd Strangwysh,[2] who wt his ij. ships & ij. other capitaynes wt owt makyng of any resistence did yelde.

Chestar.

There was so grete scarsety of corne that y{e} mayor & citizens made prouyson for wheat & rye 30000 q{rs} from beyond the se.

Harpour, mayor.

The occasion whervppon the qwene did send to New hauyn was the lorde Vidame, capitayne of New hauyn, & the bayly of Roen,[3] the treasorer of Deep[4] offered the forsayde townys to the qwenes

---

[1] Martin Bucer, and Paul Fagius ; the date of their exhumation was 6{th} Feb., 1557.

[2] Machyn, *Diary*, 206, 212-3. Strangwysh was brought to the Tower on 10{th} August 1559.

[3] Rouen.

[4] Dieppe.

magesty, if it wolde please her to further them in theire procedinges of the gospell, for that her mageste is right inheritor to y^em & to all Fraunce.[1]

Lodge, mayor.

A⁰ 5⁰ in Marche all the English marchantes wt ther goodes & shipes wer arested al Burdeus.

The men of Plymmoth did take 14 brettysshe ships wt salt & wyne.

The men of Seaton & legis from the towne of Deepe did take 15 crayers to New hauyn wt vitayll at sondry tymes.

A man of Plymmoth namyd Hawkins,[2] did take a French ship comyng from Gynys wholely ladyn.

A crayer of Rye wt 30 men in her did take a ship in Deep rode, & if there had bene more men they might haue takyn one other ship.

A passenger of Douer sayling to Dunkirk was takyn by a hayne of Diepe comyng owt of Cales, & conuayed to Calies, & there put them to their ransom.

The forsayde hayne was well knowen to ye men of Douer, that he was a comen saylor betwene Diepe and Caleis : Thes men of Douer wt a crayer well mannyd lay in wayte for hym shortly after betwen Bolen and Cales, & did take him ladyn wt canuas & howsolde stuff to Dales, whiche was to them a gode recompence.

In this somer did fall so greate aboundance of rayne in Zeland that hops were so scant that they were solde in London for liij. s. iiij. d. the C. ; & some bere breuars practised to brew wt brome & some w^t bay beries.

John Whight, mayor.

In the begynnyng of Nouember 24 western ships did toke 17 bretisshe ships laden wt wyne, and if one of the   had not bene

---

[1] This seems to be quoted by Stow, *Annales*, 1101. ed. 1605.
[2] Presumably John Hawkyns, who came home from his first voyage to the Spanish Main in Sept., 1563.

In the 30 day of August it was enacted that all soche as wolde sell their waris, plate or howsold stuff to theire most aduantage, for the paying of o^r dettes or elles for the fordell of orphans, sholde bring the same waris &c. to Ledyn hall on Monday & Friday, there to be solde to them that wolde gyue most for it.³

In this yere was browght to ye citie great plente of frute, for ther cam in one market in to Southwark ⁴ cartes wt frute, in to Graschirche strete xiiij. cartes, besids a greate qwantytie that was browght on horsbacke, in panyers and dossars : this contynuyd the moste parte of the somer.

¹ *Summary* p. 275; *Annales* p. 1103.
² No doubt a whale; it was driven ashore at Grimsby, was 19 yards long and yielded two tons of oil. See *Summary*, which is much fuller than *Annales*.
³ *Summary* with considerably more detail. Omitted in *Annales*.
⁴ The MS. is damaged.

A

Albury, 23.
Aldermary, *see* St Mary.
Aldersgate St., 36.
Aldgate, 28.
Allen, John, a priest, 14.
Allen, *or* Allyn, Sir John, 11.
Allhallows Barking, 10.
Allhallows, Bread St., 6, 7.
Allyn *see* Allen.
Amcotes, Sir Henry, 17, 45.
Andrew Moreys Quay, 3.
Antwerp, (Andwarp), 45, 47.
Arden of Faversham, 22.
Ardres, 45.
Arthur, prince of Wales, 7.
Arundell, Earl of, *see* Fitzalan.
Arundell, Humphrey, 17, 20.
Arundell. Sir Thomas, 26.
Askew, Christopher, 8.
Audley, Sir Thomas, 6.
Austin friars, 9.
Axholme, (Exsam), 10.

B

Baldry, Thomas, 2.
Bangor, bishop of, *see* Salcot, John.
Barnes, George, 26, 46.
Barns, Robert, 2.
Barton, Elizabeth (Anne) the Holy Maid of Kent, 8, 9.
Baynam, 6.
Baynards Castle, 8, 27.
Bell, a Suffolk man, 21.
Bermondsey Priory, 12.
Beauvale, 10.
Berrys, *or* Bery, a rebel, 20.
Bilney, *or* Bylneye, Thomas, 5.
Bishop Clist, 17, 18.
Black friars, 14.
Blackwall, 9.
Bletchingley, 23.
Bocher, Joan, 21.
Bockyng, Edward, 8.
Boleyn, Ann, Queen, 7, 8, 9.
Boleyn, Sir Thomas, Earl of Wiltshire, 4, 7.
Bonner, Edmund, bishop of London, 29, 31, 41.
Bordeaux, (Burdeus), 48.
Boulogne, (Bulloyne, Bolen), 7, 21, 48.
Bowes, Sir Martin, 17.
Bowler, a rebel, 18.
Boyer, William, 16.
Bread St., 6, 7, 9.
Bret, Alexander, 33, 34.
Bretons, 48, 49.
Bridewell, 2.
Bristol, 47.
Broad Causeway, Westminster, 25.
Broken Wharf, 9.
Browne, Anthony, Viscount Montague, 42.
Bryce, Hugh, 1.
Bucer, Martin, 47.
Bylneye, Thomas, 5.

4

INDEX

C

Calais, 7, 26, 48.
Cambridge, 2, 3, 27, 28, 47.
Canterbury, 8, 9, 22.
Canterbury, Archbishops of, *see* Cranmer, Pole.
Carew, Sir Nicholas, 15.
Carow, Charles, 16.
Catherine of Aragon, Queen, 7, 8, 27.
Champneys, John, 10.
Chantries, 13.
Charing Cross, 9, 42.
Charterhouse, The 10, 15, 16.
Cheap, Cheapside (Chepe), 1, 2, 4, 8, 14, 19, 25, 27, 34, 41.
Cheap Cross, 1, 5, 34, 36.
Cheeke, Sir John, 28.
Chessher, Thomas, 16.
Chester, William, 47.
Chipping Norton, 18.
Cholmley, Sir Roger, 28.
Christchurch, *or* Trinity Priory, 6.
Clarke, Griffith, 15.
Cleveland, 44.
Cobham, Lord, 31.
Cobham, Thomas, 33.
Coinage, coiners, 2, 4, 6, 14, 23, 24.
Cooke, Laurence, 16.
Corbyt, Sir Richard, 28.
Cornwall, 17.
Cotes, John, 16.
Counters, The, 34.
Courtenay, Edward, Earl of Devonshire, 29, 34.
Court-up-street, 8.
Cranmer, Thomas, Archbishop of Canterbury, 19, 22, 31, 35, 46.
Crofte, Elizabeth, 36.
Cromwell, Thomas, Earl of Essex, 9, 15, 16.
Croydon, 23.

D

Dacre of the North, Lord, 9.
Darcie, Thomas, Lord, 14.
Daunce, Hary, *see* Harridaunce.
Deryng, Richard, 8.
Devonshire, Earl of, *see* Courtenay
Devonshire, 17, 45.
Dieppe, 47, 48.
Dobbes, Richard, 24, 46.
Dodmer, Ralph, 4.
Dolman, Dr., 31.
Doncaster, 16.
Dormer, Michael, 16.
Dover, 48.
Dudley, Ambrose, 28.
Dudley, Sir Andrew, 28.
Dudley, Guilford, 31, 33.
Dudley, Henry, 28, 31.
Dudley, John, Earl of Warwick, and Duke of Northumberland, 19, 21, 24, 27, 28, 29.
Dudley, Robert, 31.
Dunkirk, 48.
Dutchmen, 2, 5, 23, 30.

E

Edward VI, King, 17-26, 29, 44-46.
Elizabeth, Queen, 27, 35, 36, 47-49.
Elsing Spittle, 12.
Esher, 4.
Essex, Earls of, *see* Cromwell, Parr.
Essex, 21.
Ewell, Thomas, 14.
Exeter, 17, 45.
Exmew, William, 10.
Exsam, *see* Axholme.

F

Fagius, Paul, 47.
Fenchurch, 29.

INDEX

Finsbury Field, 2, 4, 5, 6.
Fires, 3, 4, 7, 8, 9, 14.
Fisher, John, bishop of Rochester, 5, 10.
Fitzalan, Henry, Earl of Arundel, 27, 46.
Flanders, 25.
Fleet St., 33, 38.
Fleet Prison, 35, 39, 41.
Flower, William, 42.
Forman, William, 14.
Fostar, a heretic, 3.
Framlingham, 27.
France, 2, 48.
Francis I, King of France, 3.
Frith *or* Frythe, John, 7, 9.

G

Gambold, *or* Gambo, Peter, 20.
Gardiner, Stephen, bishop of Winchester and Chancellor, 22, 29, 31, 40, 41, 43, 45, 46.
Gates, Henry, 28.
Gates, Sir John, 28, 29.
Gavaro, Charles, 20.
Gerard, Sir William, 46.
Godstone, 23.
Gold, *or* Goulde, Henry, parson of Aldermary, 8, 9.
Gold, Thomas, 8.
Gracechurch, 4, 29.
Gracechurch (Gracious) St., 30, 38, 49.
Gravesend, 1, 28, 30, 44.
Gray's Inn, 7.
Great Conduit, The, 34.
Greenwich, 2, 6, 9, 32, 43.
Gresham, Sir John, 17, 44.
Gresham, Richard, 14.
Grey, Henry, Duke of Suffolk, 24, 28, 33, 35.
Grey Lady Jane, 31, 33, 46.
Grey of Wilton, William, Lord, 17, 18, 24, 26, 28.

Grey friars, 9, 15.
Gryffyn, Rhys, 5.
Guildhall, The, 31, 35, 46,
Guisnes, 26, 45, 48.

H

Hales, Sir James, 46.
Hall, Edward, 7, 10.
Hampton Court, 19, 20.
Harford, Thomas, 14.
Harper, William, 47.
Harman, a coiner, 2.
Harmond, a searcher of Gravesend, 28.
Harpsfield, Nicholas, 37.
Harridaunce, John, 15.
Harssam, Harry, 14.
Hastings, Francis, Earl of Huntingdon, 28.
Hastings, George, Earl of Huntingdon, 4.
Havre, *or* New Haven, 47, 48.
Hawkyns, Sir John, 48.
Hayle, John, 10.
Heath, Nicholas, Archbishop of York, 42.
Henry IV, 1.
Henry VII, 1.
Henry VIII, 1-17.
Herbert, Sir William, Earl of Pembroke, 17, 24, 27.
Heresy, and heretics, 1, 3, 5, 7, 8, 10, 13, 15, 21, 23, 41, 42.
Herne, *or* Horne, Giles, 16.
Hewet, William, 47.
Hewitt, Andrew, 7, 9.
Hill, Sir Rowland, 19, 45.
Holborn, 7, 16.
Holland, 10.
Holles, William, 15.
Holmes, Thomas, 21.
Honey Lane, 3.
Honiton, 17.
Horne, parson of St. Nicholas Willows, 24.

INDEX

Howard, Thomas, Duke of Norfolk, 29, 34.
Howard, Lord William, 26.
Hubberthorne, Sir Henry, 17, 44.
Humber, 25.
Hungerford, Agnes, Lady, 2.
Hungerford, Walter, Lord, 16.
Huntingdon, Earls of, *see* Hastings.
Hussey, John, Lord, 14.

Isleworth (Thystylworth), 10.
Isley, *or* Illisleye, Sir Henry, 31, 33.

J

Judd, Andrew, 21, 45.
Julius III, Pope, 46.

K

Kendall, Thomas, 13.
Kent, 8, 21, 31, 34.
Kett, Robert, 18, 19.
King's Head, The, Smithfield, 20.
Kingston, 32.
Knevett, Master, 4.
Knevet, William, 33.

L

Lacie, Mr., 5, 6.
Lambard, Nicholas, 5.
Lambert, John, 15.
Lambeth, 22, 39, 43.
Lambeth marsh, 9.
Langriche, Richard, 44.
Latimer, Hugh, 35, 46.
Laxton, Sir William, 16.
Leadenhall, 4, 32, 49.
Lee, Thomas, 11.

Leicester, 33.
Leigh, Thomas, 47.
Lesnes, 25.
Lincoln, 13.
Lodge, Thomas, 48.
Lombards, 9.
London, bishops of, *see* Bonner, Ridley.
London Bridge, 9, 33, 38.
Louth, 13.
Lowe, Simon, 35, 39, 40, 41.
Lucas, Emanuel, 35, 39, 40, 41.
Ludgate, 33.
Luther, Martin, 3.
Lyon, John, 39.

M

Makkarell, Matthew, 13.
Marching-watch, the, 5, 15.
Marshalsea, The, 15, 29.
Mary, Queen, 7, 27-43, 46-47.
Mary of Guise, Queen of Scotland, 25.
Masters, Richard, 8.
Mercers Hall, 19.
Mews, The, at Charing Cross, 9.
Middlemore, Humphrey, 10.
Middleton Stony, 26.
Mile End, 2.
Miles, Dr. Nicholas, 4.
Montague, Sir Edward, 28.
Montague, Viscount, *see* Browne.
More, Sir Thomas, 4, 6, 10, 11.
Morysbye, Thomas, 22.
Myryll, a tyler, 13.

N

New Abbey, London, 12.
Newark, 9.
Newcastle, 9.
Newdigate, *or* Nydygate, Sebastian, 10.

Richmond, 8, 9, 36.
Richmond, Henry, Duke of, 2.
Ridley Nicholas, Bishop of London, 26, 27, 28, 35, 46.
Risby, Richard, 8.
Rhodes, (Rodes) Master of the, 3.
Roche, William, 16.
Rochester, 33.
Rochester, bishop of, *see* Fisher.
Rode Lane, 14.
Rogers, John, 41.
Rome, 3, 42.
Rouen, 47.
Rudstone, John, 3.
Russell, John, Lord, 17.
Rycote, Oxfordshire, 18, 36.
Rye, 48.

S

St Andrew by the Wardrobe, 6.
St Antholin's, 4, 14.
St Anthony's School, 3, 11.
St Bartholomew's Priory, 12.
St Bride, Fleet Street, 4.
St George's Field, Southwark, 43.
St James' Palace, 25, 33.
St John, the Lord of, 19.
St John's Priory, 3.
St Katherine's, 25.
St Magnus, 44.
St Margaret's, Friday St., 15.
St Margaret's, Westminster, 42.
St Mary Aldermary, 8.

St Mary Overy, 7, 12.
St Mary Spittle, 12, 45.
St Nicholas Willows, 22, 24.
St Paul's, 1, 2, 3, 5, 6, 12, 15, 22, 25, 29, 30, 31, 38, 39, 46.
St Paul's Cross, 6, 8, 13, 15, 27, 34, 36, 37, 40, 44.
St Paul's School, 11.
St Sepulchre's, 13, 41.
St Thomas of Acre, 11, 13, 42.
St Thomas Watering, 15.
Salcot, John, bishop of Bangor, 8.
Salters Hall, 9.
Sandys, Edwin, 28.
Seamar, Thomas, 2.
Seaton, 48.
Seymour, Anne, Duchess of Somerset, 24, 29.
Seymour, Edward, Duke of Somerset, 19, 20, 21, 24, 25, 26.
Seymour, Thomas, Lord, 17.
Shoreditch, 42.
Skotte, John, 4.
Smith, Dr. Richard, 44.
Smith, Sir Thomas, 19, 20.
Smithfield, 3, 5, 6, 7, 10, 15, 20, 21, 22, 23, 38, 41, 42.
Somar, Thomas, 5.
Somerset, 18.
Somerset, Duke of, *see* Seymour.
Sothewell, Sir Robert, 34.
Southwark, 7, 20, 32, 34, 38, 43, 49.
Spain, 1, 43, 47.
Spencer, James, 3.
Standard, The, in Cheap, 4. 8.
Stanhope, Sir Michael, 20, 24, 26.
Stansted, 13.
Star Chamber, 39.
Steelyard, The (Stilaard), 2, 29, 38.
Stocks, The, 38.
Strangwysh, *or* Strangways, pirate, 47.
Stratford, 2.
Suffolk, 18, 21.

Suffolk, Duke of, *see* Grey.
Suffolk Place, Southwark, 20, 38.
Sussex, Earl of, *see* Radcliffe.

T

Taylor, John, Master of the Rolls, 9.
Temple Bar, 9, 33, 38.
Thame, 18.
Thames, 2, 22, 25, 45.
Thirlby, Thomas, bishop of Ely, 42.
Thomas, William, 35.
Thomson, Harry, 5.
Throckmorton, Nicholas, 35, 39, 40, 41.
Thwaytes, Edward, 8.
Tompkins, Thomas, 42.
Tower of London, The, 5, 6, 8, 9, 11, 14, 15, 16, 19, 21, 22, 24, 27, 28, 29, 33, 34, 35, 36, 45, 46.
Tower Hill, 4, 5, 6, 10, 15, 16, 17, 25, 26, 33, 35.
Tower Wharf, 43.
Towley, *or* Tolly, John, 42.
Trinity, *or* Christchurch Priory, London, 6.
Tunstal, Cuthbert, bishop of Durham, 29.
Tyburn, 2, 5, 9, 10, 13, 14, 16, 21, 36.
Tyndal, William, 5.

V

Vane, Sir Ralph, 24, 26.
Vintry, The, 4.

W

Wandsworth, 15.
Warwick, Earl of, *see* Dudley.
Warryn, *or* Warren, Ralph, 13.

LIFE OF
SIR JOHN DIGBY

GEORGES BERNARD, Licencié ès-Lettres
LATE SCHOLAR IN THE UNIVERSITY OF PARIS
MEMBER OF THE NON-COLLEGIATE BODY OXFORD

CAMDEN MISCELLANY
VOL. XII

LONDON
OFFICES OF THE SOCIETY
6 & 7 SOUTH SQUARE
GRAY'S INN
1910

The following *Life* was found in manuscript by the present writer in the course of a research connected with the history of the Royalist party in the time of Charles the First. It appeared to be worthy of interest to the scholars to whom it was communicated, because it throws some light on a hitherto not much known personality. Indeed, Sir John Digby had the misfortune to be the brother of a great man. The name of Digby is almost always associated with that of Sir Kenelm. And yet Sir John achieved no mean a reputation in his own times. The famous *Hector Britannicus* of the following pages[1] deserves more notice than he

[1] [In the Dictionary of National Biography there are lives both of the author and his hero. Edward Walsingham is there described as 'royalist author and intriguer' and said to be a kinsman of the Digbys (D N B. LIX. 230). He was also the author of Lives of Sir John Smith (Britannicae Virtutis Imago, 1644) and Sir Henry Gage (Alter Britanniae Heros. 1645). Walsingham was deeply engaged in all the political intrigues in favour of the Catholics, and also in those for the conversion of the Duke of Gloucester and the removal of Hyde from the service of Charles II. 'A pragmatical knave', 'a great babbler of his most secret employments' and 'a busy instrument of the Jesuits' are amongst the terms applied to him by Royalists of the orthodox Protestant type.

Sir John Digby the brother of Sir Kenelm who is the subject of this memoir should not be confused with the Sir John Digby of Mansfield Woodhouse, Nottinghamshire, who is so frequently mentioned by Mrs. Hutchinson in the life of her husband. The two are so confused in the index to Macray's edition of Clarendon's Rebellion. In David Lloyd's 'Memoirs of the Lives etc. of those excellent personages who suffered... for allegiance to their sovereign, folio 1968, the two personages are properly distinguished (pp. 580, 581) C. H. FIRTH.].

64   PREFACE

has received at the hands of historians. The opportunity of paying a tribute to his memory, and of making easily accessible to all this new source of historical information, was readily seized by the Royal Historical Society.

The volumes in the Camden Series being chiefly devoted to the presentation of texts, it is not possible to prefix any lengthy commentary on the " Life " itself ; it will suffice to add a few words concerning the manuscript itself

This is described as follows in the catalogue of the Bibliothèque Nationale, Paris.[1]

Hector Britannicus or Sir John Digby, late Major General of his Majestie's Western forces... Angl. Acquisitions nouvelles, No. 56. Gaignières 1034[2].

It became the property of the Bibliothèque Nationale, together with the rest of the Gaignières Collection. How it fell into the hands of Gaignières is not so surely known. It probably belonged to the library of Sir Kenelm Digby, to whom it is dedicated. When Sir Kenelm died in France, it is supposed that his books became the property of the King of France, in fulfilment of the "Droit d'Aubaine." They were bought by Georges Digby who sold them in London in 1680.[2] It might be supposed, however, that some of the Manuscripts or books remained in France, and amongst them probably the Manuscript of the " Life."

As to the author of the Life, according to Professor Firth, his name is Edward Walsingham, a Catholic gentleman very intimate with Sir Kenelm Digby. He also wrote lives of Sir Henry Gage and Sir John Smith which are printed. Verses printed at the end of the " Life " will be found to refer to these two names.

The only point in which the following printed text does not completely conform with the original manuscript concerns the use of capitals at the beginning of words. In the original manuscript, almost all nouns are spelt with a capital at the beginning. In his aim at obtaining a photographic (so to speak) reproduction of the

[1] Catalogue des manuscrits anglais.
[2] Edwards. Memoirs of Libraries ii. 116.

carried through and who has contributed
Preface. Nor can he forget to thank
Louis Cazamian, Maîtres de Conférences
ndly assistance.

GEORGES BERNARD.

TO MY NOBLE FREND AND ENGLISH MECOENAS
OF ALL LEARNING
Sr KENELME DIGBY
UPON THE VERTUOUS AND MARTIALL LIFE
OF HIS WORTHILY ADMIRED BROTHER
SIR JOHN DIGBY

Much honour'd S^r, your noble Brothers worth,
Whose Justice, Prudence, Valour were most rare
Made mee ambitious his praise to set forth,
And with the Trojan Hector him compare ¶   Fol. 1 D
For Hector-like his foes hee did with stand,
From Warlike fury to secure this Land;
I might an English Scipio have hym stil'd,
As well for skill in armes, as Modestie,
Who could not brooke to see his King exil'd
From Honour due to Sacred Majestie ;
In whose defense hee made himself a shield,
Waging for King Charles Warre in bloody field.
I might Horatius Cocles have hym nam'd,
Who, gainst Porsenna's Army, single stood
On Tibers Bridge, for which Act hee is fam'd ;
So almost sole, our brave Sr John made good
The Horse and Foots retreat against ye Scot,
At Newborne fight, W^{ch} nére shall bee forgot. ¶   Fol. 2
I might Camillas rightly have him call'd,
Who though by Rome exil'd, yet, at her need
The Gaules insulting tirannie hee gaul'd,
Winning from Victours his deserved meed.
So this our Champions Valour hath made
From foes scorching fury to frends a shade

An English Achilles I might hym call,
Whose Valour the worlds Conquerour did grace
Whose brave acts Homer in verse did enstall,
Which mov'd great Alexander to embrace
His gallant tomb, and him thrice happy stile
Whose deeds the Prince of Poets did compile.
But fearefull am I, least with rudest pen
I seeme his Gests Heroick to deface, ¶
And undervalew this Mirrour of Men,
Who did his Kingdome with his Vertues grace
Yet this my comfort is, his Brother can
Refine what doth transcend my small skills span.

Fol. 2 D

FINIS.

AND HIS COUNTRY GREAT BRITAINE.

Although the whole Life of this our brave worthy, rare type of Vertue and Valour, Sʳ John Digby may not unfitly in my judgment bee parallelled to a well polished mirrour; yet, as a looking-glasse when it is entire, doth onely represent the features of one single person at once, but if broken into severall parcells it will contract ¶ the species and will show in each small piece, shadowed to the Life, what soever visage or object is proposed before it: in like manner if you contemplate and view Sʳ John Digbie, you shall see in generall a vertuous and compleatly civill gentleman a valiant souldier, and an expert commaunder, but if you please to breake as it were this perfect glasse of his Life into sondry particles, the skilfull warriour and officer shall see his owne pourtraiture in hym lively expressed, the learned scholler, the civill bachelour, the refined traveler, and accomplished gentleman, in regarding hym may fruitfully observe what they are, or should bee, and most vertuous Ladies and gentlewomen, as well of the Court as Countrie, may with much praise and commendations paint themselves before this glasse with the well tempered Colours of his Modestie and Bashfulnesse; yea children and youth may herein behold and admire their own native Candour and harmelesse Innocency; and ¶ in a word all kind and condition of Men and Women may improve themselves by diligently looking in this glasse of Sʳ John Digby his life.

Now as for his vertues, good qualities, and speciall endowments, both of Grace, and Nature, briefly couched in a succinct character, as an Appendix, or Labell to the rest (upon designe, not to

Sʳ John compared to a looking glasse.

Fol. 3 D

Fol. 4

interrupt the series and context of his Martiall achievements) I hope I shall prove so farre from exaggerating therein, that whosoever had the happinesse to know him familiarly, will evidently perceave I come much short of what might truly bee averred in so ample and large a subject; but I wittingly and willingly rather chose to bee sparing in his due and deserved praises, then by seeming to hyperbolize to wrong both my self and him, whose knowne Worth was of so high a pitch that it needeth no flattering glasse or flourishing varnish of soothing words to set of his Vertuous comportment and admired Valour.

<small>Fol. 4 D</small>

Intending therefore with the rude pensill of my impolished pen to limme in the bright Colours of ¶ Heroicall exploits the picture of our pious and valiant souldier Sr John Digby, I will follow the example of picture-drawers, who first prepare their table, then prime it, and lastly having ground and tempered their severall colours set hand to worke, so I will summarily runne over his Noble pedigree, childhood, youth, and Mans Estate, whereby this our table will bee, as I hope, sufficiently disposed to admit the draught and picture of the most materiall and remarkeable passages of his life, which I should bee glad to see perfected by some curious Apelles.

<small>Sr John pious from a child.</small>

Sr John Digby issuing from ancient and illustrious Parentage was borne in the yeare of our Lord one thousand six hundred and five, hee seemed even with his nurses milke to have sucked piety and devotion, and was trained up under the carefull governement and

<small>The Lady Digby carefull to traine hym in Vertue and learning.</small>
<small>Fol. 5</small>

vigilant ey of his discreetly loving mother the Lady Digby of Gotehurst in Buckingham shire, who although shee laboured to her utmost to informe his tender understanding (by the best maisters shee could procure) with learning and other laudable ¶ qualities best sorting with a gentleman, wherein according to his age hee eminently advanced, yet her prime and chief endeavour from his very infancy was, to frame and mold his flexible mind to vertue, and enure hym even from his cradle, to the love and feare of God.

<small>His obedience and duty to ye Lady his mother.</small>

Wherefore from his childish years he gave a pregnant proof and hopefull presage of his ensuing Worth, when hee should write man. Though by his tractable disposition, obsquious duty, and loving

not withstanding her bowells yearned at the thought of her departure from hym, yet shee sacrifized her private content and pleasure to his greater and future good, and being now betwixt thirteene and fourteene yeares of age sent hym into Flaunders, where making his aboad three or fouer yeares hee perfected and polished himself ¶ in the liberal sciences, musique and French, in all which hee was initiated and well grounded before his going. At 14 hee is sent into Flaunders.
Fol. 5 D
Skilfull in ye liberall sciences &.

After his returne and short stay in England, where with his good behaviour and gentile carriage hee graced the places from whence hee came, hee travailed into Italy, and having deligently employed his studies in Philosophie for the tearme of three yeares, he defended his whole course with extraordinary applauses and singular opinion of a learned scholler. Having continued an other yeare at Florence and Venice the better to enable himself in the perfect knowledge of the Italian tongue and other points of civility and gentilenesse, hee returned againe into his country, where hee deservedly among all sorte and condition of people gained the generall repute and style of a rarely qualified young gentleman. He defendeth his course of Philosophy.
He is perfect in Italian.
He returneth into Eng : a compleat Gent.

Crossing Italy from Genua to Venice he fell into the hands of thieves, vulgarly best knowne there by the name of Bandits, who drawing him aside ¶ into an adjacent Wood with intention to have robbed if not killed hym, upon many questions discreetly and undauntedly answeared by hym, they were so taken, that making ostentation of great store of treasure, fruits as they said of those seemingly barren mountaines, they importunely invited and pressed hym to bee their captaine, and to joyne partner and share with them in the reaping of this their fertile and golden Harvest : but hee (inwardly disdaning in his mynd so debauched, lewd and wicked course of life) civilly excusing himself as already engaged in the warres which he could not wave in point of honour, was dismissed by them without the least losse or hurt. So great force hath a He strangely escapeth thieves.
Fol. 6

discreet civility joyntly with a manly and resolute courage to winne upon the affections of men otherwise most lewdly given and viciously bent to all villanie.

Sr John after his arrivall in England at the solicitation and earnest request of the now right Honble ¶ Earle of Portland accompanied hym in his embassie to the State of Venice, where our Young growing worthy merited the stile of a civill, courteous and well bred Cavalier, a name among them and forraine nations of singular esteeme and honour. He became so gratious in that Court, that hee was offred by the Duke and State very hon^{ble} and advantageous entertaynement and yearly large revenues upon condition hee would thinke well to stay among them, but hee thankefully and courteousley refusing their kind invitation, and desirous to use his best talents and endowments in service and honour of his King and Country if occasion should offer itself, returned with my Lord embassadour into England.

Being upon the seas betwixt Calais and Dover and encountred by a Holland man of warre which insteed of vailing sayle, discharged at the Kings ship wherein the Earle was wafted: Sr John nothing amased thereat but walking confidently upon ¶ the hatches, animated the souldiers and mariners to maintaine with the hazard of their lives his Ma^{tes} knowne right and soveraignety at sea. The Hollanders afterwards enquired what gallant young man hee was, who showed such an undaunted courage, and being told, answeared, they thought it was a Digby.

In his travailes hee seemed to have imitated the industrious bee, for whereas divers other English Gentlemen were so farre from improving themselves thereby, that they rather gathered thence the banefull Poison of vice, depraved manners and lewd habits, hee sucked the sweet and delicious honey of Vertue, Learning, and laudable and good qualities, which hee stored up in the pure Hive of his capacious and Heroicall mind.

I will not insist upon his skill at his weapon since London is a sufficient stage of dexterity therein both in jest and earnest, witnesse prime fencers and others though good sword-men, who having ¶

treated Sr John Suckling at Nottingham-Bridge in the righting of a young Lady to whome hee was then suitour, upon her complaint of being wronged by Sr John Suckling who pretended and claymed greater interest in her then ether shee or her freuds did acknowledge. I passe also in silence how Sr John Suckling, in revenge of this affront of being caned, so patiently or rather dastardly then digested, soone after most cowardly assaulted him at Black-friers, where hee attended with his owne single man and accompanied with two frends then casuallie present, without any hurt worsted and put to a disgracefull flight ¶ Sr John Suckling with his sixteen partly frends, partly hirelings who conspired basely to have murdered hym at unawares and upon so great a disadvantage, but he had pinked Sr John Sucklings doublet if hee had not bene secured from many a home-thrust of his vigerous arme by his coat of Maile. Both which actions loudly speake and sound forth his confident boldnesse, his high spirited resolution, and skilfull valour.

 So desirous was hee of some noble enterprise worthy of himself, that he put to sea in the navy Royall well manned and victualed which road upon the Westerne Coasts to cleare the ocean from roving pyrates and to hinder the incursion and inroad of forraine enemyes. He was knighted after this expedition by the right Honble the Earle of Linsey then Lord high Admirall, (who afterwards being his M^atties Generall was unfortunately slaine at Edge-Hill Battaile) according to a speciall commission which his Lord^p had receaved from his M^atie ¶ to bestow that marke of honour and preminence upon those whome hee should find to bee men deserving it. An evident testimony of the extraordinary opinion so sage, discreet and prudent a Lord conceived of hym.

[margin: neth S^r Jo· Suckling.]
[margin: Fol. 8]
[margin: He worseth Sr John Suckling wth 16 others at Blackfr·]
[margin: He goeth to sea wth ye E. of Linsey by whom he was knighted.]
[margin: Fol. 8 D]

Studious of Chivalry.

MadeCornet by yᵉ E. of Arundell.

Fol. 9

The first pacification.

Fol. 9 D

The Kings Army disbanded.

He was addicted especially in later yeares to thee frequent and diligent perusall of those bookes in several languages, whose scope and ayme was practically to handle martiall affaires, wherein he was so well seene that the right Honᵇˡᵉ Thomas Earle of Arundell Lord Marshall of England and then Lord Generall of his Majesties forces in the first Northerne Expedition against the Scots, was pleased to entertaine and harbour so eminent an opinion of his ability and sufficiency therein, that hee made choise of hym for Cornet of his Excellencies owne troop (consisting of two hundred partly knights and gentlemen of faire Estates and large yearly revenues) under his Lordᵖˢ sonne Sʳ William Howard now Lord Vis-count Stafford. In which office and employment Sʳ John so well acquitted ¶ himself, that the managing, ordering, trayning and disciplining the whole troop totally relyed upon his shouldiers, which trust reposed in hym hee discharged with singular content and satisfaction on all sides, though his paines were almost incredible, untill the seeming pacification was concluded and hastily shuffled up, and the kings flourishing Armie disbanded which if it had vigorously pursued the best advantages, would probably have put a happier issue and period to these unfortunate distempers, and stopped the swelling Flood-gates of so much innocent and christian blood, which over-flowing have since dyed in graine and empurpled these three king-domes which once were thrice-happie under the peacefull and mild Governement of his sacred Majestie, our lawfull and dread Sover-aigne King Charles who in after ages may worthily bee entitled Charles the gratious.

About the feast of Sᵗ James the Apostle ¶ this short lived pacifica-tion was huddled up and sworne unto on both sides to bee kept inviolably, whereupon the Kings gallant Army levied and maintayned with vast expence both of the Royall treasure and of private subjects was hastily dismissed, and though the Scots seemingly did the same, yet their comming into England the next yeare argued their intentions not so sincere. For when they perceaved that the cloud of so powerfull an Army which hovering over their borders menaced their King-dome, by the gracious beames of the

Scotland being hightned, a new Royall Army both of Cavalerie and Infantery is suddenly set on foot to make head against them in case of entring England. The right Honble Algernon ¶ Earle of Northumberland declared Generall issued forth divers commissions to sondry well deserving Knights and gentlemen to raise troops out of hand. Among the first hee was pleased to grace our Knight with one, which no sooner came to light and was blazed about the towne but in few days (an evident and pregnant signe how much was respected and honored) so many came flocking in to hym, voluntarily profering their service to bee listed under hym that suddenly hee picked and chose out of them a full troop of gallant, stout and proper men and resolute souldiers and furnished divers other comanders with competent numbers. Fol. 10 He is made Cap^{ne} of Horse. He speedily compleats his troop and furnisheth others.

He chose for his Lieutenant Mr John Smith, (young sonne to the noble and vertuous Lady Smith of Arshby Falloville in Lecestershire and brother to Charles Lord Carington) who then in the Low-Countries by his valour had purchased the repute and esteeme of a well experienced and skilfull Commander and ¶ was afterward knighted at Edge hill for nobly and valiantly with eminent hazard of his life rescuing the Kings standart Royall in the possession of the ennemy. His Cornet was Mr William Twingham now onely sonne and heyre to Sr Thomas Twingham of Twingham in Buckinghamshire, a hansome, civill and well bred gentleman. He chooseth Mr John Smith for his Lieutenant. Fol. 10 D

His troop in a very short tyme perfectly compleated and in fit equipage to march was mustered first in Hide Parke with generall applause, and approbation both of the men and horses, secondly soone after at Newport Pagnell in Buckingham-shire. Whence afterwards his troop hastned to Newcastle upon Tine, where hee was much esteemed both by the prime and chief Comaunders and the Nobility and Gentry of the country round about. His troop mustered in Hide Parke and at Newport.

76   HECTOR BRITANNICUS

          The Scots at Newborne nere unto Newcastle (where with little or no resistance they passed the river) felt the ponderous weight of his martiall ¶ arme, when commaunded by Commissary Generall Wilmot to assist hym in securing the retreat of the remainder of the Kings Horse, and of the body of Foot which otherwise would runne apparent hazard to bee cut of every man, he was assigned to lead up the right hand file in the charge, but those two or three troopes suddenly wheeled of and speeded after the rest to Durham, leaving Sʳ John with his single troop engaged against the whole Army of the Scottish horse to undergoe the unequall shock of the overpowering Ennemy advancing in a firme and united body. Yet his troop with their swords in hands opened and forced their way after their brave Leader, untill a Regiment of Lanciers flanking and traversing them disordered their ranks and severed them to their unspeakable grief from themselves, their colours and Captaine.

          In the interim Sʳ John with two of his stout troopers better mounted then the rest, charged thorough the Army of the Scottish Horse with extraordinary execution ¶ hee rid on a high spirited horse though easily managed, which being wounded in sondry places both of the neck and breast, frequently reared and admitted in his owne body the shot levelled at his riders head ; this gallant palfery in the second thorough charge by reason of his many mortall wounds and losse of blood began to faulter and sinking under his burthen cast his maister, yet without other hurt then losse of his helmet which could not bee recovered by his two faithfull Achates and collaterall champions with other of his troopers casually then meeting, who with much difficulty and danger in regard of the pressing ennemie, remounted hym, when the Scots perceaved hym bareheaded and without his helmet they made at him more furiously then before, but God vouchsafed to bee his helmet and overshadowed his head wonderfully with the heavenly shield of his holy protection in this day of battaile, for nether by sword, carbine nor pistol ¶ which pell-mell were brandished and discharged at his bare head, and came so near that his face glowed

any papist.

Sʳ John courageously and undauntedly replied *Sʳ I am a Roman Catholique and so am resolved to live and dy*: at which resolute ¶ answeare the coronell admiring said, *Sʳ because you are so* gallant *and noble a gentleman, the least haire of your head shall not bee touched* by whom and the rest of the scottish commaunders and nobility during his emprisonment in Newcastle hee was treated with singular respect, civilitie and courtesie. A rare president to bee imitated by all souldiers towards their prisoners. His resolute answeare.
Fol. 12 D

The Scots gallant Enemies.

Sʳ John as hee was led to the Scottish quarters, where he lay all night in the field ill accommodated of all necessaries (a cold comfort and refreshment after so hot, gallant and long service) hee saw in the way one of his footmen lying on the ground with his face downeward. *There lies*, saith hee, *dead one who living was my man* at whose voice the servant joyfully starting up, was unmeasurably glad for his maisters life whome hee conceaved also dead though sorrowfull for his captivity, wherein he was licenced by the Scots to waite upon hym as formerly. ¶ Sʳ John lieth all night in yᵉ field.

Fol. 13

In the tyme of his restraint the Scottish Commaunders highly extolled his approved and tryed valour; and much wondered at his strange and unusuall temper, adding they had never seene nor met with such a man whome they could nether see moved to indignation and wrath inticed to drinke, nor allured to speake ill of others, and free from other vices incident to many men; The Scots use hym wᵗʰ great respect.

They wonder at his temper.

6

A notable testimony of Enemies.	which elogium and commendation uttered by the mouthes of professed ennemies doth remarkeably set of the lustre of his innocent and vertuous Life, and noble worth.
His troop rallied by his Lieu-Sm.	His troop shrewdly shattered and diminished was rallied togeather by the prudent and vigilant care of their gallant Lieutenant Smith, and repaired to their unwillingly forsaken colours with sad and heavy hearts for the losse of their noble captaine, whome generall report and belief for divers dayes confirmed dead, when they were
Fol. 13 D	acertayned that hee was alive, and not wounded but prisoner ¶ they were restlesse untill they could finde some fit opportunity to fall upon some of the Scottish forces whereby they hoped to compasse his liberty by some equivalent exchange. Wherefore the brave
His troop quartereth nere yᵉ Enemy.	Lieutenant with his forlorne troop was desirous to quarter nere the frontiers of the Enemie, both to keep them from annoying the country or if upon confidence of their late successe at Newborne (where they found not such a valiant resistance as might have bene expected from true bred English men issuing from Ancestours which had erected many noble trophies of their signall Victories both in Scotland, France and elsewhere) they should presume to venture out in parties, they might perhaps come short home, which hapned not long after at Stapleton nere Richmond, where the Lieutenant so discreetly and advisedly managed his designe (as already hath bene set forth at large by a good pen) that having
Sʳ Archibald Douglas taken by his Lieutenant. Fol. 14	killed divers upon the place hee brought Sʳ Archibald Douglasse high sheriffe of Tinedale and commaunder ¶ in chief with many officers and souldiers prisoner to his Matʸ then residing at Yorke, where the gallant Lieutenant was receaved with extraordinary joy and universall acclamations, and generall applause of his Heroicall Valour.
Sʳ John is released from emprisonment.	This business so seasonably and happily atchived did much facilitate and hasten the mutuall exchange of prisoners on both sides accorded and agreed unto upon a second pacification, whereunto his Mᵃᵗⁱᵉ was pleased gratiously to condescend being loath to spill his subjects blood and engage his two Kingdomes in a Nationall Warre, hoping by his so exemplar Mercie and Indulgence to reduce

hitherto unquencheable combustion.

¶ You may more easilie conceave then I expresse in words how joyfull meeting and greeting there was at Yorke betwixt Sr John and his brave Lieutenant how cheerefull was his faithfull, though now small and shrunck troop, revived at his long desired presence. Fol. 14 D
The joyfull meeting of Sr John and his Lieutenant at Yorke.

The Earle of Straford then Lieutenant Generall expressely and peremptorily commaunded Sr John against the next muster to make his troop compleat againe with men and horses, which having donne accordingly with his almost exhausted and wasted fortunes, presently by order from both houses of Parliament hee with all of his profession and Religion was cashired out of his M$^{a\,ties}$ Army, which hard measure hee bore with great aequanimity and patience, and prudent discretion. By comaund of the E. of Straford he compleateth his troop.
Hee is disbanded.

Hee lived privatily and retiredly in the Countrie with the Lady his mother, where hee gave to all with whome hee conversed and treated no lesse evident instances of his true, solid and Christian Vertues then hee had formerly given of his matchlesse prowesse and generous resolution. Hee continued this course not intermeddling on ¶ ether side untill by his hard usage and emprisonment by the Parliament hee was enforced and necessitated thereunto and not permitted to enjoy himself and freedome as formerly at home as shall shortly appeare. His private country life.
His vertues.

Fol. 15

Now was a tyme for hym of vocation devoid of all action, wherefore loath to sit idly when probably there might bee occasion of doing his king and country service, to which hee was not admitted, but debared and discharged, willing to absent himself from the heart-piercing sight of Englands miseries which weary of the prosperous and long happinesse it enjoyed went about to engulf itself into the dangerous whirepoole of a destructive and unnaturall

Hee went wth ye E. of Arundell to wait on C: Mot: into Germ.
Fol. 15 D

warre, hee consented to the request and motion of the right Honble Thomas Earle of Arundell and his Countesse with them to waite upon queene mother into Germany where hee hoped to bee out of the ungratfull hearing of our home-bred calamities, but in vaine for it was a great heart-burning to hym to observe other nations laugh and scorne at our Feares and Jealousies. ¶

Hee is much esteemed in Holland.

When hee landed in Holland, hee was looked upon by all with the eyes of respect, honour and admiration for Fame with her sylver trumpet had alreadie shrilly entoned the high renowne of his personall deserts, and brave and heroicall atchievements especially in his late encounter at Newborne against the Scots, wherefore she had already chaulked hym out, like a diligent harbinger, against his arrivall, lodgings in the innes of Mens Hearts of all ranks and quality: yet when they saw his proper, comely and gallant personage, so richly garnished with the precious Gemmes of a courtly civility and grave modestie and graced with such singular courtesie and affabilitie, free from affectation, singularity, vanitie and ostentation, hee gained more upon their affections, and wove himself insensibly into the webbe of their high valuation and great esteeme.

Hee waiteth in the Qu: of Bohemia.
Fol. 16
The Que-Opinion of hym.

He waited upon the Queene of Bohemia (sister to our gratious Soveraigne King Charles) at her Court in Holland by whome hee was most respectfullie treated ¶ and her M^{ty} afterwards upon occasion vouchsafed to declare what an estimate shee made of hym, which is more highly to bee valewed proceeding from the princely mouth of so sage, discreet and well qualified a queene. Here he had the honour to see and admire that peerelesse Princesse her eldest daughter, concerning whome after his returne hee framed this judgment that *hee thought shee was the most modest, grave, well spoken universally learned and naturely judicious young princesse hee had beheld in all his travailes.*

The Que- of Bohemia- eldest daughter commended

Hee escapes a great danger.

Going in a Boat upon the Rhene towards Colen and discovering an Ambuscade hee alarmed with his carbin the Countesse her Convey at a good distance of, and eschieved that present danger by putting the souldiers to a fearfull flight, but shortly after both the

whome hee was specially graced and taking leave of the Earle with his noble Countesse who civilly importuned his longer continuance hee went to Aquisgrane where making his demurre a short tyme in his way to Liege hee often was endangered by thievish souldiers who way-laid hym, but hee so discreetly and couragiously ordered the busnies that hee stopped their mouthes and musquets ayming at hym and his man, with good words and a largesse, wherewith they departed content, and hee through Flanders arrived safe in England. *He escapeth robbing narrowly.*

When upon his returne hee found that the unhappie misunderstandings and differences betwixt the King and his Parliament of England were hightened by new disgusts hee retired into the country living quietly for a tyme with the Lady his Mother, and partly applied himself to his studies, and partly followed the most laudable and best Gentleman-like ¶ sports and recreations with Knights and Gentlemen his kind neighbours; who so much observed and respected hym that his presence seemed to checke and banish any lesse modest or civill word or behaviour. *His quiet Country Life.* Fol. 17 *His presence checketh Vice.*

Soone after the fight at Edge-hill which opened the Sluce as it were to so much blood-shed in this our afflicted kingdome, passing out of Rutland towards Gotehurst the house of the Lady his Mother, and not dreaming or apprehending any the least danger, riding in a peacable yea hunting or coursing garbe and posture with his men and dogs, hee was encountred on the Road nere Wellingborrow by some Parliament troopes, who in an opprobrious manner dismounting and disarming hym and his men of their swords which were their onely weapons disgracefully conveyed them to Northampton upon sory spittle jades scarse able to creep and craule under them: where Sr John by the Committee was given in charge to the provost marshall, who at exceeding charges ¶ kept *He is taken by the Parl-forces and carried to Northampton. He is committed to ye Provost Marsh:* Fol. 17 D hym in a chamber not permitting hym to stirre a foot without the Marshalls man gave his attendance upon hym, which affront hee much resenting addressed himself to the Committee and desired ether to bee set free as conscious to hymself of his owne innocency not having bene active on ether side, nor stirred scarse one night from hime for a long tyme as appeared by different certificates, or, *that I may,* saith hee, *walke in the Streets with my owne man and my sword by my side or a Cane in my hand like a Gentleman and my self, and not with the Marshalls man, the badge of a rogue at my heeles.*

<small>He is kept at great charges.</small>

<small>He requests to bee discharged of the Mar-. shalls mans attendance.</small>

The Committee promising to take his request into their serious consideration dismissed hym to the Marshalls House, and having acquainted the House of Commons with his restraint, though by letters they aknowledged they could lay nothing to his charge yet they ordered his person should bee secured. A pittifull World in the meane tyme, when Gentlemen at their sports shall without commission and cause bee seized upon and emprisoned though avouched innocent.

<small>The House of Com. have nothing against yet order hee should bee secured.</small>

¶ It was conceited it seemeth by the Committee that hee was not safe enough at Northampton wherefore they sent hym under a guard to London, and waiting some howers in the cold after a wet and wilesome journy, not admitted into the house nor questioned about any thing, was by a peremptory order from the House of Commons commaunded to the Fleet, where hee was detayned at exorbitant charges; in all which interim of half a yeare hee was never summoned to appeare before the Parliament, nor any the least reason alleaged of his undeserved restraint. At length finding his meanes daily grow short, nether the Lady his Mother nor his Brother Sr Kenelme being able to supply his wants, their Estates being sequestred by the Parliament in behalf of their Religion, fearing least hee might bee driven to great exigents, hee made a hansome and cleanely escape out of prison, and having for some space concealed himself in London till the enquiry and search was over, in a meane disguise arrived safe at Oxford, where hee was welcomed by all with excessive joy.

<small>Fol. 18</small>

<small>He is sent wth a guard to London.</small>

<small>He is committed to ye fleat.</small>

<small>He escape out of Prison.</small>

<small>Disguised hee comes to Oxf:</small>

Warres and enabled with a Commission to raise for his service a Regiment of Horse. Divers of his troopers in his absence having listed themselves under other Commaunders, with speed and cheerefulnesse repaired with hym upon the first knowledge of his longed for freedome bringing with them Armes, Horses and all the appurtenances of a souldier, who were soone imitated by sondry others of good fashion and quality which sufficiently argued the generall and great love borne unto hym by the souldiery, who were highly conceited of his solid judgment in martiall affaires, and knew his provident care in ordering and securing them from the enemie, and lastly were not ignorant of his undaunted valour where with hee couragiously led them upon any charge though never so dangerous. *His Majesty gives com: to raise a Regiment. Divers repaire to hym.*

Hee had from the beginning of his engagement in the Warres a vigilant ey that his troopers should no way wrong or prejudice the Country where they came as Newport Pagnell in Buckingham-shyre can beare ¶ witnesse, for having there mustered his troop when hee went captaine into the North, hee would not permit any of his men to stirre a foot upon their march, before all reckonings in the towne were discharged, and both then and at other tymes rather then any should suffer hee disbursed his owne money: and againe now being Colonell upon complaint from Newport and there abouts that some of his troopers had wurried the country, hee issued forth his warrant written with his owne hand to bee read there publiquely on the market day, the tenour whereof was, that if such of his souldiers who without his knowledge or permission had absented themselves from their quarters and plundered the country did not returne with certaine prefixed dayes to give an account of themselves, and to receave condigne punishment, if convicted of misdemeanours, hee declared them thereby cashired and dismissed from his Regiment, willing and requiring the constable and others in case of refusall, and upon their persisting in their former villanies to apprehend them ¶ by strong hand and bring them to his quarters to bee punished suitably *Hee was carefull not to wrong yͤ Country. Fol. 19 He send his Warrant for punismͭ of his souldiers who were unruly. Fol. 19 D* to their demerits that they might bee a president to others not to attempt the like.

Upon his comming to Newport with noble Colonell Morgan hee showed great displeasure against some of the commaunded men of other troops (who in absence of their owne officers are hard to bee civilized and well governed) when hee was informed, they had abused or wronged any, yea so zealous hee was herein that himself unhorsing some, caused the horses to bee restored to their owners, as Lathburg nere Newport can well testifie.

<small>Hee restoreth what was wrongfully taken, by his commanded men.</small>

Hee most usually was quartered in places of most eminent danger, and neerest to the enemy, and consequently most liable to a surprize by beating up quarters in the night, if his watchfull care and prudent manage of his charge had not shielded both hymself and others. In the night hys men successively and by turnes were upon their duties, and about breake-of-day, the ordinary tyme of such night-walkers exploit hee in the head of his men would bee at a Rende-vous in some common or field out ¶ of towne, in fit posture to receave the ennemy if hee would or durst approach, in the interim sending out scouts several wayes, upon whose returne understanding all coasts were free hee commaunded his Men to betake themselves if they would to their rest interrupted by their necessarie and nightly duties. Which course if it had bene taken by all the Kings Commaunders since the dismall beginning of these unfortunate and uncivilly Civill Warres: London-Pamphleters would not so much have vapoured and insulted over the drowsie and lesse vigilant Cavaliers then the duty of their place and Office justly required.

<small>Hee quarters nere the Enemy.</small>

<small>His care to prevent a surprize.</small>

<small>Fol. 20</small>

I will not so much wrong his never dying memory to silence that remarkeable victory achieved by his Maties Forces against Sr William Waller at Round-way Downes nere the Vize in Wilt shire (the same day and hower as Naworth learnedly observeth when in their Maties the King and Queen happily met at Edge-hill after her returne out of Holland) In which Victory the Regiments of Sr John and ¶ gallant Colonell Morgan bore a great share, who at the speciall solicitation and procurement of his Highnesse Prince

<small>Fol. 20 D</small>

<small>Sr John and</small>

OR SIR JOHN DIGBY   85

Maurice marching day and night united themselves (beyond all Col. Morg:
expectation and belief of the Ennemy who thought all sure and the Reg. share greatly in yᵉ
day their owne) to the body of the Kings Horse though farre Victory against
inferiour to the number of the Enemy. SʳW.Waller.

In this famous Battaile Sʳ John commaunded a strong Body of
Horse, where-with hee fell upon Sʳ Arthur Haslerigs Cuirassiers Sʳ John rouseth Sʳ Arthur
with such resolution and dexterity that many being killed upon the Haselrigs
place hee put the rest to a shamefull route in which encounter Cuirassiers.
Sʳ Arthur himself was grievously wounded, but soone after these
Cuirassiers rallying againe at a distance upon a second charge made
by Sʳ John were forced to trust more to their horses heeles then
their owne hands, yet many made more hast then good speed, for Hee chargeth them
in their swift horse-race riding upon the spurre downe the then againe.
slippery hills some broke their owne necks, or their horses or both.

Our Martiall Knight ¶ on the plaine following the chase in the   Fol. 21
poursuite with some of his best horsed over-topped them and
compelled them sore against their Will to an ungratefull stand, He pursueth them.
necessitating them ether to fight or yield themselves Prisoners.

Sʳ John observing the maine body of foot to stand on a neigh- He and his
bouring hill in Battaglia, resolved to give them also a full charge, single man ride about a
wherefore ranking in their files and marshalling his men, hee com- Body of foot.
maunded that when by making a circuit they had gained the hill,
and were come at a competent distance, they should suddenly ride
in with full speed upon them and disorder their ranks, but it
seemeth, they mistaking his commaund wheeled on the contrary
hand to his directions, notwithstanding which errour, hee accompanied but with one man confidently marched up close unto them
and almost round about them; (though in the meane space many
fierce voleys though in vaine and without hurt played upon them)
and returned to the Body ¶ of horse which stood in the bottome   Fol. 21 D
and gazed with admiration of his resolute and venturous attempt.

The foot now seeing themselves abandoned by their Army of The foot
Horse which was long since fled out of the field, and amated with disarming themselves
the confident boldnessse of Sʳ John whome they saw making ready fly.
for a charge, throwing downe their musquets, swords, bandeliers

and coats made them selves as light as they could to runne for their lives. The King Horse in part giving them as it were law, (like eager grayhounds let out of slips) broke forth into speedy poursuance of them; but the pittifull heart of his Highnesse Prince Maurice could not brooke it to see voluntarily disarmed men to bee exposed to a bloody massacre of the victorious conquerours, wherefore he strictly commaunded to receave them to mercy and give them faire quarter, wherein hee was obeyed. Many prisoners were brought unto his Highnesse, whome understanding to bee pressed men, after ¶ that by his appointment they had gathered up their owne and their horse-mens armes which lay thick scattered in the field, and had loaded them in carts, upon Oath never to fight against their Sovereigne, hee set them free licencing them to repaire to their homes. The Kings Army in this wonderfull Victory consisting but of Horse onely, and but a handefull in comparison of theirs both horse and foot, became hereby absolute Maisters of the field, armes, Ordinance Carriages and all their amunitiou; wherefore this Victorie so successefully and seasonably pourchased saved or rather wonne the whole west which then lay at stake.

· So great was the opinion generally conceived of Sr John in the Kings Army that whatsoever enterprize was difficult and hazardous the Commaunders in chief usually imposed upon hym, which hee never refused nor waved but cheerefully embraced, for they well knew his often tryed valour, relyed upon his solid Judgment and discretion in ordering and managing ¶ warlike affaires and were most confident of his unquestionable trust and Fidelity.

Wherefore when the Earle of Essex was on his march towards the relief of Gloucester then besieged by the King in person Sr John was commaunded by his Highnesse Prince Rupert to stay behind upon the advance of the Kings Cavalierie to bring up the reare with about three hundred troopers and Dragons, and to hinder the Ennemie if possible from falling upon them in their march. Sr John his Sergeant Major Brookebanke (a gallant man and skilfull souldier afterwards taken at Grafton and shot to death at St Albans by the Earle of Essex his order for having deserted the

Parliament service after the Battaile at Edge-Hill) made earnest suite to Prince Rupert then Commaunder in chief to accompany his much respected Colonell in this enterprize of so great concernement and liable to so eminent danger, wherein hee behaved himself most courageously and wonne deservedly much ¶ praise and commendations and merited his lasting renowne should live among men by an honourable mention of his Prowesse and Valour. That brave vertuous, and flowre of English Gentry Colonell Morgan much endeared to Sr John solicited hee with his men might bee licensed to joyne with hym but his boone to his great resentment was refused.

Shot at St Albans.

Hee accompanieth Sr John and behaveth himself valiantly.

Fol. 23

Col. Morgan refused by P. Rup. to goe with Sr John.

Before Sr John his arrivall the Parliament forces had already maid them selves Maisters of Peddington Bridge in Oxford-shire, and had manned it with a strong guard of troopers and Dragooners, with whome they had also lined the hedges and lane. Sr John endeavoured to possesse himself of the Bridge but not at first prevailing hee used many notable and souldier-like stratagemes to draw them if hee could compasse it from their great advantages; wherefore hee cunningly disposed certaine Dragons privily in an Ambush behind a Banke bordering upon an adjacent meadow then sent a small party of Troopers into the Meadow to flourish and skirmish slightly with their troopers ¶ and dragons in the lane and hedges, who apprehending the great ods they had against so few as it were hemmed in on each side and exposed to the butcherie as they thought, fell furiously in great number upon them, but Sr John his men, as they had in commaund by little and little gave backe retreating towards the ambuscade, and suddenly making a stand and lane, the Parliament forces now within a proportionate and fit distance were unexpectedly from the ambush saluted with an ungratefull peale of musquets so well levelled that some fell, the rest were eagerly followed in their flight by the troopers in the meadow.

Peddington Bridge manned by ye Parl.

Sr John disposeth an ambush.

Fol. 23 D

The Ambush succeedeth prosperously.

Which advantage Sr John skilfully improving to the hight with his entire body made an onset upon the Guard at the Bridge with so resolute and well ordered a charge that after some dispute hee

Sr John beateth a triple number to his.

gained it though most advantagiously possessed by a triple number
to his, and forcing them thence poursued them fiercely through the
lane and towne almost to their mayne Army with more feare and
confusion of ¶ the Enemy then losse of their men

Here making a halt and marshalling his men in Battaile-array
and fit posture to receave the Enemy if approaching, but seeing
them in along tyme not advance a foot towards hym, hee caused
most of his men to march away after the army who some miles of
by mediation of Colonell Morgan to Prince Rupert made a stand,
where this gallant Colonell hearing that his entire frend Sr John was
dangerously engaged with the too powerfull Enemy, used such
efficacious perswasions that relief was agreed upon to rescue
hym but the whole busnies was first happily passed over.

Sr John with his small remainder faced the whole Army of the
Enemy, but last seeing no appearence of engagement hee also
drew of the field, and returning againe back thorough the towne
was entertained in passing with great and generall acclamations
and singular applause of His Heroicall exploit, and going over the
bridge so bravely wonne without ¶ losse of men, overtooke the
Army where hee was welcomed on all hands with excessive joy
and admiration all giving hym and his men for lost.

The Kings Army of Horse marched still almost in view of the
other to keep them from straggling, annoying and wronging the
Country, wherefore there were daily and almost howerly skirmis-
hes of strong Parties encountring each other, in many whereof
Sr John was and still came of nobly and courageously and like
himself, hightening the conceit already framed of his Worth,
Valour and skill in feates of Armes.

After Gloucester was relieved by the Earle of Esssex (which
was his Maister-piece) when hee thought by his long night-marches
to have stolne away to Reading unfought with, Sr John was in company when hee was overtaken by the Kings Cavaliery and worsted
at Auborne Hills, in which fight the two Honble Lords Digby and
Jermin charged most gallantly (as witty and learned Mercurius
Aulicus well observeth) and came of with slight hurts ¶ but great

noble penitent and pious end ; to whome may bee joyned that pily.
vertuous, learned judicious, discreet, and civill Gentleman Colonell
Thomas Morgan who shot with a field-piece, had onely tyme to The pious
say cordially and affectionnately *O God what is man!* and shortly Death of
after speaking inwardly to himself, which might bee discovered by Col. Morg.
the continuall motion of his lips, his soule made hast ¶ to take pos- Fol. 25 D
session (as wee confidently hope) of the eternall reward and Crowne
of glory in Heaven correspondent to his exemplar and innocent
Life.

Sr John in this dayes Battaile, with his owne Regiment and other Sr John
commaunded men charged bravely first severall tymes whole bodies chargeth y^e
of horse whereof hee killed manie and routed the rest ; hee charged Canon.
likewise the Canon passing by hedges strongly lined with musquetiers, where God extraordinarily protected hym from evident
danger, for no sooner was hee marched by but a field-piece
discharged, out right killed two his troopers stout, proper and
valiant men whereof one had bene for many yeares Servant to his
brother Sr Kenelme Digby but the gunner could not long brag Kenelme
and boast of his fact ; for hee was suddenly slayne by the rest Goodman.
who revenged their companions death ; and the next day was
found with 17 wounds upon hym, when they bestowed decent
Buriall upon their fellow-troopers. ¶ Fol. 26

Lastly Sr John charged also the foot and that so close that for a Hee charges
long tyme togeather hee lay his sword upon their Pikes which ye foot.
goared his horses breast, which was shot under hym ; here hee His horse
receaved a slight hurt by the grazing of a musket-Bullet a little hym.

above the wrist of his right Arme, which notwithstanding shot through his coat and doublet sleeves ; and although hee stood almost from morning to night as a marke for the Canon and musquet to play upon, yet hee sustained no hurt other then newly specified ; so strangely was hee defended by the powerfull hand of God.

Hee is slightly hurt.

After Newbury fight Sr John having waited upon the King in his royall march to Oxford, hee with his men repaired to their old quarters at Heford in Oxford-shire, where hee and his were most lovingly still and kindly welcome, (no usuall thing among the most of souldiers) when hee had refreshed himself, men and horses after so long and wilesome service, his Ma^{ty} ¶ was gratiously pleased to give Sr Lewys Dives and hym a commission to garrison for his royall service Newport Pagnell in Buckingham shire but two miles distant from Gotehurst the mansion-house of the Lady Digby his mother.

Hee returnes to his quarter at Heford.

Fol. 26 D

Hee is comanded with^1 Sr Lewys dives to garrison Newport.

His highnesse Prince Rupert with good strength both of horse and foot unexpectedly by Bedford came before them to Newport, which busnies if it had bene well followed, and not so suddenly let fall by drawing the Kinges forces out of the towne, it would probably have proved very prejudiciall to the Parliament and advantagious to his Ma^{ty} by stopping in great part their road for the succour and relief of their more Northernely Garrisons, and also by hindring provisions going to London, the inexhaustible magazine both of men and money with armes and other necessaries, for the keeping on foot these unnaturall warres betwixt the Kings Ma^{ty} and his liege people. ¶

P. Rupert comes to Newport.

Of what consequence Newport had bene to the King.

Fol. 27

In the few dayes of his stay at Newport with Sr Lewys Dives, hee infinitely gained the affection and good liking of the People; as hee did also at Bedford ; where at the first summons the Country flocked in with great cheerefulnesse and alacrity joyfully declaring themselves to stand well affected to his Ma^{ty} and his cause which afterwards cost them deare upon the retyring of the Kings forces and giving leave to Major Generall Skippon with his Cittie-strength to enter without a blow the towne forsaken by them and perfect

Hee gaines ye love of ye Country.

Bedford cheerfully obeyeth Sr Lewys ^{s}ummons.

Skippon wth his Lond:

the workes modelled and traced out for them, which they to the great disparagement of the Kings party in a scoffing way commended as well delineated ; who if they had insteed of casting up slight trenches at Tocester, thoroughly fortified, manned and victualed Grafton-House, which might with ease have bene donne, it would have courbed if not wholy foiled their rising garrison at Newport. enter Newport forsaken by ye Kings men whom they mock for leaving it.

Few dayes before his Highnesse Prince Rupert went from Tocester with the greatest part ¶ both of the horse and foot, Sr John was commaunded to stay behind in quality of Governour of Grafton House which hee was to fortifie, with faithfull promise of Prince Rupert to bee relieved within a very short space if besieged, which was not performed accordingly. Grafton well fortified had much annoyed Newport.

Fol. 27 D

Sr John appointed Governour of Grafton, which hee was to fortify.

Sr John in the short continuance of his office wonne to hymself much Love and esteeme in the Country round about, which hee did not suffer to bee wronged by any under his charge if hee ether knew it or could redresse it, as even those can and doe witnesse and give evidence, who were publiquely and openly knowne by their owne actions and profession to bee great stickless against the King, yet they give such a singular testimony of the integrity and faire comportement of him and his men that passing and repassing most frequently and almost daily by their houses and grounds, they were not endomaged to the valew of a farthing. No small commendation from the mouth of such, who would not have bene sparing in aggravating any the least ¶ trespasse or offense committed in that kinde. Sr John and his men commended by their Enemies.

Fol. 28

By his favourable, courteous and gentile usage, hee wrested deserved praise from the mouthes of the Parliamentary prisoners which hee tooke, for they released highly extolled their entertaynement aknowledging they had fallen into the hands of a gallant Enemy, which hee and his afterwards could not verifie when it was their unluckie disaster to become prisoners of Major Generall Skippon as in the sequele of this narration shall bee notified. Comended by ye prisoners hee tooke.

The neighbouring garrisons of Northampton Alisbury and Newport conceiving by these small beginnings how offensive and annoying Grafton house would in all likeliehood prove unto them, if well fortified and manned especially under so judicious valiant, and active a governour, they used all possible care to assault, and crush hym before hee and his house grew too strong for them.

<small>All ye Garrisons conspire against Sr John.</small>

<small>Fol. 28 D</small>

Sr John like a vigilant Commander and ¶ well understanding his charge, apprehending the danger wherein hee lay, to prevent any suddaine surprize commaunded a Sentinell to watch all day by turnes on the top of the steeple nor farre distant from the House, thereby to discover farre of, any bodie of approaching ennemies, and in the night gave order, that all the horse ready saddled, foot and troopers with their armes should bee within the walles of the House.

<small>His vigilant care.</small>

Wherefore Major Skippon with his Londoners seing hee could not prevaile against hym by any suddaine surprize or beating up his quarters in the night, because Sr John was alwais in a ready posture to welcome hym ; hee resolved to attacke hym by maine strength not doubting but with ease and without losse of men to make himself maister of so unfortified a house. Upon which designe all the garrisons of thirty or fourty miles compasse were drayned to patch up a Medly-Army of at least seaven or eight thousand as is generally ¶ reported and believed.

<small>7 or 8000 combine against Grafton.</small>

<small>Fol. 29</small>

Though that very morning they sate downe with their Army before the House, Sr John with safety might have retreated with his horse and men into Tocester, yet hee so much stood upon his honour which hee judged would be nerely concerned therein if hee should desert his charge ; and so confidently hoped relying upon Prince Rupert his promise to bee relieved upon notice with in fowre and twenty bowers, that hee determined not to forsake the trust reposed in hym by his Matie but to make good this weake hold of his honour of Grafton if hee could possibly against their strongest forces and Attempts even with the hazard of his life, and so courageous were his men that some sallied forth upon the reare of their past Army and brought back divers troopers well mounted and armed prisoners.

<small>Sr John relying on P. Rup : promise intends to stand out ye siege.</small>

<small>His men sally out and take some prisoners.</small>

The Parliament horse faced Tocester and Eston a house of the

were drawne in competent distance of Grafton thinking perhaps as it was boasted that the compassing of their worke would bee so easie that they should breake their fast at Grafton, dine at Eston and sup at Tocester, but it seemes, they reckoned according to the proverb without their host, not dreaming at what a deare rate they were to buy this their intended breake-fast. *Vaine brags.*

At first in a full body the musquetiers charged the House, but they were resoluted with so well levelled a voley from within that they retreated in disorder leaving many of their companions gasping upon the place ; this so unkind greeting so abated the edge of their appetite that they had but small stomach to come on so thicke againe, but first by fower and fower and that at a distance, and from an other, then in single files, one by one dropping but even so they found the service so hot, and so perfect markes-men within (though they had no other but musquets and fireling-pieces) that they could ¶ not bee entreated nor scarce hired to discharge against it by day, so farre were they from storming it. Many of the foot and horse very valiantly retreated and sheltered themselves behind the ordinance which played almost continually by day and the musquetiers grew also bold and hardy, covered as they thought with the sable wings of a darke night yet the fire of their musquets discharged most commonlie in vaine, to the stout Defendants within gave ayme, who so well plied their musquets that the first day and night, five or six carriages of dead bodies, are credibly reported by neighbours who saw them to bee secretly convayed away and privately buried not to discourage the besiegers, an ordinary course among them since the first beginning of these bloody and intestine warres, for according to the ordinary computation of their weekely Pamphleters and New-mongers few of their men are killed wherefore it seemeth an aenigma or Riddle worthy of an other Oedipus how then it commeth to passe that they have made so many thousand comfortlesse widdows and fatherlesse children onely in London itself. ¶ *The foot find hot service. Their courage is cooled. No ordinance at Grafton.* Fol. 30 *Many killed of Skippons men.* *A Riddle.* Fol. 30 D

When Major Skippon saw hee could doe no good upon the

house nether with his musquets nor gunnes brought from Newport hee sent for a great battering piece from Northampton which beeing planted at a distance was frequently discharged, yet without any great hurt untill in the night it was secretly drawne into a farme close over against over the house, whence making a hole through the wall, by severall shoots they made such a breach in Grafton-House that it could not bee repaired or made up, but endangered the fall of that part if continued.

<small>A Battering-piece from North: make a great breach.</small>

Perhaps since these unhappie warres begun there hath scarse or ever bene so long and hot service so gallantly maintayned on the part of so few defendants, not 200 in a house so ungarrisoned and slenderly provided of all things, besides victualls stored up by the carefull foresight of the wachfull Governour. The siege endured three dayes and two nights without any the least respit or interruption so that it is a great wonder how the troopers and musquetiers not relieved in their continuall and hard duties were ¶ able to hold out. The troopers had no use of their horses, wherefore every one according to their ability and skill turned musquetiers; some charged the musquets and made them ready for others to shoot, some were otherwise employed so that none was idle. In the whole siege there were not about two or three killed outright in the House and as many mortally wounded who dyed afterwards.

<small>Grafton stoutly defended.</small>

<small>Fol. 31</small>

Upon notice of the danger wherein Sr John and his men stood engaged if not tymely relieved his Ma^{ty} expressely comaunded Prince Rupert that aid should bee hastened to him forthwith, but such speed was not used as the Nature of the exigent worthily might seeme to require, whereby so valiant and gallant a Comaunder with so many stout and brave souldiers was exposed to inevitable hazard of loosing ether their lives or liberties to the great discouragement of others who upon like occasion hereafter will rather yield upon the first summons though to the Kings great disservice, and their owne disgrace then after a stout resistance for want ¶ of relief to fall into the cruell and mercilesse hands of an insulting and domineering Ennemy.

<small>The King ordreth aid to be sent which was not hastened.</small>

<small>Fol. 31 D</small>

The siege began on friday morning the two and twentith day of December, and the Canons in a manner incessantly played by day and the musquets sometime by day but most fiercely by night, so that such hard and never ceasing duty without rest or refreshment exceedingly wearyed and exhausted the defendants; but the assailants were still reenforced with new and fresh supplies; yet Sʳ John with his other commaunders and officers so heartened and encouraged them by their words but much more by their example, that as forgetfull of their wearinesse they persisted in constant defense. *The Siege began the 22 of Dec:* *The Besiegers recruited.*

Upon Sonday in the afternoone his Major Brooke-banke (not dreaming how deare it would after cost hym) importuned Sʳ John to a parly, upon hope, as hee said, ether to gaine bonᵇˡᵉ conditions, or in case of refusall to get that tyme of treaty free from Acts of hostility, whereby they might refresh themselves and save their amunition, which now ¶ began to grow some what short, or finally that succour so long expected might perhaps in the interim arrive which infallibly had come to passe if there had bene so great forwardnesse and readinesse in those whom it most concerned as his entire and deare frend Sʳ John Wake showed who solicited most affectionately and earnestly in his behalf. *Major Brooke-b: adviseth a Parly.* *Fol. 32* *Sʳ John Wake solicited relief.*

With these reasons proceeding from so able a commander, Sʳ John inclined though otherwise not willing condescended to the sounding a parly wherefore sending a drummer to the top of the house when hee began to beat it against all lawes of armes was shot by them, whose roome in other supplying it was admitted. *A Parly is sounded.* *The drumer shot against law of armes.*

When honᵇˡᵉ conditions of marching away with bag and baggage horses, armes and other appurtenances were demaunded by Sʳ John, but refused by Major Skippon; and upon second demaunds that hee his captaines and officers might bee allowed their horses and armes and the troopers and foot souldiers, batons in their hands, when this also ¶ would not bee hearkened unto but that hee with the rest of his men should yield themselves prisoners onely upon quarter for life; hee absolutely refused it and encouraged his men to stand to their armes and sell the house at the dearest rate they could even to the shedding of the last drop of their blood. *Demaunds of Sʳ John.* *2 Demaunds.* *Fol. 32 D* *Major Skippon will onely grant quarter for life.*

His manly troopers were most readie and willing but the foote-
souldiers like dastardly animals daunted at the view of so great an
army both of horse and foote which not suitably to the conditions
of a parly had gotten close under the walles and all the while of
the treaty had menaced the foot with a most cruell death and not
affording them quarter if they made but one shot more, they nether
with words nor blowes of the officers could bee perswaded or forced
to fight, but threw downe their musquets and armes threatning their
commaunders in a mutinous manner if they persisted in pressing
them to fight against their wille and refusing quarter now offered. ¶
Which being overheard by some of the officers interested in the
treaty and notified to Skippon made hym so absolute and peremptory in yielding to no conditions proposed by Sr John for seing the
great advantage hee and his men had gotten who swarmed thicke
about the walles sent to Sr John for his finall and suddaine answeare,
whether hee would yield up the house himself and men upon the
proposed conditions of quarter for life onely, otherwise hee should
expect a fierce storming, and bee exposed to the fury of the violent
and enraged souldiers.

Wherefore Sr John wisely considering what a sad exigent hee
was driven unto the consent and advice of his officers, and moved
by the mutinous importunity and outcries of the Foot, made a
surrender of the house, himself and men to Skippons mercy which
rather degenerated into unchristian cruelty and barbarous and
unhumane usage for the souldiers under his commaund, entring
the house like so many ravenous wolves plundered and risted all,
and unstripped many souldiers and ¶ the gentlewoman of the
house with other women most immodestly to their naked skin.

Sr John comming out of the house with his sword by his side
and looking into a sterne and unamated countenance upon the
commaunders and souldiers present, couragiously told them that
if his foot would have stood to hym and their armes as resolutely
as his troopers the best man amongst them should have found hot
entrance into that house though unfortified and so sorely battered
that it was almost ready to drop downe upon their heads, but that

Margin notes: The Foot refuse to fight. False Play in Sk. Army. Sr John foot mutiny. Fol. 33. Skippon peremptory summons. Sr John yields himself pris: Hard usage of the Enemy. Fol. 33 D. Sr John his resolute speach.

hee and they would have maintayned it, and opposed their owne bodies as rampires against their utmost fury with the hazard of their lives. *Wherefore I request,* saith hee, *faire quarter and civill usage for my officers and troopers who behaved themselves so gallantly and like gentlemen, but for the base and cowardly foot, who shrunk and failed mee in my greatest need and use of their service, I ask no favour, treate them as you please, for they will nether doe the King nor you, service.* ¶

This so resolute speach though frowned at and distasted by some, was so well relished by others of the more civill and gentleman—like commaunders that one calling Sʳ John by his name, highly extolled his gallantry therein adding *it were a thousand pitties such a brave gentleman and valiant commaunder should bee ill used or wronged.* Whereby you see true worth and a generous noblenesse pourchaseth respect and Honour from gallant Ennemies. Many of the common souldiers were over-heard to avouch that no man living could have more courageously and judiciously discharged his part and office in defending so weake a house unfortified, then hee did, and that it was pitty and shame so worthy and deserving a man was suffred to perish for want of timely relief.

Sʳ John seing Colonell Bartlet a Scottish gentleman and then governour of Newport, well knowne unto hym for his civill and courteous usage beeing the Scots prisoner at Newcastle, desired to become his prisoner, which was graunted by whome he was used very ¶ respectfully, nether would hee permit hym or his man to bee searched but commaunded a sergeant with two musketiers to guard and secure his portmanteau from the violent and plundering hands of the unruly and rude souldiers, which hee did so long as Sʳ John was in his custodie.

Few howers after the house was delivered there came a messenger from Tocester with a letter to Sʳ John, the contents whereof was that if hee could but hold till such a tyme without failed relief should come : this poore man not knowing what had passed, met with one of the Parliament Commaunders who enquiring and understanding his busnies said he was Sʳ John Digby,

Fol. 34

Sʳ John praised by his Enemies.

He is commended and pitied by his Enemies.

Hee desires to bee Col : Bartlet Prisoner.

Fol. 34 D
Col. Bar: useth hym civilly and defendeth his Portmanteau.

which the other simply believing delivered hym the letter, who having read it, caused the bearer to bee kept in strait hold ; and this mistake hee brought afterwards at a deare rate for shortly after the innocent wretch was hanged at Newport by appointment and order of Major Skippon. Which act if it had bene performed ¶ by any of the Kings Commaunders, what bitter invectives would Britannicus and other weekely London-Intelligencers have maid against them.

<small>A messenger hanged for his mistaked.
Fol. 35</small>

Major Skippon commaunder in chief having given order that the Kings mannour-House of Grafton first pillaged and plundered to the bare walles (a pious worke for Christ-masse day in the morning) should bee fired in severall places marched to Newport with the foot and foot-prisoners.

<small>Major Skippon fireth Graft :</small>

Sr John with his Captaines and officers rode in company of Colonell Bartlet and Colonell Twell who since these tymes hath alwais bene ready and willing to doe any neighbourly and frendly courtesie to the Lady his Mother they both courteously and civilly conversed and treated with hym.

<small>Col : Bartlet and Col : Sivell respectfull to John.</small>

Major Skippon led up the foot among whome Sr John his troopers and musquetiers prisoners with much cheerfulnesse and alacrity in the depth of winter, each step to the mid-leg, forced often to wade the waters being then out, many almost naked (so mercifully had they bene used at Grafton) divers ¶ of them being gentlemen of good quality and breeding, who in former tyme had kept better men for their servants then many of the commaunders.

<small>The Prisoners durty march to Newport.
Fol. 35 D
Many troopers of good quality.</small>

They were scornfully taunted and reviled by the souldiers as they went in the hearing of their commaunders who accompanied and conveyed them, who seemed rather to countenance then checke it, being farre from imitating herein their Brethren the Scots who when Carlile (so gallantly and so long beyond expectation kept by Sr Thomas Glemam and Sr Henry Stradling to their lasting fame and renowne) was at last surrendred to the Scots upon most hon^{ble} tearmes and conditions, they conveyed the Kings Souldiers (horse and foot which came out of the towne) into the Kings quarters about Worcester side, and most civilly treated them punishing

<small>The prisoners scoffed at and railed.
The Scots comended for civill using their Enemies.</small>

bury where they were but very meanely accommodated of all things necessary. I can not omit one particular which happened here not unworthy as I conceave of your knowledge, for when certain officers appointed by Major Skippon to register their names and tamper with them to draw them if they could to side with them, one of Sʳ John his troopers a stout, proper young man summoned to appeare before them, and privately warned by one of his fellow-troopers not to take notice that hee was a Roman Catholique, angerly replied unto hym *I will not conceale nor deny my Religion though I dy for it;* who comming before them and among other questions being demaunded whether hee not a Papist, *I am,* hee answeared, *a Roman Catholique and so will bee by Gods grace though you hang me for it* for which resolute answeare they commended hym and when further they urged hym to take up armes for them, hee undauntedly said *though you have already disarmed mee as a souldier yet I thanke God* (spreading his hands abroad) *I have yet these armes left mee, which I intend never to employ in your service, nor to lift them up against my King:* after which words hee presently voided the roome leaving them in a great amazement of his resolute and confident boldnesse. Which example if it had bene imitated by many, these unfortunate and bloody warres long since had bene ended and this distressed Kingdome enjoyed againe a happie and flourishing peace.

Sʳ John having lodged with Colonell Bartlet one night in Newport, the next day with his officers ready for London, bidding adieu to one of his men who had wayted upon hym, commaunded hym to wish his troopers ¶ to bee of good courage and not to bee dismaid at this present disaster being confident they should come of with credit and honour.

Hee writt a letter to his Highnesse Prince Rupert by leave of

Marginalia: A Remarkeable passage. — Fol. 36 D — A brave resolute speach. — Sʳ John encourageth his Men. — Fol. 37

Colonell Bartlet with whome hee left it, engaging his promise it should bee sent wherein hee gave his Highnesse an exact account of the whole busnies of the siege and upon what tearmes hee was necessitated to a surrender, concluding that his present state and condition should in no manner dishearten hym from doing his Ma^{ty} hereafter the best and most faithfull service hee might bee capable of, as hee maid evidently appeare by his after actions.

Before hee was gonne two miles out of Newport hee was overtaken by a party of troopers sent after hym by Major Skippon, who carrying hym into a House at Broughton seized upon his Port-manteau wherein was nothing but his wearing apparell ¶ and linnen and tooke from hym all his money and a most curious watch. Which was but small credit to Major Skippon who authorized these souldiers to use a Knight of his quality and condition in so base and opprobrious a manner. His Officers escaped no better then their Colonell.

When Sr John came to the Earle of Essex then lying at St Albans with his Army hee was treated by him with much affabilitie, civilitie and respect, discoursing familiarly a good while with hym, and the Earle being informed that the Captaine of their Guard threatned and attempted to take from some of his companie their upper garments as his pretented due, hee checking hym said, *Hee had as good bee hanged as touch the least haire of their head* which made hym afterwards forbeare to urge his claime. Which example of this noble Earle if like a president it had bene followed by all the Inferior officers in their severall armies from the first beginning of these warres they would ¶ not have bene so justly taxed and charged with such outrages, wrongs and Injuries committed against their prisoners and others who have long pittifully groned under the heavy burthen of their hard and mercilesse usage.

Arrived at London, as they passed the streets some miscalled and reviled them, others seemed to pitty their present distressed condition; but the couragious prisoners nothing deceited by this disaster changed not their countenance, but rode on confidently, so that one might read in the serenity of their visages, the quiet of

you easily may guessse how narrowly Major Skippon with his harpies hands (I meane his troopers who rifled them at Broughton) had formerly searched and picked their purses. ¶

About ten at night they were led into New-Prison in Mayden-lane where they were put all togeather in a low Parlour at little ease for they had nether bed nor straw to ly on but the bare floore : and yet these men forsooth complaine and raile against the Cavaliers for abusing their prisoners of Warre. The next day Sr John was conveyed to the tower and delivered into the hands of the then Lieutenant thereof Mr Isaac Pennington.

Wherefore for the present leaving him we will returne and accompanie his troopers and foot souldiers in their wet, weary and ill appointed march to London who the next day after Sr John his departure were brought from Lathbury to Newport. It would have grieved any compassionately pittifull heart to see so many brave stout men well borne and bred, and among the rest one Gentleman with his fower sonnes comely proper young men lately worth some hundreds a yeare, to bee treated like poore beggers or worse and bee glad to accept a small pittance of course hard bread to save ¶ them from starving ; and when some of the standers by repaired upon the courtenesse and badnesse thereof the souldiers of their guard were heard to say *Hang them rogues if it were worse then horse-bread it were much too good for them*, yet I doubt whether they upon like tearmes would rest satisfied and content with such hard faire and meane usage.

They were driven like a heard of beasts or drove of sheep and forced often to march faster in the deep, durty foule wayes, then their weake and almost hunger-starved limbs would give them leave tyed three and three togeather.

The first night comming to Ouborne they were all shut up in

the Schoole-house without ether fire or straw to ly on, or meat but what charitable people afforded them and that privately least if discovered they should bee wronged by their Guard as being guilty of assisting the King in befrending his Cavaliers, for now alas the more is the pitty and shame Loyalty and allegiance to ones Kings and Soveraigne is stigmatized and branded with the names ¶ of malignancy and delinquencie.

<small>The foot almost starved.</small>

<small>Fol. 39 D</small>

The second night they lodged at Dunstable in the church (and these are the Religious zelots who make churches which are the houses of God and Prayer to become their prisons and often stables) where they were accommodated much in the same nature as at Ouborne; but these scrupulous souldiers their guard seemed to reverence the church, wherein they feared to commit sacrilege for seeing some better coat or suite then their owne which they aliking unto to have taken as it were sanctuary in the Church upon the backe of some prisoner, they subtily called hym out pretending as if their Captaine sent to speake with but bringing hym to their Companions who on purpose lurked in some by-corner, stripped hym and returned hym backe accoutred in their nastie rags, having served divers in this manner, at last others warned by their fellowes harme would not obey their pretended summons, which had like to have caused a mutiny. ¶

<small>The Prisostript of their cloths.</small>

<small>Fol. 40</small>

They had but two good meales meat provided them all the way to London, the one at Barnet, the other at Higate and these at the charge of some well affected people commiserating their cruell and evill usage I hope God from above will reward their charity.

<small>A poore refreshment.</small>

<small>Sailers blamed.</small>

When they came nere London they were lodged a night or two upon a Court of Guard at the six wind-milles, a small refreshment after so tedious, long and hungrie a march; thence they were distributed into sundry prisons, where most of them might have starved if some freuds and well-willers both in city and country had not supplied their pressing wants for twelve that were committed to the Fleet had no allowance afforded them, whatsoever was in other prisons. I can not frame so meane and undervaluing a conceit of the Parliament that they would have their prisoners of warre to perish in prison for pure want of food precisely necessary to sustayne nature, yet I thinke it strange if they allow any thing, that they permit the hard-hearted Keepers to purse it up. ¶   Fol. 40 D

I could wish they would appoint some Committee to looke into these abuses and see them exemplarly punished and to procure there bee not such extortion by the keepers upon the poore prisoners, who have no other maintenance nor liveliehood but what their frends exhausted with daily losses, plunderings and continuall taxes can afford them.   *Extortion of Keepers.*

In new-prison in Mayden-lane ten shillings weekely for above half a yeare together was unconscionably exacted by the keeper from two of Sr John his troopers who lay both in one bed, which kind of abuses if they bee not timely redressed by due care and punishment of the offenders, it will ly heavy upon the Parliament who frequently stile themselves the highest Court of Justice.   *A true example of it.*

Now it is high tyme after this needfull digression to visit Sr John in his new lodging in the tower and observe whether hee was better treated then his troopers. The Lieutenant consigned hym to the custodie of one of his warders who kept a very strict hand over hym and for some moneths locked ¶ hym up day and night in a close chamber, not suffering hym all that while to set his foot over the threshold: this course continued till one day Sr John seing the dore open set his table against it and resolutely told his keeper hee would have his chamber-dore locked no more.   *Sr John long kept under lock and key.*   Fol. 41   *The strictnesse of his Warder.*

The Lieutenant would not give way that Sr Johns man should waite upon hym, but a little boy who was sometymes searched to the skin at his comming in and going out, and hee after a while must bee discharged and a stranger put in his place so full of jealousies and feares was the Lieutenant, who admitted none, not so much as his taylour to speake with hym but his keeper must bee present and bee privy to their discourse. Hee could not bee private in his owne Chamber but the keeper ever and anon through loop-holes made upon designe would bee peering and peeping what hee did.   *His man not admitted to wait on hym.*   *His boy oft stript and searched to ye skin.*   *His taylour not admitted to his speake wth out ye Keeper.*

Hee used to sit up late in the nights at his studies, which it seemeth distasted the Lieutenant in whose... (?) ¶ Wherefore one night hee sent unto hym to put out his candle, goe to bed and keep more orderly and seasonable bowers, to whome Sʳ John returned answeare that therein hee was not to bee directed by hym, for hee would observe what bowers hee liked best of going to bed and rising, after which hee was never intermeddled with in that kind.

<small>Fol. 41 D
Not private in his owne Chamber.</small>

Sʳ John suffred this his hard restraint with great and admirable patience without any the least pusillanimity or dejection of mind, for the space of full three quarters of a yeare, and although in the meane season the Kings Maᵗʸ had dispatched severall trompeters to the two houses at Westminster proposing exchanges for hym, yet upon one pretense or other they were still rejected, so loath they were to set hym at large whome they conceived would prove an active and stirring Ennemy against, and that they were not deceaved in their expectation and judgment of hym Sʳ William Waller and many others who afterwards experienced it, will beare hym witnesse. ¶

<small>Many exchanges proposed by his Maᵗʸ for hym rejected.</small>

<small>Fol. 42</small>

A little before the Kings famous Victory at Lishthiell(?) in the West, Colonell Buttler, Lieutenant Colonell to the Earle of Essex and his Ensigne taken prisoners were released by the King, upon their parole to procure the exchange of Sʳ John Digby against them to bee ratified by the Parliament, which after much suite and importunity they did : yet for many weeks after Sʳ John was not released by the Lieutenant pretending hee had not his passe from the Earle of Essex.

<small>Hee is exchanged for Col : Buttler.</small>

But this proved onely a colourable pretext to have cunningly still kept hym in hold ; wherefore when Sʳ John understood : that Lieutenant Colonell Buttler was committed to the tower to bee questioned for their overthrow in the West, hee with his keeper going to the Lieutenant boldly demaunded his Libertie so long due unto hym, to whome it was replied that his exchange was void because Lieutenant Colonell Buttler was not free beeing now questioned by the Parliament and committed to his custody ¶ *what doth that concerne mee*, answeared Sʳ John, *since hee was released by*

<small>Col : But- pretended to bee questio- ned for yᵉ lᵒˢse in yᵉ West.</small>

<small>Fol. 42 D</small>

persisted in demaunding his exchange and the Earle of Essex his passe, which hee knew was in his hands and would have it. The Lieutenant seeing hym so round and resolute and impatient of delay, mildly and gently entreated hym to respit it till the next morning, and hee should have his desire.

Sʳ John having payed his fees, wherein the Lieutenant to say the truth was favourable, the next morning his passe being delivered to hym by the Lieutenant, who courteously accompanied hym out of the tower and sent a guard of souldiers with hym to passe hym out of the line of communication after three quarters of a yeare hard and chargeable ¶ imprisonment, in a Coach hee went out of towne towards Oxford where hee arrived safely and was entertayned and welcomed by all sortes of people with great signes and expressions of Joy for his long desired release. *Sʳ John released goes to Oxford.* *Fol. 43*

The King having fought the second battaile at Newbury upon his comming out of the west commaunded Sʳ John at Oxford to waite upon hym in his returne to disengage his Canon lodged under the shelter of Dennington Castle, and fight with the Ennemy if they had a mind to encounter, but it seemes they had enough of the last, for they looking on and not offering or daring to oppose, the ordnance were drawne of and conveyed to Oxford, whither after some stay, seeing hee could not invite the fearfull enemy to come into the field, the King with his brave and Royall army marched backe to Oxford. *Hee waites on yᵉ King to Newbury.* *The Canon are disengaged and drawn to Oxford.*

Many of Sʳ John his Regiment formerly freed from prison, after some expectation of their Colonell had put them selves for present entertaynement under other commaunders, but upon his release repaired to hym ¶ whome with some others Sʳ John one day trayning the King passing by asked whose men they were *Mine,* saith hee, *my Liege to do your Maᵗʸ service,* the King gently smiling com- *Fol. 43 D* mended and encouraged hym saying *It is well donne Sr John I will provide you more horse ere long.*

The Obedience of a Souldier.

Among other duties in the life of a souldier one is an exact and punctual Obedience to the commaunds of their superiour officers, which is so precise that they judge a disgrace and disparagement unto them not onely to refuse, but even to wave any difficult or lesse pleasing enterprize if imposed. Sr John was alwais most pliable to the orders of his commaunders wherefore hee renounced whatsoever particular commodity or private Interest to obey them.

Hee is commaunded to gather contribution at Swanburne in Buck:

Fol. 44

He was appointed with a strong party of horse to gather certaine contribution due and unpaid at Swanburne and there abouts in Buckingham shire and although hee could not but thinke that his beeing employed therein would probably give distast to ¶ Alisbury and Newport, two Parliament-Garrisons of that County, which perhaps thereupon might fall heavie upon the Ladie his Mother who liveth under their lash, yet being commaunded hee could not in point of Honour (which a souldier and gallant gentleman stands nicely upon) refuse to obey; though otherwise it went against the hayre to doe any thing which might seeme grievous or burdensome to his Country as his fore-past Actions at Grafton may well testifie.

This businesse with as much sweetnesse, gentlenesse and moderation as the nature of such an Action might require, for it is alwais a hard taske and ungratefull employment to wrest money from people refractory and unwilling.

Hee pursued 60 Alisbury horse to the Walls.

Fol. 44 D

Having performed what hee came for, upon his returne hee discovered a Party of about threescore Alisbury horse, whome hee in the interim faced, while secretly hee drew of some of his men to get behind them and intercept their passage home-ward, intending then with his other troopers to have fallen upon them ¶ but they discovering the intended stratageme put spurres to their fresh and unfoiled horses and ride for it. Sr John with his best horses (for many with their long marches were much haltered and out of heart) rid pell-mell among them, wounded many killed some and pursued the rest to Womens-bridge close by Alisbury.

There was not one drop of blood drawne from any of his, but with their spurres from their horses sides. That night by the carelessenesse of the keepers to whome they were entrusted some prisoners stole away in the darke night; but next day hee brought about sixteene into Oxford with their armes and horses, whither the report of this so well managed ¶ exploit arrived before hym, with singular commendations of his discretion prudence and valour.

Fol. 45

Soone after hee was sent with his Ma^{ty} to joyne his Regiment to the Lord Gorings Army in the West, where first hee was made Commaunder of a Brigade then Major Generall in place of Sr Marmaduke Langdale, who so bravely relieved Pomfret Castle besieged and got such a great Victory over them with inconsiderable number of men.

He is made by ye L. Gor: Com: of a Brigade then Maj: Gen:

The Lord General Goring understanding that the Enemy had possessed a towne called Christ-Church, which they had partly fortified, hee sent Sr John, with the commaund of five hundred foot and nere upon a thousand horse and Dragons to beat them out of it, and make it good for his Maties service; hee marched on horse-back at the head of the foot, and though a gallant Major of foot was killed ¶ at his stirrop, yet hee still advanced on and with the foot beat the Enemies out of their workes with their great losse into the Church nere which his men gained a house. Hee still sit on horse-back encouraging the foot in their assault of the church, and escaped narrowly many dangerous shots made at hym. But seeing the Church could not bee wonne by force of foot but by famine or ordinance of which hee was not provided, and beeing acertained that a great body of Souldiers were upon their nere march to releave their fellowes gonne to church against their

At Christ-Church hee rideth at ye head of the foot.

Fol. 45 D

will by appointment and order hee drew of his men without any considerable losse and repaired safe to the mayne armie.

Sr John in his Office of Major Generall was so carefull of his charge that what others usuallie entrust to their Adjutants and subordinate officers, upon whose weake shoulders they disburthen ¶ the heavie load of their weighty affaires, hee would alwais attend to them himself : and the chief Commaunders were so confident of his vigilancy and care that when they saw hym present, they conceived they might bee dispensed withall to absent themselves for some howers from their severall Offices, not doubting but hee would supply what might bee wanting in their absence.

Sr John well knowing in his discretion of how dangerous a consequence it was for souldiers upon duty to bee carelesse and negligent, especially the Ennemie being at hand and ready to lay hold upon any the least advantage given, whereby often whole armies and townes relying upon them, have bene at unawares surprized by undiscovered ennemies till it was too late to prevent : hee severall tymes in the day and night, as occasion served, went to observe how the out-guards (of whose care and diligence depended the safety of the whole army) discharged their duty, and the trust reposed in them, and if hee ¶ marked any neglect hee would mildly put them in mynd of the danger both themselves and the army incurred thereby which gentle admonition more prevailed with them then the menacing words, fearfull oathes and often severe blowes of some other commaunders lesse maisters of themselves and their passions then governours of their souldiers.

He was still very close in carrying on his designes, keeping them in his breast and not imparting them to any till the necessary tyme was of putting them in execution, which course if it had bene punctually observed in his M^{aties} Armies by the chief commaunders and others privie to the mysteries of warre since the beginning thereof, their resolved intentions had not bene so frequently prevented nor their ₁secret counsells anticipated by the Ennemy to the great domage of the Kings once flourishing armies, to the discouraging of his faithfull souldiers and heartning of his Ennemies.

If this example of Sʳ John had bene put ¶ in practise both in the army and Court, the close Committee at London would not with their golden key have opened the Kings Cabinet and the Results of Councells of warre, nor would their armies in all probability have had such prosperous successe in their undertakings, as of late, but if some notoriously detected in this kind by an exemplar punishment had bene made a president to others it would have kept them in their duty and courbed them, for reward and punishment are as it were the two axel-trees whereon the wheeles of a well governed Kingdome or common-wealth are turned.

_{Fol. 47}

Taunton in Sommerset-shyre having bene long besieged and distressed by the kings forces under Sʳ Richard Greenfield the parliament sent Sʳ William Waller Westward to relieve if hee could his afflicted brethren with his army; but hee found it a harder taske then hee conceited for the right Honᵇˡᵉ the Lord Goring attended his motions and ¶ his no lesse vigilant then valiant Major Generall Sʳ John Digby gave him leave to rest nether night or day, but still plied hym and wearied hym out with almost continuall alarmes falling upon his quarters not onely in the night (beating hym at his owne weapon) but in the morning, at noone-day and at all howers even in the view of his head-quarters, where notwithstanding hee lay couchant not daring peepe forth to the rescue of his men who were struck with such panick feare and amazement and terrour that they have rid through townes full speed with their naked swords in their hands, where their fellowes without giving them an alarme whereby within an hower after their quarters perhaps have bene beaten up. Wherefore in the space of three weeks at the most, Sʳ William Wallers whole army was killed partly and taken by Sʳ John partly dispersed, and put to a shamefull flight.

_{Taunton besieged by Sʳ Rich. Green.}

_{Fol. 47 D}

_{S. W. Wallers Armie defeated by beating up his quart: in 3 weeks.}

Then Generall Goring joyning his forces to Sʳ Richard Greenfields in a short tyme had so ¶ straitned Taunton and driven it to such exigents that without speedy relief it was upon the tearmes of capitulating and surrending, when unluckily the Lord Goring horse beeing called away under pretense of securing the Kings march out of Oxford towards the relief of Chester then besieged, in the

_{Fol. 48}

_{The L. Gor: Ho: called from Taunton.}

8

meane season for all the Westerne horse and foot left behind to make good the siege, Taunton was relieved by an inconsiderable number of the Enemy to the small credit of the Westerne men, who if as willing as able might with ease have hindred it

Taunton relieved for all y⁺ Westerne forces.

Cromwell had beseiged Faringdon but withdrew upon the approach of the Lord Gorings forces, yet some of his men possessed themselves of New-bridge with intention to have interrupted the Lord Gorings passage; notwithstanding which opposition by the Heroicall courage of the Lord Generall who in person charged them most resolutely and of gallant Major Generall Sʳ John Digby ¶ and part of the Regiment of the brave Lord Carnavon whose valour still breathed in his men, after a sharp dispute at sharp for above half an hower with disgrace and much losse they were beaten from the bridge and forced to runne for it. Which hapned even in the nick of tyme for otherwise if they had made good the bridge and joyned with their other forces beyond the water they would have endangered to have fallen upon the Lord Gorings quarters that night.

Cromwell draws from Faringdon.

Fol. 48 D

His men beaten at Newbridge.

The relievers of Taunton in their returne homeward were encountred by the Kings horse at South-Petherton bridge which they had strongly manned, yet by the Valour of the Lord Goring and his Major Generall Sʳ John they were forced and pursued in great disorder and confusion to Taunton, where they were besieged togeather with their brethren whome they had so lately relieved, and helped them more speedily away with the provisions laid in, but they were unwelcome because uninvited guests.

The Relievers of Taunton driven back againe into y⁺ Castle.

Fol. 49

¶ But Taunton now growne more confident by reason of the unexpected supplie of these new forces driven in against their will, made frequent sallies and often fell upon the guards of horse and foote with different successe. Wherefore Sʳ John desirous to redresse these inconveniences was carefull often in his owne person to observe and see how the guards discharged their severall duties in which the whole army was so much interessed, and having one afternoone certaine intelligence that the Ennemy with a strong party of horse was abroad hee drew forth three score musquetiers,

Taunton falls on y⁺ Kings gards.

and himself would needs have the leading and ordering of them hee disposed them in an ambuscade in a place very advantagious for their owne security, whence without danger they might have killed most of the Enemies horse as they were of necessity to passe by ; but the musquetiers stood not to their armes and their hearts, or honesly or both failed them and they hym ¶ in his greatest need of their service, for the musquetiers would not shoot at but slowly, though encouraged and commaunded by Sr John, till the Enemy was now out of distance ; and then they discharged a whole voley, which cowardlinesse or rather wilfull neglect of their duty the Enemy out of their reach observing, returned againe and let freely fly their pistols and carbines at the foot not able to approach with their horse by reason of a deep dick and banke betweene so well the ambuscade was chosen for the security of the foot and certaine annoyance of the Ennemy, if they had showed themselves couragious souldiers and men of their hands.

<small>Sr John leadeth 60 musquetiers to an Ambush.</small>

<small>They stand not to their armes.</small>

<small>Fol. 49 D</small>

They killed the Captaine of the foot a gallant resolute man, and shot Sr John in the right arme somewhat above the elbow, which wound nothing amated his undaunted courage, hee drew of thinking at first hee had receaved but some slight hurt and rid with his men pleasantly and ¶ merrily at a good distance of, where being dressed the wound appeared greater then was apprehended where taking no rest that night in regard of the extraordinary anguish and paine, the next day in a souldier-like litter hee was conveyed to Bridgewater the next towne of safely from the danger of the approaching Ennemy.

<small>Sr John is shot in ye right arme.</small>

<small>Fol. 50</small>

<small>Hee is carried to Bridgewater.</small>

The right Honble the Lord Generall Goring with the chief Commaunders often visited hym and seemed much to lament his sad case, and resented the want they found of hym in their army which was more particularly taken notice of by all and found at the unfortunate Battaile not long after at Lamport.

<small>He is visited and lamented by ye prime Commaunders.</small>

Among their great advantages the Parliament hath had of his Ma^{ty} I conceive the least hath not bene that they have had so great choise both of sea and land-chirurgions whereby it hath happened that many of their men though grievously and dangerously wounded,

<small>The Parliam. have great advantage of ye King in good chirurgions.</small>

Fol. 50 D have bene strangely and beyond ¶ expectation cured as might bee instanced in Major Skippon and others ; and on the contrary his Majesties men have miscarried and dyed of slight seeming hurts for want of good, experienced and skilfull chirurgions, whereof there hath bene too frequent and wofull tryall.

The Lord Generall Goring was pleased to leave for his cure the chirurgion Generall of his army who though it is hoped did his endeavour, yet ether too confident of his owne skill, or not fully apprehending the danger or for some other reasons would not permit other chirurgions (after the 2 or 3 tyme when there appeared no danger) to bee present at the opening and dressing of the wound, which was never thoroughly searched nor launched to find and take out the bullet and when hee was often importunely desired to have the opinion and advise of some other chirurgions hee would not heare of it saying it would bee a disparagement to hym to consult with any who were under hym although all sufficiently

Fol. 51 know that even the best ¶ Doctours and chirurgions who conceive their patients in danger doe usually admit a Councell of those of their profession, the better to administer to them what by the unanimous consent of all is conceived most fitting. Which course if it had bene taken in ordering of S\u02b3 John his wound it would have given his freuds and the world better satisfaction and had cleared the chirurgion himself from suspicion of any neglect of his duty according to his place and profession, to which now thorough too much an overweening conceit of his owne sufficiency and skill in rejecting the advise of others, hee hath made himself liable.

It is generally believed that the hurt had not proved mortall if the wound had bene well searched and ordered from the beginning and afterwards by a skillfull, honest and carefull chirurgion ; for the bullet as it was discovered after his death, having made its way through the bone of the arme lay but little under the skin, which the chirurgion, launcing when it was too late without difficulty tooke out.

Fol. 51 D S\u02b3 John lay day and night in unspeakable and ¶ excessive paine which hee endured with invincible patience, the anguish of his wound debarred him almost of all rest, hee was kept at a very spare dyet under pretence least hee should fall into a feaver ; his wound never disposed to gangrene or swell upward.

The one and thirty dayes hee kept his bed in small rest and great paine of his wound, hee spent most piously and religiously in the frequent and continuall exercice of true solid and christian Vertues to the great edification of those who gave their continuall attendance upon hym ; hee was most exactly and punctually observant of the prescriptions, orders and directions of the Doctour and chirurgion.

The weaker hee daily grew in body the more vigorous hee became in spirit, and finding himself in a declining condition hee carefully used the best and wholesome meanes his languishing state worthily required ; wherefore practising invincible patience and perfectly resigned to the will of God, hee piously breathed forth his pure soule ¶ into the hands of his Creatour the sixteenth day of July, in the yeare of our Lord one thousand six hundred forty five about fower in the morning ; and released from the prison of this wretehed mortality, is rewarded in Heaven, as wee confidently hope and piously believe for his Life so innocently and vertuously led on Earth.

Bridgewater had now bene closely besieged by Sr Thomas Fairefax about a fortnight, wherefore his funerall exequies could not very solemnly bee performed. Hee was buried in the Chancell of the Church, his herse was carried and accompied that night by the chief Commaunders and prime Gentry then in towne, who by their unfamed grief gave evident signes and testimonies how much they resented his Death. The next day, the Besiegers it seemes having good intelligencers within the walles cryed out in an insulting and upbraiding manner to the Defendants. *Where is now your stout Champion Digby hee can no more ¶ defend you for hee is dead and buried last night.* Within few dayes after the towne fell into the hands of the Ennemy.

To the never dying Memory of the Vertue and Valour of this brave and gallant champion of his King Sr John, not onely at the desire and solicitation of some frends who have interest in mee, but much more out of my respects and knowledge of his worthy person and deserts, I was willing to contribute these my grosse materialls wishing and hoping some more able hand will bee pleased to order them, and some more expert artificer will polish and square them by their more exact Line and Compasse of skill into an historicall Monument wherein his Vertuous and valiant exploits may bee enregistred and engraven. My earnest desire is that these my rude draughts may at least serve as an obscure and darke foile to set of the bright lustre of better pens in the same subject ¶ whereby I shall deeme my small paines happily bestowed if never so little I may assist to express the deserved praise and Noble Worth of hym, whome living I affectionately loved, and gloriously dead in defense of his soveraigne, I honour.

Fol. 53

I can not in testimony of my sincere and true respects to so well deserving and gallant a worthy, but inscribe upon his monument this Epitaph.

Sr John Digby late valiant Major Generall of his sacred M$_a^{ties}$ forces in the West (under the right Honble L. Generall Goring) sprung from noble and renowned Ancestours, embellished with the most radiant gemmes of Vertue, Learning Education and Valour, which shined in the whole course of his life, like a bright Sunne having enlightened this our little world of England with his bright rayes, overshadowed at Taunton in Sommerset shire with a ruddy or rather bloody cloud ¶ set at Bridgewater in the west the sixteenth of July one thousand six hundred fourty five by a noble death in defense of his Soveraigne Liege King Charles ; and shall, wee hope rise againe in the East of a blessed and endlesse Eternity in company of all the Saints and those glorious Martyrs, who having washed their stoles in the sacred blood of the Immaculate Lamb, have dyed them in graine with the rich Cochenell of their owne blood and togeather with them shall sing an immortall and victorious Pœan and in triumphe to this never dying Generall Christ Jesus under whose Royall Standard of the holy Crosse hee so manfully and vertuously fought during life.

Fol. 53 D

FINIS.

¶ A SHORT CHARACTER OR MODELL OF THE OUTWARD AND INWARD MAN OF Sir JOHN DIGBY

I will imitate herein a famous artist who being requested by a frend to paint hym a great and fierce Lyon according to his perfect and full proportion and dimensions, not having at hand a table large enough, with few draughts of his skilfull pensill limmed but one of his pawes with this Motto under it Ex ungue Leonem, that is by this one pawe guesse and make an estimate of the whole Lion. In like manner I avouch in the present subject we handle Ex ungue Leonem by this short abstract of Sr John Digby gather his greatnesse and Worth if hee were set forth at the full with the lively and well mingled Colours of his vertues, Valour, and Innocency.

¶ Sr John Digby nobly descended, was even from a child, religiously pious and devout towards God, obedient and lovingly dutifull to his mother the Lady Digby of Gotehurst in Buckinghamshire affectionately observant to his tutours, respective to his equalls, affable and courteous to his inferiours and finally amiable and loving to all with whome hee did consort.

Hee was well seene in the liberall sciences; hee studied and defended his whole Course of Philosophie in a frequent Assembly of Princely and Honble Personages with generall applause and singular honour to our English Nation, hee was skilfull in Musique and naturally perfect in the Italian and French.

Hee diligently reaped the true fruits from his travailes by carefully and exactly polishing and civilizing his exterior man by the quaint gentilenesse of foraigne Nations, but not in the least tainting his inward, though in the midst of dangerous allurements, with the staynes of their vices.

HECTOR BRITANNICUS

Fol. 55 ¶ Hee was rarely endowed with a singular and solid Judgement, a quick apprehension and perspicacious understanding : hee was maister of a faithfull and tenacious Memory, which served hym as a safe magazine to store up so rich treasures of different learning. His mynd was still busied and seriously employed in most laudable objects, and generously disdayned whatsoever might seeme less suitable to one of his profession, breeding and quality.

His Conversation was judicious and modest, his Recreations innocently and harmelesly pleasant, and no way offensive, but rather cheerefully gratefull, and gratefully cheerefull, his discourse was never lavish and extravagant, but grave, moderate, substantiall and confined within the bounds and limits of a rescrued discretion; his Words but few, yet such and so fitly couched that every one might seeme to have passed the touch-stone of a prudent circumspection being poized in the equall and just balance of a sage decorum ; accommodating each sentence and word to the

Fol. 55 D ¶ parties humour and disposition with whome hee treated, yet without any affectation, Vanity or singularity.

This his so well tempered comportment rendred hym acceptable and kindly gratefull not onely to his frends and domesticks with whome he lovingly and familiarly conversed, but even to strangers and forraigners who were ambitious of his acquaintance and frendship, of which though hee was not at all nice yet after a civill entertaynement hee discretly let it fall on his part when hee saw any inconvenience might accrew thereof.

Hee refused noble proffers of hon^{ble} advancement in forraine States and Warres, being desirous to stand disengaged to strangers in case his King might have occasion to make use of hym, as hee did in an eminent Manner, in whose service and defense hee willingly and couragiously afterwards pawned his Life.

Fol. 56 And thus much for his outward man obvious ¶ to the view of all, much more might bee said touching his inward, but my prefixed brevity will not licence mee to exceed my bounds proposed to my self in the beginning, yet I will give a slight hint thereof which may serve as a small scantling of a larger piece which I hope will easily gathered by the whole tenour of his Life, but espacially by that publique, and constant profession of his Faith being surrounded with the whole Scotish army when hee was taken prisoner by the Scots at Newborne fight nere Newcastle in the North, for being demaunded of what Religion and faith hee was, I am, saith hee, a Roman Catholique and so am resolued to live and dy.

¶ From this so firme, constant and lively faith sprung his stedfast hope and confidence in Almighty God, that though frequently tossed, with boisterous waves and violent surges of afflictions, miseries and Imprisonments which hee most resolutely and patiently suffered for his Love to God and his King yet hee was never seene to bee dejected or dismaid but cheered both himself and others with Hope to see the storme blowne over, and enjoy the quiet calme of a better condition. Fol. 56 D

His ardent charity towards God hee maid brightly shine by his carefull observing of his holy Commaundements and keeping his soule and conscience free from the staynes of sinne as much as humane frailty would permit, using speciall care to eschiew occasions of sinne, and applying seasonable and convenient remedies both to preserve from falling and to raise hym being fallen.

Hee exercized frequently with much devotion and attention the highest and chiefest acts of ¶ Religion, and when hee was to undergoe an enterprize which might imply danger and difficulty hee advised with discreet and wise vertuous men how hee was to behave himself therein ; and in an exquisite manner for many dayes togeather sequestring himself from others wordly employments, recommended to God the successe thereof, craving most piously his divine assistance for the well ordering and managing the businesse which hee tooke in hand. Fol. 57

Though his prudence, Judgement and discretion was great, yet hee would not rely upon them but in matters of greater moment and higher concernement hee permitted himself to bee overswayed by the opinion of others, whose dictamen and Verdict hee would humbly follow, though the party otherwise was not so well able to advise as hee hymself, so farre was hee from overvalewing his owne and undervalewing other mens opinions, which is a rare thing and seldome found in one in whome so many prerogatives both of grace and Nature were in their prime.

Fol. 57 D ¶ Hee was faithfull, sincere and loving to his frends and kind, affable, gentle, civill and courteous to his neighbours. Pitty and Compassion seemed to bee inbred and naturall to hym. Hee was still very wary not to taxe the defects of others yea though hee heard any enveigh against some persons absent, hee would ether excuse them or utter some thing to their praise or at least modestly hold hys peace. Hee was never given to those three most ordinary and hatefull vices of Lust swearing and drinking which beare so great sway in the world and most frequently spoile and drowne other good and commendable parts. Much more might and perhaps hereafter may at a more seasonable tyme bee recounted concerning these and other Vertues which were singular and remarkeable in hym, which may serve as a patterne for all to imitate.

But that which did most adorne these and such like Graces, Vertues and good qualities in hym, was, his being free from Pride
Fol. 58 and an ¶ overweening conceit in regard to them.

Hee was alwais void of singularity and affectation, and behaved hymself with such modestie that his diserved praises uttered by any in his presence did stayne his cheeks with a bashfull blush so farre was hee from being trumpeter of his owne commendations.

What shall I say of his Magnanimity and generous Valour? of which hee hath given ample testimonies to the whole Kingdome: shall I speake of his Judgement and knowledge in martiall affaires? It were in vain for it is notoriously knowne both to frends who highly prized hym for it, and to Ennemies who tryed it in severall encounters to their owne cost. Yet I can not omit in conclusion his unstayned Loyalty towards his King, whose cause hee espoused

FINIS.

POEMS
WRITTEN IN HONOUR OF
Sir JOHN DIGBY
Sir JOHN SMITH
Sir JOHN GAGE
AND OTHERS

Sʳ JOHN DIGBY

¶ You three brave Impes of gallant Digbies race   Fol. 59
  Whose Fathers worth through Europe doth rebound
  Your unkles Vertues in your Lives enchase.
  Which will your names to after Ages sound,
  For Vertue is a Gemme most rich and cleare,
  Which men to God and the World doth endeare.

  Paint upon the tables of your pure soules .
  Apelles-like in Colours mingled well
  The Pourtrait of his Vertues, which controules
  All soule-killing Vice which guides to Hell,
  This will your Unkle's soule in Heaven rejoyce
  This will you make high Heavens Darlings choise
  The Noble Romans caused their Children beare
  About their necks the Picture of some rare
  Ancestour, which should to their eyes appeare
  With whose brave acts they might their lives compare
  With whose bright lustre they might darknesse chase
  Of Vice, which would their noble names embase
¶ So in your Breasts your Unkles picture weare   Fol. 59 D
  Garnished with unstain'd faith and Loyalty
  To God and his King, and zeale hee did beare
  Unto his countries weale and honestie

AN INVITATION

Which Vertues make hym live in each Mans breast
And yield hym a prime place among the blest
And when you are allur'd to uglie sin
Like that Roman your unkles image kisse
Which you should find lodged your breast within
And say *farre bee't from us to doe ought amisse
Or of thy name unworthy,* this will bee
A Bridle to Vice a spurre t' Honestie.

FINIS.

Madame, the lost is great you have sutain'd
By the Death of your Sonne, whose Vertues gain'd
Him Honour with his frends and Foes, his Fame
In future Ages shall enhance your Name.
I must not wonder that your eyes doe powre
Fountaines of teares for so choise a flowre
Cropt from your garden in his highest prime
Of Worth and Vertues unblemish'd with Crime
Yet give mee leave t'avouch, those teares should run
Not in griefs channel for your pious Sonne
Stint then those floods of grief, let teares of Joy
Supply their place, hoping hee doth enjoy
¶ Without all feare of loosing, Heavens blisse   Fol. 61
And you in Glories expecting is.

FINIS.

Englands Funerall Teares shed upon the Tomb
of
Sr JOHN DIGBY

All mourners sad consigne your teares to mee
Who have just cause my self to moane, since hee
Who was my Joy is dead, my gallant Knight
My martiall Digby, and true Valours Light
And is hee dead? my Heart tells mee hee lives
And ever shall in it, my eyes it gives
A check for being Fountaines of sad teares
Since hee is gonne to dwell above the spheares.
Why should you weep saith it? though hee is dead
Envie can not cut his Vertues Lifes thread.
Hee Phœnix-like from his fragrant nest
Of Vertues Baulmes, is flowne to perfect rest.
¶ His noble goodnesse and deserving Parts
To enstall hym a Worthy moves Mens Hearts.
His zeale and Valour link'd to his loyall mind
Shall render hym the Darling of Mankind,
His love to his King and Country shall ly
Enroll'd in times eternall Memory.

FINIS.

DAPHNIS You mournefull Westerne Nymphe of Britaines Ile
         Whither is fleeted all your wonted Joy!
         Why to sad ruth is chang'd your gladsome smile?
         Your teares proclame some heart-launcing annoy :
         Vouchsafe to open the source of your grief,
         And I, if able, will afford relief.

¶ NYMPHE Hath not the dolefull Eccho pierc'd thine eares   Fol. 62
         That gallant Digbies shining sunne is set
         In Westerne Deepes, this makes out brinish teares
         Streame in full tides, this doth our grief beget
         Wise, grave, discreet was hee, and humbly low
         And for his country weale endur'd much woe
         His prudence, Worth and Valour did excell,
         His sage and watchfull Prowesse were most rare,
         His wisdome did foresee and eke foretell
         The wretched state wherein we plonged are
         Since then our Digbie's dead why should not I,
         In wayling hym, sound forth our Miserie.

DAPHNIS I can not but beare part of England Crosse
         In parting with her Digby, in whose Death
         The West must needs resent heavy losse,
         For hee to their Armies did courage breath
         I can not but sad Nymph your grief commend
         I cannot but condole such a Frend

Fol. 62 D ¶ NYMPHE His sunne dispersed Wallers armies cloud,
Hee was the Anchore of our Westerne trust,
Hee was the Bowre wherein we did us shroud
Hee was our Prop whereof was no distrust,
Our sunne is set, and our Anchore is burst,
Our Bowre is faded and our Prop is crusht
Hee was the starre which our Armies guided,
The Commaunders staffe which did direct their pace,
His Valours tree from foes them shade provided
Hee was a Leader did his Country grace,
Our Starre is fall'n and our staff is broke
Our tree and Leader felt Deaths fatall stroke
Our sunne, our Anchore, our Piller, our Bowre
Is set, is crushed, is shrunk, is decay'd
Our Starre, our staffe, our tree our Leaders powre
Is fallen, broken fell'd and hath Death obay'd
Yet Death thou striv'st in vaine from mee hym to part
A living tomb He raise hym in my Heart.

FINIS.

What is 't I heare ecchoing in myne Eares?
A dolefull sonnet fountaine of sad teares
Gushing from the flood-gates of weeping eys,
Which with heart-throbbing sighes thus mournfull cries
Brave Sr John Digby flowre of Valour, dread
Of his Foes, fightings dead in Honours Bed
Is Digby dead? can's Martiall Prowesse dy?
Can's Vertue, Wisdome, Innocency dy?
How is hee dead? whose undistained fame
Shall blazon unto Mortalls Digbies name,
His name which never can obscured bee
By thickest clouds of Envy, nor shall hee
Eclypsed stand through malice of his foes,
For his sun-shine of Vertue will disclose
¶ His Worth and Valour, whence both frend & Foe   Fol. 63 D
Hee rich & poore endear'd, both high and low
Is Digby therefore dead? whose better Part
In Heav'n enjoyes his Maker and whose Heart
Fountaine of Life, on Earth enshryned lies
In the devoted Breasts of frends, whose eys
Witnesse their grief yet cease, o cease those teares
Which sad tributes of bleeding Hearts appeares
Attend what his blest soule from Heav'n doth sound
And let it from your Eares to Heart rebound
Why mourne you mee who have quit Worldly toyes
To bee possessed of immortall Joyes!

      FINIS.

AN INVECTIVE AGAINST DEATH
FOR UNTIMELY CROPPING THE FLOWRE OF
Sr JOHN DIGBIES VERTUES

Fol. 64

O Death how fatall was thy dismall blow,
For when brave Digbies flowre did shoote & grow
Thou cropt it in his early Vertues bud,
Was it perhaps because thou saw'st hym good,
¶ Sage, grave, discreet, humble, just and devout
Thou thought old Nestors glasse hee had run out
But this thy custome is, a man that 's rare
Thou scarce gives leave, old ages gowne to weare.
De : 'Vaine man why gainst my deed dost thou complaine?
Why dost thou Godd accuse? under whose raigne
I but a servant am, hee bid mee seaze
Digby's rare flowre because it did hym please,
I cropt it, put it in his hand, whose sent
Of choisest Vertues gave hym prime content.
If longer it in earthly mold had staid
His leaves had fall'n wither'd and decay'd
But in Gods hand hee shall securely rest
And never fading spring among the blest.'

FINIS.

Did in their proper Center lodged stand
His Breast a Mag'zine was of Vertues treasure
Wherewith God hym endow'd in great measure
His spirit enrich'd with Vertues choisest Gemmes
And quaint endowments of Gods heav'nly grace
Distasting Earth and all vaine Honours stemmes
Repaired againe oft soone to the place
From whence it came and doth admiring sit
His makers essence who created it
To soone alas for those who did affect,
His humble Mildnesse and deserving Parts ·
Too soone for those, who now sadly reflect.
How hee by Love hath stolne away their hearts
Their Hearts which hee to Heav'n hath captives led
In loves sweet Bands fast ty'd & manicled
But first hee dy'ed for his Sov'raigne King
Whose Cause hee espoused in many a fight
Whence his fame will in future ages ring
And make hym shyne with Vertues radiant Light,
A sacrifize for's King and Countrie's Good
Hee made hymself by shedding of his Blood
At Taunton Deane his right arme was shot
Which had supported long the Westerne Crowne
Witnesse is Wallers Army which could not
Rest from Hym secure in field nor in towne,
But now his Army lost, Waller did hie

Fol. 65

To London to raise hym a new supply
But while our Knight did at Bridgewater ly,
Sore wounded, at Lamport in that sad day
The Kings Army mist his **Vigilancie**
And sage conduct, which did his foes dismay
Soone after fell the **Westerne Crowne** to ground
Because hee dy'd who did their foes confound.

FINIS.

One day as I did musing sadly stand,
With pensive thought casting in my Mind
How many gallant Champious of our Land
Since these unnaturall Warres, death unkind
Hath strucken with his fierce & fatall Dart,
Which deeply hath launc'd many bleeding heart
I seem'd to see a comely portly Knight
Mounted upon a stately prancing steed
Whose Armour dazled myne eyes with ye light
Which sparkled from it that I scarce could read
Who it might bee who to my sight appear'd
And of his Valour had such trophies rear'd
Upon his shield in azure field hee wore
A white flowre de luce, which from heav'n was sent
For France to beare in her Armes long before,
Which at this day is that Crownes Ornament
The white flowre show'd his Life Innocency
Th'azure that his thoughts soar'd to God on high
¶ I saw an Estridge on his Helmet's Crest   Fol. 66
That bird so much famed in Historie,
Because his stomach Iron can digest
This Motto *nul qu'un* was thereby
Which to mee seem'd not void of Mystery,
Wherefore I wish'd some scene in Heraldry
Who mee the hidden secrets would unfold
Of his so strange a Motto *None but one*,
When suddenly I found my thoughts grow bold
To dive into the meaning that as but one

Bird could Iron, but Digby could digest
Such Iron-dangers which hym still opprest
His Love to his dread Sov'raigne was so great
That nothing to hym seem'd to bee so hard,
Which like **Waxe** melted not before this heat,
This Perills from his gen'rous mind debarr'd.
This, this maid hym undaunted gainst his foes
This did his Valour to the hight disclose.

Fol. 66 D ¶ Upon his head a Laurell did appeare
A Wreath well purchased for Victorie
On his left Arme more girlands did hee beare
Then noble Scœna Valours Prodigie
But what is 't did I see on his right arme?
My fainting heart presaged some great harme.
I saw him beare his right arme in a string
As if hee wounded were in bloody fight,
Which hee endur'd in defense of his King
Opposing his Foes with all powre and might,
The wound above the elbow seemed to bee
Which nought amated his stout **constancie**;
I saw the Blood trickling downe amaine,
Which purpled all his garments with its **dy**,
It gush'd as if broken hee had some vayne
Or for a skillful surgeon did I cry
In vaine I call'd for too soone alas
Tyme warned cruell Death to turne his glasse
Have you not seene some choise flowre in its prime
Parched with scorching Rayes of Titan bright

Fol. 67 ¶ Hang downe its drooping head before full **tyme**
Faire flourishing i'th morne fading ere night
Then thinke this but a type of our sad case
And with your teares his tomb bee pleas'd to grace,
But why should I thus wish you teares to shed,
" Since that his soule **releas'd** from **mortall shryne**
With divine Nectar and Ambrosia fed

Sr JOHN DIGBY
his Soule by Angels carried to Heaven

When I one night gazed upon the skie
Inly lamenting Sr John Digbies Fate
I seem'd from the Westerne Coasts to espie
A starre shoot towards Heav'n which did-abate
My weake ey-sight with its lustre cleare
And light some made all things nere hand appeare
¶ As I stood wondering what this might imply
Mee thought I heard this Voice sound in myne eares,
The starre which thoe beheld, doth signifie
The Soule of Digby mounted bove the spheares
There to receave guerdon of his paine
Which for his God and King hee did sustaine
At which voyce joy'd I cast againe my sight
Towards the Heav'ns which ore Bridge-water lies
When suddenly appear'd a wondrous light
Which did illustrate all the bordring skies
In midst whereof I saw a Beauty rare,
Wherewith no Worldly Beauty can compare.
A Damzell faire accoutred all in white
Yet this her garment sprinkled was with blood
Which Rubie-like had embroder'd it quite
And enlightned the place wherein shee stood,
Then from Heaven two Angels did descend
This beauteous Bride to her spouse to attend
On each side these heavenly ushers guard
This spotlesse Virgen towards Heav'ns high Court
¶ To reape of her pure life condigne reward
And with the Saints and Angells to consort
Ascend my thoughts and see her crown'd wth Blisse
Where still in the spring Joy unfading is.

Most Poets to their help their Muses call,
That unto them assisting they would bee
When they some Heros in Verse would install
And raise a tomb t' his lasting Memory
But I no muse, but Digbies genius will
Call to vouchsafe to guide my Novice quill
Come then, o thou blest Genius and inspire
My Love-incensed myud his Worth to sing
That I may warme mee at his flaming fire
Of Love and Loyalty to God and 's King
¶ Open mee the Garden of his pure Soule   Fol. 68 D
To call his Vertues flowres without controule.
Then help mee to compasse a Girland faire,
Wherewith crowne I will his Conquerours Brow,
And though unskillfull yet I will prepare
The Matter, where better Poets may show
Their polished art and well experienc'd Pen,
In painting forth his Picture for brave men.
Forthwith into a Garden was I brought
Most strongly walled and with five dores kept
Still locked that no salvage beast or ought
Might enter, the Allies weeded and swept
The Hedges and the Borders cut, no tree
But well proyn'd and order'd could I see
In midst hereof there stood a fountaine deep
Whose waters were as any crystall cleare
Which sprinkled on the flowres them still did keep
In their first prime and made them fresh appeare

This Garden seem'd a type of Edens Bowres
Which garnished was with choisest trees & flowres
¶ There you might see the azure Violet
Hung downe its humble head & there hard by.
The white & purple gilliflowre were set
The red and white Rose grew unto them nigh,
All which breath'd forth so sweet a fragrancy
That in them I admir'd Gods Majestie
Here first I cropt the humble Violet,
The White Gilliflowre of's Innocency,
The red of Charity which shall bee set
Next to his white Rose of Purity
The red Rose blushing in its scarlet dy
Breath'd Love unto his King and Country
These five sweet flowres ranked in order fit
And ty'd with the crimsen-silke of Gods Love
And of his Neighbours in a Chaplet knit
Shall crowne his Temples in that happie Grove
Where with the blest Angels hee sings his part
And praiseth his God with an humble Heart.

FINIS.

Stay gentle Reader and vouchsafe to cast
An ey on hym with whome this tomb is grac'd
And if thou faine would'st know whose grave it is
Brave Digbies genius tells thee it is his;
Hee was a man justly by all admir'd
Whose Vertuous frendship best men still desir'd
Mild, grave and gentle was hee in his port
And humbly with all mankind did consort
Pious hee liv'd still to Gods will resign'd
His life and manners Heav'ns just Laws confin'd
Meeke in his suffring, patient in his paine
Grace taught hym malice gainst foes to refraine
In brief hee was a man whose noble Parts
Wrested respect and honour from foes Hearts
¶ His frends hee left Example how to trayne
Their Lives in Vertues love Heaven to gaine.

A POSY

FRAMED OF THE NEVER FADING FLOWRES OF VALOUR
THE EARLE OF CARNAVUAN, Sᵣ JOHN DIGBY
Sᵣ JOHN SMITH, Sᵣ HENRY GAGE
Sᵣ JOHN BEAUMONT, COLONELL MORGAN
COL : MARKLAM & EVERS

Some Skilfull gard'ner planting choisest flowres
Which cast their fragnant sent on verdant bowres
Where Titans rising rayes with guilded Beames
Powres on their short liv'd Beauty quickning streames :
When hee observeth they are in full prime
Hee crops the fairest and watching his tyme
Them in a nose-gay tenders to his Lord
Who to them kind acceptance doth afford
¶ This Garden in Christ Church, the Gard'ner is
Jesus himself, each soule a faire fllowre is
Bedew'd with Christ owne blood and doth admit
The bright Rayes of his Grace which nourish it.
Christ daily walking in this Gardens pulls
Now one sweet flowre, now an other culls
Witnesse Carnavuan Digby, Smith and Gage
Beaumont, Evers, Morgan, Markham, who wage
Warre for their King, and nobly dying live
Never to dy and us Example give
To combat gainst our ghastly foes till death.
And never yield although wee loose our Breath
The eight faire flowres Christ pleas'd to gather
And in a Posy present his Father
Who cherishing them for his sweet sonne's sake,
Vouchsafeth them into his hands to take

Gentle Reader

Give mee leave here to joyne in my Praises with Sr John Digby those two gallant Worthyes Sr John Smith and Colonell Morgan, who with hym on Earth were straitly linked with the golden chayne of entire Loue and frendship indissoluble even by Death it self and are now, as wee hope joyned in Heaven among that happie Society in *end lesse glory, never to part.*

AN ENCOMIUM

OF THAT BRAVE CHAMPION OF HIS KING CHARLES AND NOBLE RESCUER OF HIS STANDARD ROYALL AT EDGE-HILL
Sr JOHN SMITH

Fol. 71 D

When all alone I musing stood
Mee thought I saw a Warlike Knight
¶ Whose Armour embrew'd was with blood,
Which hee had shed in cruell fight
Hee seem'd a second Mars in Field
And to his King prov'd a shield
His visage was both sterne and mild
Sterne to his foes, mild to his frend
His manly face nicenesse exil'd
Er'n Foes his noble Worth commend
By's Vertue from freuds, love hee gain'd
By's Valours courb Foes hee restrain'd
Willing to know who this might bee
Who of his Valour trophies rear'd
My thoughts sharply seem'd to check me
Not knowing who to mee appear'd
This is brave Sr John Smith say they
Who hath for Valour wonne the day
Hee pawn'd his Life for Charles his King
At Alsford in that bloody fight
England shall still his Prowesse ring

Fol. 72

¶ And blazon forth his Valours might
His Vertues shall registred lie
In Gods eternall Memory.

His Name was Smith, who for his King fighting
Unto his foes seem'd a flash of Lighting
Whereat enraged Mars with deadly ire
To his hellish Engine presenteth fire
Which swiftly cutting th' ayre with fiery wing
Kills brave Smith stout Champion of his King
" Whose happie soule franchiz'd from mortal shrine
" *In Heav'ns high Globe like a bright starre shall shine.*

FINIS.

UPON THE UNTIMELY THOUGH HAPPIE DEATH OF THAT RENOWNED AND VERTUOUS GENTLEMAN
COLONELL THOMAS MORGAN
SLAYNE IN DEFENSE OF HIS SACRED MA^{tie} KING CHARLES IN THE FIRST BATTAILE AT NEWBURY

Since Morgans Vertue, Modestie, Renowne
His Learning, mildlenesse, Honour weare the Crowne
His prudence, Wisdome, Justice win Heav'ns goale
Why should his Frends with teares his Death condole?
His Death to his pure soule a Passage is
To bee partaker of eternall Blisse
Among the quires of Saints hee sings his Part
Praising his God with a devoted Heart
Hee pray's for frends to whome on earth his Love
Was bounded with Gods Will, in Heav'n above
Tenders their finall good expecting when
¶ Hee there shall meet them nere to part agen
His Barke hath past secure these wordly seas.
And in Heav'ns Harbour rides at quiet ease
But we alas are tost on boist'rous waves
Which poast us day & night unto our Graves
Yet if true glory bee the onely scope
Of all our Actions wee may firmely hope
At length to anchore in that happie Port
Where none but chosen Vessells doe resort
Such as brave Morgan was ah let us then
Hoise saile for Heaven with such gallant men

FINIS.

SIR HENRY GAGE

Fol. 73 D ¶ I will adde a fourth to these three gallant comaunders to wit Sʳ Henry Gage famous for the relief of Basing the Mansion-House of the right Honᵇˡᵉ the Marquis of Winchester.

> Where Vertue lodgeth it doth often prove
> In Iron-breasts the true Load-stone of Love
> When Wisdome meeteth with a gentile mind
> It doth endeare that subject to mankind
> If Valour in some Worthy makes demurre
> To blazon forth his Praises all concurre
> Doth Prudence lustre joyne to noble deeds
> Of brave achievements hee reaps worthy meeds
> Where Learning doth set of a high-borne Race
> Th'one the other embellishing doth grace
> But when true Goodnesse guildeth other Parts
> Deservedly it ravisheth Mens Hearts
> If one of these singly imparts such praise
> Gage grac'd with all well may weare the Bais.

FINIS.

Clarendon's rebellion, 63.
Cologne, 80, 81.
Cromwell, Oliver, 110.

D

Devizes (the Vize), 84.
Digby, Lady, 70, 90, 98, 106, 115, 125.
Digby, George, 64, 123.
Digby, Sir John, of Mansfield Woodhouse, 63.
Digby, Sir John, 63, 64, 67, 69, 70, 72, 76, 77,'79, 81, 85-86, 87, 89, 94, 95, 96, 97, 99, 100, 101, 102, 104, 105, 108, 109, 110, 113, 115, 123, 126, 127, 129, 130, 131, 133, 134, 136, 137, 139, 141, 142.
Digby, Sir Kenelme, 63, 65, 67, 82, 89, 123.
Dives, Sir Lewys, 90.
Donnington, (Dennington), 105.
Douglasse, Sir Archibald, 78.
Dunstable, 102.
Durham, 76.

E

Easton, 92, 93.
Edge-hill, 73, 81, 84, 87, 142.
Essex, Earl of, 86, 88, 100, 104, 105.
Evers, Colonel, 140.

INDEX

F

Fairfax, Sir Thomas, 112.
Faringdon, 110.
Farmer, (Fermor) Lady, 92.
Florence, 71.

G

Gage, Sir Henry, 63, 65, 121, 140, 146.
Gage, Sir John, 121.
Genoa, 71.
Glemham, Sir Thos., 98.
Gloucester, 86, 88.
Gloucester, Duke of, 63, 64.
Goring, Lord, 107, 109, 110, 111, 112, 114.
Grafton, 86, 91, 92, 93, 98, 106.
Greenfields,(Grenvile),Sir Richard, 109.

H

Haslerig, Sir Arthur, 85.
Heyford, (Heford), 90.
Highgate, 102.
Howard, Sir William, 74.

J

Jermin, Lord, 88.

L

Lamport, 110, 111, 132.
Langdale, Sir Marmaduke, 106.
Lathbury, 84, 99, 101.
Lindsey, Earl of, 73.
London, Maiden-Lane in, 101, 103.
—, Fleet prison in, 102.
Lostwithiel (Lishthiell), 104.

M

Markham, Colonel, 140.
Maurice, Prince, 86.
Morgan, Colonel, 83, 84, 87, 88, 86, 140, 141, 144.

N

Newbury, 89, 90, 105, 144.
Newburn, 67, 76, 78, 80, 115, 117.
Newbridge, 110.
Newcastle on Tyne, 75, 76, 77, 97, 117.
Newport Pagnell, 75, 83, 90, 91, 92, 94, 98, 99, 100, 101, 106.
Northampton, 82, 91.
Northumberland, Earl of, 75.

O

Ouborne, *see* Woburn.
Oxford, 82, 105, 109.

P

Peddington Bridge, 87.
Pennington, Isaac, 101.
Portland, Earl of, 72.

R

Reading, 88.
Richardson, John, 76.
Roundway Down, 84.
Rupert, Prince, 86, 87, 88, 90, 91, 94, 99.

S

St. Albans, 86, 100.
Shelton, 73.

ITER BELLICOSUM
1685

HON. FELLOW OF TRINITY HALL CAMBRIDGE
VICE-PRESIDENT AND HONORARY SECRETARY
OF THE ROYAL HISTORICAL SOCIETY

CAMDEN MISCELLANY
VOL. XII

LONDON
OFFICES OF THE SOCIETY
6 & 7 SOUTH SQUARE
GRAY'S INN
1910

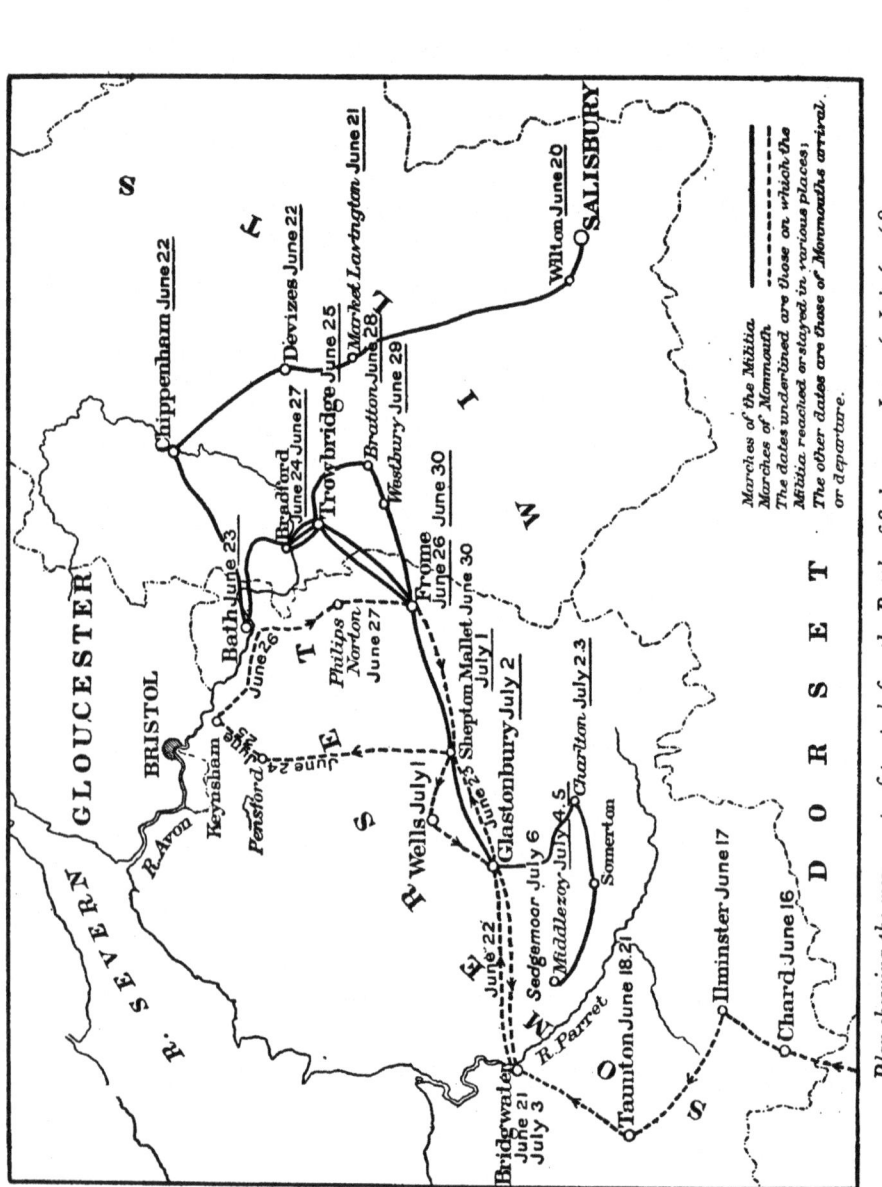

Plan showing the movements of troops before the Battle of Sedgemoor, June 16–July 6, 1685.

PREFACE

This MS., called on the outside " Adam Wheeler, His Account of 1685," was found in Corhampton House, Bishop's Waltham, Hampshire, by Mr. A. R. Malden of Salisbury, M.A., Trinity Hall, Cambridge. It has been put into the hands of the Society by the kindness of the owner, Mrs. Campbell-Wyndham-Long. The history of the writer has not been recovered. Adam Wheeler occurs in the rate-book of St. Edmund's parish, Salisbury, in 1661, but is more likely to be this Adam's father than himself. He was a man of some education, who not only could write and spell but could quote Virgil, *Sic vos non vobis*, and could compose two very indifferent Latin elegiac couplets. Very possibly when not drummer to the Wilts Militia he was a Schoolmaster. He seems to have been rather specially attached to Colonel Wyndham, for whom no doubt he wrote the account. This was John Wyndham, of Norrington, M.P. for Salisbury in 1681 and 1685, father to Thomas, created Lord Wyndham, Chief Justice of the Common Pleas. His direct male line is extinct, but he was a relative of the owner of the MS.

Evidently Wheeler put down some matters as they occurred; for instance his enumeration of the prisoners marched by his regiment was made then and there upon the top of his drum. The account was written up generally after the campaign. The dates are wrong at the beginning. He starts on Wednesday, June 16th, but June 16th in 1685 was a Tuesday. His days of the week are more likely to be right than his days of the month. On what he calls Saturday June 19th, really the 20th I believe, the regiment marched from Salisbury to Wilton. They left Wilton in the afternoon of what he calls Sunday the 20th. He does not mention going to church in Wilton, probably they did; at any rate he would know that it was Sunday morning when they were there. We may take it therefore that the Regiment was first called together on Wednesday June 17th. On the previous Monday the Lord Lieutenant, the Earl of Pembroke, had come to Salisbury, for the Churchwardens' account of St. Thomas' shew 6/- for ringing the bells for his arrival. Two days later is full short time for his forces to be mobilised. On the day when they assembled Monmouth, who had landed at Lyme on the 11th, was at Ilminster. On Saturday June 20th when they marched to Wilton, Monmouth was at Taunton. The dates are wrong by a day till they came to Frome on what he calls the 29th; then 30 appears in the margin, and on Wednesday July 1st they march from Frome to Shepton Mallet, the dates henceforth being correct.

The general reasons for the marches appear fairly clear, if we consider the movements of the enemy. On the afternoon of June 21st and on June 22nd, they made long marches from Wilton to Market Lavington, thence to Devizes and Chippenham. On the 23rd they went to Bath. Monmouth in these days was marching from Taunton to Bridgewater, Glastonbury and Shepton Mallet, evidently aiming at Bristol, or at least a passage of the Avon. Churchill had only a few regulars yet on the spot; and the Militia, though not highly trusted, might be necessary for want of better troops. On the 24th Monmouth was at Pensford, and the Militia marched to Bradford. Circumstances had altered. Feversham was at Bath on the 24th, some cavalry had been pushed on to Bristol, and the main force of the regulars was closing up. They concentrated about Bath on the 26th. There was some idea in Monmouth's army of a dash into Wiltshire as an alternative to attacking Bristol, and at Bradford the Wilts Militia guarded their own frontier, and the Royal Artillery which was still at

murderous weapons of which the drummer disapproved. On the 27th Monmouth beat off an attack under the Duke of Grafton at Philip's Norton. The Wilts Militia were drawn up with other troops in support, in case the rebels should attack in turn. Monmouth however retreated, and the whole royalist force followed slowly.

The Militia were not actually under fire at Sedgemoor. They seem to have turned out at "the alarum" more promptly and steadily than the Bradford experience might have shown to be probable, and were complimented on their smartness. They were well commanded, and not allowed to break their ranks for plunder after the battle. The prisoners were led by them to Weston Zoyland Church, and were counted and described by Wheeler. He says 228 in all, but he really counted 238. The Parish register of Weston Zoyland gives another estimate of prisoners and of losses. No doubt some prisoners were brought to the church another way. This account is as follows :—" An account of the fight that was in Langmoor.[2] The ingagement began between one and two of the clock in the morning. It was continued near one hour and a half. Their was killed upon the spot of the King's souldiers sixteen, and five of them buried in the churchyard, and they all had Christian Buriall. One hundred or more of the King's souldiers wounded, of which wounds many died; of which we have no certain account. Their was killed of the rebels upon the spot about 300 ; hanged with us 22, of which 4

[1] See Lord Wolseley's *Life of Marlborough*, vol. i, Ch. 37. But the reader must observe that Lord Wolseley's dates are as muddled as Wheeler's.

[2] The battle was on Langmoor, not on Sedgemoor properly so called.

weare hanged in gemmaces. About 500 prisoners brought into our church ; of which there was 79 wounded, and 5 of them died of their wounds in our church."

Feversham writing to Sunderland, directly after the battle, says that he lost not 50 killed and about 200 wounded.[1] Of Officers and men 208 survivors were compensated for wounds in the campaign.[2] The Wilts Militia lost two men in the campaign, by accidents. The bells of St. Thomas' Salisbury were rung, at a cost of five shillings, "when Colonel Wyndham came home from the Army," and no doubt Wheeler shared his triumph.

H. E. M.

[1] Hist., MSS. Comm., Ninth Report, p. 21.
[2] Col. McKinnon, *Origin and services of the Coldstream Guards.*

OR

A PERFECT RELATION OF THE HEROICK MARCH OF HIS MAT^ies TRUELY LOYALL SUBJECT AND MAGNANIMOUS SOULDIER COLONELL *JOHN WINDHAM ESQRE.* WITH HIS REGIMENT OF FOOTE INTO THE WESTERN PARTS OF ENGLAND FOR THE SUPPRESSING OF *JAMES SCOT* AND HIS ACCOMPLICES IN THEIRE REBELLIOUS INSURRECTION. TOGETHER WITH SOME REMARKABLE OCCUR RENCES HAPPENING IN THAT EXPEDITION.

*Faithfully set down by Adam Wheeler
one of the Drums of his Hono^rs, owne Company.
An° Chrs^ti 1685.*

Being Wednesday[1] I was summoned by a Comand from his Honor to appear in the Market-Place of New Sarm in the County of Wilts by eight of the Clocke in the Morning in his Regiment compleatly armed according to my place as a *Drum*. Where the Regiment being drawne together was dischardged till the next Morning. When againe met, being the Seventeenth day. They were dischardged untill Fryday the eighteenth of June; and ye nineteenth being Saturday;[2] The Regiment was exactly com-

1685.
June 16.

[1] June 16th was Tuesday.
[2] Saturday was June 20th.

pleated by his Honor and accomodated fitt for Warre according to Military Discipline, and that day by his Comand, about sixe of the clock in the Evening, the Drums beating and the Colours displayed, leaveing the Citty wee directed oure March to Wilton, beinge about Two Miles distant and Quartered there that night; where his Honor ordered his Carridge and Amunicon to be brought to him.

June 20. The next day being Sunday[1] on W^{ch} day in the Afternoone leaveing the Towne of *Wilkton (sic)*, we continewed oure March to Market Lavington.

June 21. Early the next morning his Honor marched to the Devizes, and there refreshed his Regim^t for the Weary and hard Afternoones March they sustained the day before.

In the Afternoone by Beate of Drum the Regim^t marched as farre as Chippenham and June the 22, being Tuesday,[2] They marched from Chippenham to the City of Bath, where They Quartered that night.

June 23. The Regim^t leaveing the City of Bath went as farre as Bradforde. *That Night* being very darke there was an *Alarum*. By reason of which the Regim^t could not unite into a Body till They came to Trowbridge, wch was

June 24. Where, for the better security of his Honors Carridge, I desired some assistance being Resolued to hazzard my Life by Ball or Sword, rather than loose any part thereof here the whole Regim^t lay.

June 25. The Rt. Hon^{rble} the Ld Lieuten^t *Earle* of *Pembrook* gave Comand for some of the Regim^t and some of the Militia Horse to goe wth him to Froome, Where he forced the Rebells to lay downe theire Armes, and brought away with him the Constable of that Towne to Trowbridge who proclaymed the Duke of Monmouth King, and severall cruell and New invented murthering Weapons as *Sithes* and ye like.

[1] Probably Sunday June 21st.
[2] Tuesday was June 23rd.

From Bath the Regim^t was led by his *Honor Col^{ll} Windham* June 27. to Trowbridge, Where They made noe stay but Marched forwards into Bratton Lane, and there by an *Alarum* of the Enemies being neere caused the Regim^t to incampe in that Landsend, and the Blew Regim^t alsoe, and the yellow Hampshire Regim^t encamped in a ground neere the said Lane.

The Regim^t marched into Bratton Fields, and was there drawn June 28. up, and after some small stay moved to Westbury. and thence directed its March neere to Froome ; Where his *Hono^{rs}* Tent was erected, and wee encamped there in a certaine Ground neere the Towne.

Dislodging from thence, wee marched directly into Froome; June 29. Where the *Kings Mati^{es}* Gracious Pardon was proclaimed to all such as had taken up Armes against him, if in 8 daies They 30. would come in and accept thereof. Some Persons onely excepted, who were therein mentioned.

Being Wednesday[1] his Hono^{rs} Regim^t tooke theire March to July 1. Shepton Mallet ; Here not farre from the Towne, a Ground was shewne which lay within Prospect, where *Monmouth* and his Army was drawne up and exercised.[2]

[1] Correct date.
[2] Monmouth was that day retreating to Wells. It means where his army had been drawn up, not that it was then there. But the armies had come very close together on July 1, 2, and if Churchill had been in command Sedgemoor would have been anticipated by four days.

July 2. Being Thursday we marched from Shepton Mallet to Glastenbury, and from thence wee removed and went fowards Sumerton. In which March wee had the sight of *Kings Sedgemoore* being about One Mile distant from us; And here Wee received a Comand to Returne and March back to Charleton.

July 4. From whence wee Marched to Kings Sedgemoore, marching Eight Miles in the Moore soe farre as Middlesey; Where being Alarumed;

July 6. The Rh^t Honor^{ble} The *Earle* of *Pembrooke* Lord Lieuten^t in great hast came rideing to the house where his Hono^r Colon^{ll} Windham was quartered, it being betweene Twelve and One of the Clock in the Mornening, calling out *Colon^l Windham Colon^{ll} Windham the Enemy is Engadged*, and askeinge for his Drums; The Colon^{lls} answer was that he was ready, and soe forthwith prepared himselfe.

There being then noe Drum in the house but Adam Wheeler, who opened the doore and answered his Lorsh^p that he was ready to obey his Comand; Soe his Lor^p immediately comanded him to beate an Alarum, wch he presently performed.

(Although some of the Regim^t did endeavor to have the Credite of that peece of Service ascribed to Themselves; One saying it was I that did first beate the Alarme; Another in like manner saying the same, soe that *Wheeler* may iustly complaine as the *Poet Virgil* did concerneing his, Sic vos non vobis, and somewhat after The same manner as he spoke, superscribe, Hos Ego Versieulos feci tulit alter honores.)

When the *Alarum* was beaten by Adam Wheeler in Middlesey according to the Lord Lieuten^{ts} Comand; The Regim^t marched through Weston into Weston Moore with as much expediĉon as possible could be, where They were drawne up Three deep in order to engadge if Occasion required.

The Aforesaid Sixth of July, the *Fight* began very early in the morneing which Battell was over within the space of Two Howers, and the Enemy received a totall Rowte.

Here Adam Wheeler (being then at his Post) was one of those

of the Right Wing of his hono[r] Colon[ll] Windham's Regim[t] who after the Enemy began to run desired Leave of his Hono[r] to get such Pillage in the feild as they could finde ; But his Hono[rs] Answer and Comand was ; That upon Paine of Death not a Man of his Regim[t] should move from his Post saying ; That if the Enemy should rally together againe, and the Regim[t] be in disorder, every man of them might loose his Life.

The *Battell* being over the Right Honor[ble] the Earle of *Feversham*, Generall of his Matie[s] Army, came to the Head of Collon[lls] *Windhams* Regim[t] and gave him many Thanks for his readynesse, Saying, his *Matie* should not hear of it by Letter, but by Word of Mouth ; and that he would certfy the *Kinge* himself of it.

An Account of the Prisoners that were brought along by the Right Wing of his Hono[r] Colon[ll] Windhams Regim[t] to Weston Church as they were tyed together : Adam Wheeler writeing them downe on his Drumhead as they passed by.

The first Number was Fifty and five, most of them tyed together.

The Second Number was thirty and two tyed in like manner.

The Third was Two wounded in theire Legs, crawling uppon the Ground on theire Hands and Knees to Weston Church.

The Fowerth was Thirty seven in number, many of them tyed and pinnackled together.

The Fifth was One alone being naked, onely his Drawers on.

The Sixth was One Single one more.

The Seventh was One more running, being forced along by Two Horse Men with Blowes, and rideing close after him.

The Eighth Number was Fowerteene most of them being tyed together.

The Nineth was Forty Seven most of them tyed as the former, such of Them as had a good Coate or any thinge worth the Pilling, were very fairely stript of it.

The Tenth Number was Eight tyed by Two together Arme to Arme.

The Eleventh was, Twelve tyed and pinnackled.

The Twelfth was Seventeene tyed and pinnackled as the former.

The Thirteenth One more.

The Fowerteenth in Number were Seven more.

The Fifteenth, One more.

The Sixteenth, One more.

The Seventeenth was One more, Hee was very remarkeable and to be admired, for being shot thorow the shoulder and wounded in the Belly ; Hee lay on his Backe in the Sun stript naked, for the space of Tenne or Eleven Howers, in that scorching hot day to the Admiration of all the Spectatours ; And as he lay, a greate Crowde of Souldiers came about him, and reproached him, calling him, *Thou Monmouth Dog* How long have you beene with youre Kinge *Monmouth ?* His answer was, that if he had Breath, he would tell them : Afterwards he was pittyed, and they opened round about him, and gave him more Liberty of the Aire, and there was One Souldier that gave him a paire of Drawers to cover his Nakednesse : Afterwards haveing a long Stick in his hand he walked feably to Weston Church, where he died that Night, and two wounded men more.

The Number of the Prisoners that were led by the Right Wing of his Hono^{rs} Regiment did amount to 228.[1]

The Country men that gathered up the Dead slayne in this Battell gave an Account of the Minister and Church Wardens of Weston of the Number of One Thousand Three hundred Eighty and Fower ; Besides many more they did beleeve lay dead unfound in the Corne.

Where Adam Wheeler saw of dead Men lying in One Heape One Hundred Seventy and Fower ; which those that were digging a Pit to lay them in gave the Number of.[2]

From Weston Moore the Regim^t marched to Weston, and thence to Middlesey, and from Middlesey againe to Weston, and thence to Weston Moore : *Where* a Dutch Gunner, and a Yellow-

---

[1] The total is in fact 238

[2] There used to be a mound, now levelled, near what had been the left wing of Monmouth's army, where the men were buried.

coate Souldier that ran out of his *Matie⁵ Army* to *Monmouth* were hanged on a Tree in Weston Moore not farre from the Church.

This Day *Adam Wheeler* went into the Campe and tooke an Account as neere as hee could of his *Matie⁵ Carridges* and Great Guns where were neere One Hundred and forty of them : Of these there were nineteene *Guns* some haveing sixe Horses. Some seven, and some eight Horses a peece to draw them.

Here his *Honoʳ Collˡ* Windham received Orders to Guard his Matieˢ Guns and Carridges with his Regimᵗ : from Weston Moore to the Devizes, it being a peece of service of noe small Trust and Credite, and soe much his Honoʳ was pleasd to informe his Souldiers of.

This Afternoone an Accident fell out to be lamented : One of His Honoʳˢ owne Souldiers, being in Exercise, and quitting his Armes, A musquett went off as it lay on the Ground, and shot him thorow both of his legs, soe he died in a short time after.

From the Camp in Weston Moore his *Honoʳ Collˡ Windham* marched with his Regimᵗ to Glastenbury : Heere at the signe of the White Hart a *Duell* was fought betweene Captaine Love and Major Talbot. The Major fell, and Captain Love fled for it.

Heare alsoe were sixe men of the Prisoners that were taken hanged on the Signe Post of that Inne, who after as They hung were stripped naked, and soe left hanging there all night.

Here Alsoe at this towne of Glastenbury there was an Alarm, where uppon the Regimᵗ was comanded to the Abby Cloyster.

His Honoʳˢ Regimᵗ Marched from Glastenbury (where those sixe men were left hanging on the Signe-Post) to Wells ; Thence they marched to Embetch and soe to Philips Norton.

The Regimᵗ left Philips Norton, and Marched to the Devizes (guarding his Matieˢ Carriages and Guns where his *Honoʳ* was dischardged of that Trust And here his *Honoʳ* dischardged the Regimᵗ likewise, till the next Summons by Beate of Drum.

July 8.

July 9. This is the best account I can give yor Honor of that successfull March : and doe humbly beg yor Honors pardon for this Presumption, and with leave subscribe my selfe Sir,

        Yor *Honors* most dutifull *Drum*, and most humble and
                Obedient Servant,

                        ADAM WHEELER.

Anglorum vivat semper Prolesque Jacobi,
Rex : fugiant Hostes non remorante pede.
Atque diu vivat stirps Nobilis inclyta Wyndham
Detque Deus pueris Gaudia Multa suis.

Ilminster, 154.

K

Kingsdowne, 161.

L

Langmoor, 154.
Love, Capt., 165.
Lyme, 154.

M

Market Lavington, 160.
Middlesey, 162, 164.
Monmouth, Duke of, 154, 160, 161.

N

56, 161,

New Sarum, 159.

INDEX

P

Pembroke, Earl of, 154, 155, 160, 162.
Philips Norton, 155, 165.
Prisoners, list of, 163, 164.

S

Salisbury, 154, 159.
Sedgemoor, 162.
Shepton Mallet, 154, 161, 162.
Summerton, 162.

T

Talbot, Major, 165.
Taunton, 154.
Trowbridge, 160.

W

Wells, 165.
Westbury, 161.
Weston Church, 163, 164.
Weston Moor, 162, 164, 165.
Weston Zoyland, 155, 162.
Wheeler, Adam, 153, 162, 163, 165, 166.
Wilton, 154, 160.
Wyndham, Colonel, 153, 156, 161, 162, 163, 165.
Wyndham, Lord, 153.

Y

Yong, Colonel, 161.

COMMON RIGHTS AT
COTTENHAM & STRETHAM
IN CAMBRIDGESHIRE

*President of the Royal Historical Society
and Archdeacon of Ely*

CAMDEN MISCELLANY
VOL. XII

LONDON
OFFICES OF THE SOCIETY
6 & 7 SOUTH SQUARE
GRAY'S INN
1910

COTTENHAM

	Pages
Preface	173
Articles of Agreement 1596	193
Orders made 12 Jan. 1639	230
Extract from the decision in regard to Subtraction of tithe (1630)	246
An account of the Tithing of cattle (1820)	250

STRETHAM

Extracts from a Decree in the Court of Exchequer (1607)	253
A coppie of an Affoedavit, 25 Maij 1609	260
Orders made for Stretham by Commissioners, 28 June 1609	261
Orders made for Thetford by Commissioners, 28 June 1609	263
Orders made by the Leet, 29 April 1614	265
Orders made by the Court Leet, 29 April 1614	267
Orders made by the Inhabitants of Stretham, 24 Feb. 1622	275
Libell for Tithe of Herbage	288
Libell for Tithe Milk	289
Index	291

PREFACE

The papers here printed furnish materials which are of considerable assistance for the study of one great department of English rural life. During the Middle Ages the management of land was collective, as it was carried on by the co-operation of the lord and the various tenants within the manor. So far as tillage is concerned, we are fairly informed, as we can picture to ourselves the open fields with their intermingled strips, and know from the surveys of many manors the precise obligations in week-work and boon work which the villeins were bound to render, and the amount of free time which they had for their own holdings. But the information we possess about the management of the common waste is apt to be scrappy and incidental. It must have been a matter of supreme importance in every manor, as the inhabitants were always dependent on the waste for the pasturing of the stock with which they worked their land; and they might rely on it for building materials and fuel as well. In those districts where, from the conditions of climate and soil, cattle feeding and dairy farming were specially remunerative, the good management of the resources of the common waste must have been a far more important factor in the prosperity of a township than the tillage of the common fields. Much of the land on the south west of the fens, which lies along the valleys of the Cam and the Ouse, between Cambridge and Ely, was peculiarly adapted for pasturage and was of no use for tillage. Here the collective management of the common waste survived in a fashion, which is interesting as a matter of local history, while it is still more important as an illustration of a system which was once generally prevalent and has now died out.

PREFACE

In modern times enclosure has been carried on by act of parliament, and the parish has generally been the unit dealt with; but before the eighteenth century this was not usually the case. There were instances of ruthless enclosure when a whole parish was depopulated and the land used entirely as sheep-run;[1] but occasional incidents of this kind, which made a deep impression on the minds of contemporaries, such as John Ross and Sir Thomas More, can hardly be taken as typical. Throughout England generally, enclosure was a process which went on piecemeal within one parish after another, and it was a constant cause of irritation from the manner in which it interfered with customary rights. Sometimes a few contiguous strips in the common fields might be enclosed, either by the Lord, or by a tenant with his permission, to be tilled in severalty; in such a case the ground was withdrawn from the area over which cattle pastured in winter, and was to this extent lost to the community. Besides this, the lord might encroach on the common waste by applying more and more of it for use in severalty, so that the opportunities of the tenants for pasturing their stock were seriously interfered with. The grievance from the increase of sheep farming evidently took this form in some cases where there was no evidence of deliberate depopulating. Both Cottenham and Stretham afford cases in point, and there is a chorus of complaint on this matter during the sixteenth century. It is plain too, from such writers as Fitzherbert, Hales, Tusser, and Norden, that farming in severalty was generally regarded as the system by which the most was made of the land. As this improvement was adopted there was a tendency for the common waste to diminish not only in area but in importance, so far as the lord and his more progressive tenants were concerned; the neglected waste was sometimes given over to an undesirable class of squatters.[2]

[1] Cunningham *Growth of English Industry and Commerce*, I, 404, 448, 529.
[2] See my *Growth of English Industry*, II. 570. A bill was introduced in 1656 which provided for the regulation of commons and commonable grounds, but it failed to pass. E. M. Leonard, *Royal Hist. Soc. Trans.* XIX, 130.

PREFACE

The Tudor enclosures seem to have affected Cambridgeshire but little. Wholesale depopulation does not appear to have occurred to any great extent, though there had been complaint on this score against Barnwell Abbey in 1414, on the ground that 'great waste of housing' had been made at Chesterton, and that no housing was left standing on the manor "but if it were a Shepe Cote or a berne or a swynsty and a few houses by side to putt in bestes."[1] Sir John Cutts' depopulation at Childerley is a later instance of a similar kind, though he may have aimed at creating a park for deer, rather than a sheep-walk; but throughout the high lands of Cambridge generally, there was little temptation to enclose the common fields. The colleges at Cambridge offered a convenient market for food stuffs, both corn and dairy produce[2]; and as landowners they were interested in having plentiful supplies. The corn rent act which "passed the houses before they were sensible of the good consequences of it,"[3] was apparently intended to enable the colleges to obtain supplies on reasonable terms, though it also served to maintain their revenues, as the value of money fell. There was less motive in this district than in other places to engage in sheep farming in the sixteenth century; and agricultural improvement went on in the seventeenth and eighteenth centuries without the breaking up of the common fields. In the southern part of Cambridge the enclosure of common fields was delayed; and we have, as a consequence, unusually full records of the actual changes which ensued when it at length took place.[4]

In the Isle of Ely, the conditions were entirely different whereas in the high land every part of a parish was fit for use as arable land—and in the case of some parishes, e.g. Hildersham was actually so used, the land in the Isle of Ely, which was fit

---

[1] *Rot Part.* IV. 60. b.

[2] Vancouver. *General View*, pp. 193-198. W. Gooch. *General View of the County of Cambridge* (1813), pp. 56-94.

[3] 18 El. c. 6. Compare Kennett, *Parochial Antiquities*, II 295.

[4] Vancouver. *General View of the Agriculture in the County of Cambridge*, (1794), p. 87.

PREFACE

for tillage, consisted of occasional islets and ridges in a great area of country, much of which was flooded in winter and could only be used for pasturage in summer. The work of draining the fens, which served as common pasturage for the men of one village or for several villages together, was pushed on in the seventeenth century ; and as it proceeded, large areas were allotted in severalty to the Duke of Bedford and other undertakers.[1] The direct interests of the Bedford family were chiefly in the valley of the Nene, and the Russells became a dominating influence there. Somewhat similar conditions prevailed in the parishes, such as Cottenham, Stretham, Waterbreach, Willingham and Haddenham, which lie near the junction of the Ouse and the Cam[2] except that this district was in much[3] less need of drainage, at all events for purposes of pasture farming, than the rest of the fens. The undertakers and wealthy improvers had not such a footing that they could carry everything before them ; the owners of common rights were able to hold their own, and they continued to pasture the herd of milch-kine on the common waste.

In this district we find several instances of legal proceedings with the view of limiting the lord of the manor's power of interference and of defining and securing common rights over the waste;[4] and the records of these recurring disputes give very full information about many details of life in a district where dairy farming was the main avocation. But there were also frequent differences

---

[1] For the areas of enclosed and unenclosed land in different parishes see Vancouver *op. cit.* 193.

[2] On the old course of this river see Vancouver *op. cit.* 29 also my paper in *Camb. Antiq. Soc. Communication XIV*, 75.

[3] Badeslade *Lynn* p. 29 R. Atkins has interesting allusions to pasture farming in several instances : he notes that " there be usually 3 heards of milch cattel at Soham, each consisting of 700 beasts, as Jefferie the host of the Bull informed me, yet is there in this Towne in winter Scarcitie of Butter and cheese, and not so mutch as will suffice the Towne." Harl. MS. 5011 f. 21 b.

[4] An interesting parallel from a similar district in Lincolnshire is afforded by the agreement at Epworth in 1359, printed by W. Peck. *Topographical Account of the Isle of Axholme.* Ap. i.

between manorial lords and the tenants, and among the latter there were some substantial men who were not alarmed at the cost of legal proceedings. Taverner writing in 1653 remarks of Haddenham that "many of the inhabitants had competent estates, who wanting a full imployment in tillage, they of ancient custom make it a part of their recreation to discourse of law cases."[1] The frequency of such legal proceedings in this district has been the occasion for putting on record a mass of details that would otherwise have been likely to pass out of mind altogether. When a difference of opinion arose between the lord and the tenants the usual course appears to have been to submit the matter to arbitration, and then to obtain a decree in Chancery which might make the award binding on the successors of those who signed the agreement; or the difficulties might be settled by a commission from the Court of Exchequer. Every decision which enabled either the lord or any of the tenants to hold more land in severalty was a permanent step in the progress of enclosure; but this was not the only matter in dispute, as difficulties arose about the levying of tithe, and gave occasion to acrimonious litigation.

Very full information has been preserved in regard to affairs at Cottenham, and it is possible to trace the course of the successive disputes which arose; the story goes back to the Tudor period when sheep farming was the most profitable use to which pasturage could be put. Sir Francis Hinde of Madingley, the lord of the manors of Lyles and Crowland and of the moiety of the manor of Sames in Cottenham, came to an agreement with the "greatest number of welthiest and substancyalist inhabitants and tenants of Cottenham in the behalfe of themselves and of all the rest of the inhabitants of the said town," at Easter 1580; he and his tenants were to enjoy sheep-walk for 2000 sheep in severalty,

---

[1] They failed in their attempt to establish common rights over the Delfs and Ouse-delfs, an area of about 800 acres which had been kept as severalty and let for grazing by the Bishop of Ely from the time of Edward III. F. Taverner. *A Vindication of the Jurie who upon the twelfth day of May 1653 gave their verdict in the Upper Bench at Westminster against the inhabitants of Hadenham*, pp. 18-22.

while he gave up his right of joisting[1] sheep or cattle on the common fields of the parish, and allowed the tenants to pasture the town flock and to fold their sheep on these fields. Chancery proceedings were taken in 1584, and Edward Coke argued on behalf of George Pepys and others of the same family that this agreement was a very onesided affair; that the lord and the principal farmers were encroaching on the common rights and had not left sufficient pasturage for the poorer inhabitants, and that the right of joisting cattle on the town fields, which the Lord had given up was much more limited, and therefore of less value than he alleged. The dispute was not settled by the arbitration which took place in 1583, when the Dean of Ely, the Master of St John's, the Master of Christ's and other eminent men were called in to adjudicate. Subsequently, in 1585, a Chancery decree, enforcing an award by the Bishop of Peterborough, seems to have set the matter at rest for the time. Unfortunately the record of his decision appears to have been lost, so that it is difficult to get at the result of the case, in regard to which the Bill of Sir F. Hinde, the Answers of the Pepys family, and the Replication of Sir F. Hinde have been preserved.[2]

When the disputed pasture rights at Cottenham came into court again in 1596, the whole situation seems to have changed, for there is no mention of the Lord's sheep walk, or of the town flock, but the resources of the place were evidently being devoted to the herd of milch-kine. The same families were again the principal parties in the dispute. Sir William Hinde of Madingley, the son of Sir Francis, exhibited a bill in Chancery, and an answer was made by Pepys. The matter was referred to Lord North, the Lord Lieutenant and Custos Rotulorum of the County, who " upon hearing of the matter *in variante* hath sette down certain articles of agreement with their mutual consents."[3] This award, unlike its

---

[1] To joist or agist cattle is to allow the owners, in return for a payment, to feed them on common pastures.

[2] Record office, Chancery Proceedings, Elizabeth H. $\frac{19}{58}$.

[3] Decree in Chancery in 1669.

PREFACE 179

predecessors, stood the test of time : for the *Articles of Agreement* then drawn up were confirmed by a Decree in Chancery[1] and continued to be the basis on which the management of the common waste at Cottenham rested, until the enclosure in 1842.

We have a contemporary reference to this agreement in a description of the Fens by Richard Atkins of Outwell in 1604 · and as he was according to Dugdale[2] a person " whose observations on these fenny grounds were very notable, " it may be worth while to print his description at length.[3]

Cottenham. Lord there Sr. William Hynd. It hath veric good Fennes and great ; viz from a Fenne by Awdrich causey called Sechell to Chittering on the East. The names of Cottenham fennes be thes.

1. Sechell right over against Outlawes Cote, it begynneth at the gate by the River on the west and cometh downe to Robbins lode.

2. Michellee about 200 acres lieth est of Sechell, Robins lode parting Michellee and Sechell on the one syde.

3. Topham more about 150 acres lyeth more Est Michellee towards denney.

4. Awbrose is about $\frac{3}{4}$ of a mile square it butteth on michellee on the north and the field to the south, and vppon smethy fenne to the west. Memorandum, the Lottes there about 200 acres wherin everie howse hath an acre. It lyeth north Est from Awbrose.

5. Smethy fenne is that wherto they passeover a bridg. It containeth 500 acres and more. It contynueth from Cottenham to the were at the howse next Aldrith Calsey.

6. Charefenne common Fenne, and a pece called xx. *d*. lie more Est to denney Ward, the Common is a turfe fenne 20*d*. leadeth to the Riv^r and is aboute 30 acres, Charefenne is next denney and ther goeth the heard commonly.

On the Est side of the Towne next denny, the Lord hath taken in certeine pastures called Woolfes pastures, by reason wherof he

---

[1] 9. May 1597. Mr. Bacon was counsel in this suit.

[2] *Embanking.* 378.

[3] The MS. is among Dugdale's Collections in the British Museum: Harl. MSS. 5011 f. 23, 3. It has been summarised by Badeslade : *Navigation of King's Lynn.* 74.

doth not Common but is excluded by composition, some say this is for his life onely. The Fenns of Cottenham be at least 4 miles long Est and West, and about a mile di. broad or more one place with an other, and have the River of Owse all the way on the North. They be all imbancked and provision made to convey there water away, more then any Fenne towne theraboute, yet be the banckes in many places defective, in so much as Charefen lyeth [waste] and long drowned and overfloweth into Chitteringes. Note that in Awbrose Fenne, ther is a pece of high ground about 200 acres, it hath a pece adioyning to it called Cuttes lying betwene yt and Topham more. Memorandum, a pece of an 100 acres of Common for which the Towne gave Sr William Hynde 200li. Item the Calves pasture there aboute 20 acres nere to the Cote in Stretham called the white house. there is a were called poole were 16 foote deepe etc., and below the same within a stones cast there is a grave[l] layd by Stretham men to cart ther foder[1] out of willow fenne, where the water commeth not above 2 foot deepe, a great cause of drowning those Fenns.

Some sixty years later the dispute broke out again; Sir William Hinde had disposed of his rights at Cottenham to Hobson, the Cambridge carrier; he died in 1630, and the representatives of this family endeavoured to set the award of 1596 aside. Katharine, the widow of Thomas Hobson (the carrier's grandson) and her son, denied that the commoners in Cottenham had any right of common whatsoever within the marshes, fens or waste grounds of Cottenham. As a result of the litigation which ensued, a decree was issued from Chancery in 1669 confirming once more the award which had been made by Lord North, and establishing the position which had been maintained by the owners of common right.

Beside the conflict with the manorial lords there were other legal proceedings which throw additional light on the economic and social conditions of Cottenham. The Rectory was a valuable piece of preferment, especially after Lord North's award had come into effect; and the claims of the clergy in regard to tithes, especially in regard to small tithes, were frequently resisted. A certain Walter Male had subtracted tithes of apples and of hay in

[1] Compare Sir Clement Edmunds, Report on Badeslade. *op. cit.* p. 30.

PREFACE 181

the years 1623, 1624 and 1625 when Dr. Leonard Maw was rector, and was sued in the ecclesiastical court by his executors,[1] with the result that the Vicar General decreed that he should pay 6d. for the tithe of apples in each of the years 1623 and 1624 and 2d. for the tithe of apples in 1625, as well as 24/5½ for the tithe of hay in the same years. The schedule of tithable things which was annexed to this decision serves to shew that the fruit-growing, for which Cottenham is now famous, is a thing of long standing: damsons and plums seem to have been produced as well as pears and apples.

An embittered dispute arose as soon as the puritans came into power. Dr. Richard Manby, who had been presented to the living by the Bishop, was a decided high churchman of the school of Laud; he soon became the subject of high handed proceedings, as the parliamentary committee deprived him of his living in 1641; and Mr. French, who had married Robina the daughter of Cromwell, entered on the enjoyment of the preferment. The rector retired to a living of which he was patron in Yorkshire, leaving Mrs. Manby and the children to live with his sister Mrs. Cass; Mrs. Cass had a "little house in Cottenham which gave her a right to the Common, but having no cattle to put upon it, the Doctor bought some cows for her to keep a dairy, the better to support herself and his own family;[2] but the barbarous villains presently drove the cows from the common to the market, where they sold them and put the money into their own pockets."[3]

At the Restoration Dr. Manby still survived and re-entered on the enjoyment of the emoluments of his benefice, but it was only by legal process that he was able to eject Mr. Nye, an intruder

---

[1] A similar action was brought against Henry Graves.

[2] Mrs Cass was apparently treated as guilty of colouring Dr. Manby's cows (article XXXIII), and the cows may have been sold to pay the fine. See also article XXIX.

[3] J. Walker: *Sufferings of the Clergy*. 304. Compare also Brit. Mus. Add. Mss. 15670, f. 117, 149ᵇ, 180ᵇ, 230, 338.

who had succeeded Mr. French, and who practically secured another year's income by his tenacity.

As the work of drainage proceeded, and land which had formerly been used for pasturage came to be employed for tillage, the question of tithe again became the subject of litigation.

In 1780 the tenants of Soame Jenyns, who owned the undertakers land in Cottenham, took a crop of oats, and Dr. Ward, the Rector claimed the tithe, though this was in excess of the tithe allowed in Lord North's award.[1] His attempt in 1811[2] to set the award aside altogether was unsuccessful; and when the claim to the tithe of crops on the Undertakers piece was brought into court by the next rector, Dr. Sparke, it was disallowed in 1821. The award of 1596 proved to be the corner stone of village economy both in regard to manorial and ecclesiastical claims.

The story of the maintenance of common right by legal procedure has in some ways less interest than belongs to the *Orders* which remain in the parish chest at Cottenham with regard to the manner in which the common rights should be exercised. The lords had had days of drift, when they took account of all the cattle, and saw that no persons, who could not claim common rights, fed their cattle on the waste. The risks of infection and damage were reduced by insisting that the cattle should be properly sorted out, and rules were laid down as to the times at which they might feed in different parts of the common waste.

In the seventeenth century this practice survived at Stretham where the orders were issued in the court leet, though powers were given to the commoners of Stretham and Thetford respectively to make by-laws for their separate cow-pastures.[3] But the case of

[1] Article XXVI and schedule.

[2] The only record of this dispute which I have seen among the papers in the parish chest is a draft of the pleadings in the Rector's favour in 1810.

[3] Vancouver, writing in 1794, commends the Stretham Fen Reeves for their attention to drainage, (*Op. Cit.* 150). Further details of the working of a similar system are to be found at Willingham where the accounts of the Fen Reeves during several years in the reign of Elizabeth have been preserved. Compare also the sustom of Whittlesea. W. Nelson, *Lex Maneriorum*, Ap. 79.

PREFACE 183

Cottenham is of special interest: it may be that the owners of common right felt especial need of effective administration so that the banks which protected the fens might be kept in good condition, but they bargained to take the whole matter into their own hands. The responsibility for the management of the herd and the waste was transferred to twenty four order makers chosen according to specified proportions from among the copyholders in the various manors. This system of government was maintained with success till the parish was enclosed in 1842 and the kine could no longer be pastured as a common herd; but a tradition still lingers of the picturesque procession which was formed at milking time by the herd of two thousand kine which moved from the fen, past the church, and along the village street with each cow turning into her own byre as it was reached.

The machinery for managing the common waste at Cottenham, which was introduced in 1596¹ is of interest in its constitutional aspect, as it furnishes an instance of a democratically governed township successfully carried on for two hundred and fifty years. The system has interesting analogies with the townships which were springing up on the Borders as the country became more peaceable, and in the colonies which were soon to be planted in Ulster and in New England. The owners of common right at Cottenham formed a village community which had become free by the buying out of the manorial rights: and this type of social organisation had a great future before it. The circumstances of the New England settlers gave the opportunity for the reproduction of similar institutions for the regulation of economic affairs. The system in vogue in Massachusetts, at Chelsea in 1638,[1] at Malden in 1678,[2] or at Lexington[3] was closely allied to that which existed at Cottenham in 1596, and the township, in a new atmosphere and in new surroundings came to play an important part in the constitutional and political history of the United States.

[1] M. Chamberlain, *History of Chelsea*, I, 89.
[2] D. P. Covey, *History of Malden*, 352.
[3] C. Hudson, *History of the town of Lexington*, 33, 63.

PREFACE

Though the story of Cottenham possesses a unique interest, it does not stand alone, as analagous difficulties in regard to pasture rights arose in several of the neighbouring parishes, at one time or another; still the proceedings in each case had special characteristics. The course of events at Stretham was so closely parallel as to be very instructive: the inhabitants of Stretham and of Thetford intercommoned to some extent, and there had been long controversies and diverse suits between Sir Miles Sandys lord of the manor of Stretham and his tenants. In 1597 Sir Miles Sandys was the complainant; but on June 22 1607 the Court of Exchequer on the complaint of the Lord of the Manor of Thetford, the Rector of Stretham and other tenants, granted a commission; and an award was made on the adjudication of Francis Tyndall, Henry Bynge and John Batisforde. The scheme of these commissioners was that of granting Sir Miles Sandys 100 acres out of Stretham Fen, of bringing the intercommoning of the Stretham and Thetford herds to an end, and of excluding Sir Miles from interference of any kind in an area of 1600 acres of fen. Occasion was taken at the same time to secure the copyholders from arbitrary exactions: heriots were abolished and the fines were to become certain, but it is remarkable that even at this late date the obligation of the copyholders to give personal service in ploughing and reaping was reinforced.

The orders which were made immediately in consequence of this decree have not been preserved. They gave rise to complaint, which was exhibited to the Court of Exchequer on 25 May 1609, as the requirements of the tenants for pasturing the stock with which they worked the land had not been allowed for sufficiently, and a new set of orders were issued by the commissioners on June 28 1609. Subsequent orders and bye-laws were made in 1614 and 1622. The question of tithe was also a cause of dispute at Stretham, and the libels which have been preserved are instructive as showing the manner in which the tithe was claimed in regard to pasturage and to milk.

At Willingham the same Sir Miles Sandys, who had entered on

the estate by grant from the crown dated 8 Nov. 1601 on a payment of £2069, came to a similar agreement with the tenantry, after they had "unlawfully, ryotously, routeously and in forcible manner" pulled down the fence of an enclosure. In accordance with the award of the Bishop of Ely, Sir John Cotton, Anthony Page, Mark Steward and Francis Tyndall, it was agreed that Sir Miles should be allowed to enclose, but that he must leave a sufficient way for 'a great herd of cattle in the same place where formerly the way hath been for the drift of cattle,' and that he was not to have any rights of feeding cattle on the common pasture. It was agreed to have this award confirmed by a decree in Chancery at the joint expense of the two parties, but this does not seem to have been carried out. At Willingham also Sir Miles abandoned some of his claims over the copyholders, and in 1611 remitted the hen rent, egg rent, days works and heriots to which they had been liable.

Similar action was taken at a later date at Waterbeach: an agreement had been come to between Peter Standly, Lord of the Manor of Waterbeach cum Denny in 1740 and this was confirmed immediately afterwards by act of parliament. The Lord of the Manor gave up his right to joyst cattle in consideration of a payment of 2/- each from the commoners; the rights of each commoner as to the number of horses, sheep, cows &c., which he might pasture were defined, and arrangements were made for the election of Fen Reeves.[1] An amending act was passed in 1790; and an admirable picture of Waterbeach in the last decade of the eighteenth century, with its activities in the way of pasture farming and market gardening, was put on record by the Rev. Robert Masters who had been Vicar of the parish.[2]

A large number of papers bearing on the management of common pasture are preserved in the parish chests at Cottenham

---

[1] An act passed in the fourteenth year of his late Majesty, George II, entitled "*An Act for the effectual draining of Waterbeach Land.*"

[2] *A Short account of the parish of Waterbeach in the Diocese of Ely* by a late Vicar. 1795.

and Stretham, and in the Public Hall at Willingham, and through the kindness of the Rev. R. P. Moline, Rector of Cottenham, of the Rev. S. S. Stitt of Stretham, and of Mr. Few of Willingham, I have had opportunities of examining them; but it has not been altogether easy to make a selection of the documents which are likely to be of most interest to members of the society. There could be no doubt, of course, about printing Lord North's award, and the articles of agreement on which the whole authority of the Cottenham order maker was based. The orders for 1639 are the oldest which survive, and these are printed; they were reissued annually with insignificant alterations and copies exist for 1645, 1662 and 1665. The schedule of tithe owing by Walter Male at Cottenham is also given in full.

Extracts have been made from the decree of the Court of Exchequer which enforced the award of the commissioners at Stretham. The orders and bye laws at Stretham are so varied, that they are given in full, as well as the complaint of 1609 and the papers in regard to tithe.

The members of the Society are much indebted to Mr. Arthur Bull, Church Warden at Cottenham, for making transcripts of the papers in his charge and for his careful notes upon them; to the Rev. Evelyn Young of Fen Drayton for discharging a similar task at Stretham, and to Mr. Hubert Hall for the additional information which had been preserved in the Record office.

THE COTTENHAM ARTICLES OF AGREEMENT

There are four manuscript copies and one printed copy of the articles of agreement in the parish church at Cottenham, but so far as is known the original document no longer exists.

In the Chancery decree " It was ordered that the complainants should at the Defendant's request deliver the defendants a copy of the said Articles... and should also suffer the defendants to examine such copy with the original articles, which copy... etc. "

It does not appear that this original document was ever pro-

PREFACE 187

duced in any of the various law trials that have taken place from time to time.

The copies from which these "Articles" have now been printed may be described as follows—

I. The parchment copy.
On the inside page of the outer cover are these entries—viz.
"Nov. 25. 1735. I bought this copy of W. Hayhow of Ely, who had it among a parcel of old parchments of Mr. Barnes, whose ancestors had an estate there and are in the list of the first contractors in the agreement." and—
"July 1870. Mr. Wyles of Denney Abbey gave this copy to me to place in the parish Chest.

SAMUEL BANKS.
Rector of Cottenham."

At the foot of this copy is written
"Scriptum per me Richd Robinson apud villam [de C......] quarto die Aprilis et anno D^{ni} 1615."

II. The paper copy. (1638).
This has at the foot—
"Written by mee John Clarke in the yeare of our Lord God one thousand six hundredth and thirtie eight."

There are several notes in seventeenth century handwriting on a spare sheet at the end of the book, as follows

(A) "The Officers have two bookes of these orders fairlie writ, one in parchment of fifteen leaves[1] the other in paper of twelve leaves."

(B) The Decretall Order.
"IX die Maii Anno Regni Elizabethe Regine XXXIX. Inter Willelmum Hynde et alios querentes, Georginam Pepes et alios defendentes.

---

[1] This is not the same as the existing parchment copy which consists of ten leaves.

Forasmuch as the matter in question betweene the said parties hath been by all their mutuall assents referred unto the hearing and ending of the said right honorable the Lord North one of her M^a^ties most honorble privie Counsell and Treasurer of her Highnesse houshold, according to agreement heretofore made betweene the said parties. Which agreement was, that if anie ambiguitie did arise on ether side touching the premises then he to have the determining thereof. Who upon hearing the said matter *in variante* hath set downe certen Articles of Agreement with their like mutuall assents. Whereunto as well the plaintiffs as defendants have subscribed their names as verie well content there unto. And humblie desired by Mr. Bacon, being of their Councell, that the same may be by this Court decreed accordingly. It is therefore ordered and decreed by the right honorable Sr. Thomas Egerton Knight Lord Keeper of the Great Seale of England with the assent of all the said parties on both sides That all and everie such matter Thing Clause and Article as is set downe between the said parties by the said Lord North in the said Agreement shall be perfurmed fulfilled and kept by all and everie of the said parties whose names are to the said Agreement subscribed according to the tenor and true meaning of the same in as ample and forcible manner as if the said Agreement had been judiciallie pronounced and set downe by this Court." par 75^a (?)

Li. A. fol. 897.

Signatur Manibus.

This copie was taken out of the Registrie. Termino Michælis Anno regni regis Caroli 17 Anno domini 1641. (paying for it 2s. 6d. that is XVIII^d the first folio and XII^d. the next.

Bacon pro querentibus
Ellis pro defendentibus
Rotheram pro querentibus
Evelin pro defendentibus

per Henrie Stobell
deputatum Registrarii.

(C) " Decretum inter Hynde et Pepys. Anno Elizabethe.

The inhabitants subscribers to these articles are 111. towards the latter end of them is the Master of St. Johns but not his name which makes me doubt it is not a true copie of the subscription or subscribers. Amongst whom is not the parson of Cottenham, or Dr. Fleming. But in the beginning of them the inhabitants parties to these articles are about 60.

So it seems all of them subscribed not. Neither is the Master of St. Johns name in the begining of the decree. The inhabitants parties to the decree are 98 and defendants 4 in all 102. So more are made parties to the articles than are to the decree which makes me thinke it a counterfeet copie."

(D) "I conceive the parsonage of Cottenham to be improved by the Composition.
1. The inclosures granted to the parson by the same is worth £XXX per an.
2. The benefit of keeping 20 milch cows upon the common £X per an.
3. His Easter booke improved by poundes per an.
4. Tithe corn improved £LX per an."

"This is a copie of the note was given me by Jo. Wright."

(E) "Dr. Fleming was Instituted into Cottenham vndecimo aprilis 1581.
Robert Telnie quinto Februarie 1601."

III. A copy of the Articles of Agreement is inserted in the Decree in Chancery—probably from the paper copy.

IV. About the time of the last law trial, concerning matters more or less connected with these "Articles," (circa 1820.), the articles were printed. A few copies of this (incorrect) edition exist: and also what is most likely the written copy made for the printing of the book.

The first two of the above mentioned copies have been carefully collated for this edition of the "Articles of Agreement."

STRETHAM PAPERS

The Rector of Stretham, in the Isle of Ely, has in his custody a number of papers of the 16th and 17th centuries, relating for the most part to the tithes and common-lands of that place and of the Chapelry of Thetford, and to a long succession of disputes and law suits arising therefrom, covering the greater part of the 17th century.

PREFACE

Amongst these various papers is a thin paper book, endorsed on the cover as follows ·

"Stretham 1623

Copies of several ancient Documents relating to the Rectory of Stretham and the Byelaws for regulating the Commons: including a Terrier of the Lands belonging to the Parsonage in 1571."

The book, measuring about 11 by 6½ inches, is stitched in a cover of thin parchment. It had originally 80 pages, numbered; 8 of these pages have been removed, having been apparently blank. On the last page is a table of contents, which is here reproduced; the items marked with an asterisk are those which are now printed in whole or in part.

"A table of the cheif things contained in this Booke.

The Decree of the Exchequer in 1607 relating to the Mannor of Stretham.	page [1]
A Terrier of the glebe of Stretham Parsonage. [12 Nov. 1571.]	27
* Orders made 1622.	35
Orders made 1614.	49, 50
A note of the Seuerall fens in Stretham. [1626.]	57
A coppie of Wisbeach Barton Lease. [1538.]	58
A terrier of meddow and marrish in Stretham. [1614.]	60
Orders made 1609.	63
* A coppie of an Affœdauit.	64
A Coppie or Proesident of a Libell for Herbage of Steers for tythe milke.	65 } 66 }
An Inuentarie of Euidencies beelonging to Stretham. [1573.]	78. "

[1] The numbers are those of the pages in the MS. book.

PREFACE

There is no doubt that these copies were made for the use of the Rev. Nicholas Felton; about half of the book is in his own handwriting. He was the eldest son of Nicholas Felton, Bishop of Ely, who presented him to the Rectory of Stretham, to which he was inducted 10 March $162\frac{1}{2}$. It is stated in Carter's "History of Cambridgeshire" that he was ejected by Manchester's warrant dated 19 March 1644. There are two other copies of the Decree of the Court of Exchequer, one of them being a certified copy, with which the copy here printed has been carefully collated.

Considerable interest appeared to be aroused among the members of the Royal Historical Society who were present when I alluded to the contents of these papers at the last Annual Meeting, (*R. Hist. Soc. Trans.* Third Series, IV. 12) and I am glad that an opportunity has so soon arisen of putting them in type.

Trin : Coll : Cambridge.   W. C.
Dec. 1910.

IRELAND QUEENE DEFENDER OF THE FAITH &c.

TABULA

Article		Page
I.	That Mr. Hinde shall have and enjoy in severalty the great Inclosures upon Mare-hill.	[196]
II.	Christ College to have Sixty Acres and one Close belonging to the Manor of Harlstons.	[198]
III.	The Parson to have his Moor-closes and two Closes in Alborough.	[198]
IV.	The Heirs of John Peyps, deceased, to enjoy in severalty certain Closes.	[199]
V.	Christ College to have one Acre next their Close.	[200]
VI.	Richard Scott to enjoy in severalty certain Grounds.	[200]
VII.	St. John's College to hold and enjoy their Lands at Stone-ditch.	[200]
VIII.	The Dean and Chapter of Ely to enjoy Pelham's Cross Close.	[200]
IX.	The Lords excluded from keeping sheep	[201]
X.	Mr. Hinde to have no Sheep, with a proviso for Westwick.	[201]
XI.	That Alborough shall be fed and be Common.	[202]
XII.	No Cattle taken into Jeest, Joist or Adjist.	[203]
XIII.	The Holme Closes allowed Twenty Acres.	[203]
XIV.	No Houses to be built upon the Common, and those already built to be pulled down.	[204]
XV.	The Inhabitants to enjoy the Commons which were Common for Sixty years past.	[204]
XVI.	Allowance for Ditches and Banks, &c.	[205]
XVII	The Lords may Plant the Banks with Wood, &c.	[206]
XVIII.	Officers may levy Penalties and despend the money	[206]
XIX.	For Robert Rivers fourteen Roods in Smithy Fen, &c.	[207]

COMMON RIGHTS AT

Article		Page
XX.	The Town to have the Wood in the Fens.	[207]
XXI.	The Inhabitants to have the leavings in Smithy Fen.	[208]
XXII.	How twenty Customary Tenants, Order-makers are to be nominated and chosen.	[208]
XXIII.	How the sums of Money levied by reason of pains and penalties are to be paid.	[210]
XXIV.	Orders are to be wrote and Published within fifteen days after they are made.	[211]
XXV.	No Orders to be made in any Court.	[212]
XXVI.	No person to Common not being Inhabitants, except.	[213]
XXVII.	What Cattle shall be put upon the Common.	[215]
XXVIII.	For dividing the Lots and Weanling Calves.	[215]
XXIX.	When and by whom Two Men are to be chosen.	[216]
XXX.	Concerning Cow-way.	[218]
XXXI.	For Common Drain and Tillage.	[219]
XXXII.	When Sheep to go in Smithy Fen	[219]
XXXIII.	For Coloring of Cattle.	[219]
XXXIV.	Forfeit of Swine.	[219]
XXXV.	For Bye-Herds.	[220]
XXXVI.	For appointing Fieldreeves and Officers.	[220]
XXXVII.	For Pales and Walls.	[221]
XXXVIII.	Suits againt Officers, how to be borne.	[222]
XXXIX.	About those who willingly break this Agreement.	[222]
XL.	No Benefit to be had till Subscribed.	[223]
XLI.	For Charges of passing this book.	[223]
XLII.	For Droves and Drifts.	[224]
XLIII.	Mr. Hinde to make his drifts.	[224]
XLIV.	To consent to Ratify to bring this decree to an Agreement.	[224]
XLV.	To pay or give security for the 300£. to Mr. Hinde.	[226]
XLVI.	King's College Tenants to enjoy the Common as others.	[228]
XLVII.	How any mistake which may arise may be rectified.	[228]

Betweene Willm Hinde of Maddingley in the County of Cambridge Esquire lord of the Manor of Crowland and Lyles and the moyety of the Manor of Sames in Cottenham in the said County of Cambridge on th'one parte, And the Master or Keeper of Christes Colledge in the Universitie of Cambridge and the Fellowes and Schollers of the same Colledge, The Deane of the Cathedral

Church of the holy and undivided Trinity of Ely and the Chapter of the same place, the Provost of the Kinges Colledge of Blessed Mary of saint Nicholas in Cambridge and the schollers of the same Colledge, The Master of the Colledge of Saint John the Evangelyst in the Universitie of Cambridge [and] the Fellowes and Schollers of the same Colledge, Samuel Flemynge parson of the Rectorie of Cottenham aforesaid, Thomas Allcock gent, John Russell gent, Thomas Pepis the elder, gent, Thomas Pepys the younger, gent, Robert Pepys the elder, gent, George Pepys, gent, Richard Scott, gent, Edward Scott Master of Artes, William Lovell, John Taylor, Thomas Watts, John Pepis, gent, Rob'te Barnard, Frauncys Browne, William Treeve, Richard Whitinge, John Fanne, Thomas Vale, Edward Cambridge, Thomas Badcocke, Thomas Barnes, William Brigges, Richard Brigges, Richard Mayze, Thomas Ryvers the younger, Richard Caverley, Thomas Humphery, Thomas Haddowe, William Fordham, John Brigham the younger, Richard Norman, Henry Gylate, John Ewesden the younger, Nicholas Haylocke, Thomas Roger, William Walker, John Mayle the younger, George Pepys the younger, Thomas Howleton, Richard Townsende, William Webbe, William Phillippes, Robert Fordham, Robert Wimple, William Roger, William Halden, John Brigham the elder, John Ewsden the elder, Thomas Ryvers the elder, Izabell Browne widowe, William Denson, Walter Reeve, John Fletcher, Thomas Jackeson the younger, Anthony Greene, Thomas Wimple, Henry Langham, gent, John Thacksteede, Rob'te Pepis de Norff[olk], Edward Norman, John Essex jun, Elizabeth Norman widowe, Richard Bridgeman, John Reade, John Essex sen, Thomas Jackeson the elder, John Denson, William Lambe, John Glover, Edward Rymer, Edward Reeve, John Haddowe the elder, Thomas Bankes, William Phillippe, John Phillippe, Thomas Hawkyns, Thomas Smyth, Elizabeth Essex, widowe, William Ivatt, Robert Rivers, John Maile sen, James Mayle, Edward Mayle, William Emerson, Thomas Awsten, Clement Cropwell, John Haddowe the younger, Robert Norman, John Norman, William Jackeson als Tabram, John Roger, John Maize, Raphe Mullinex, George

Huddlestone, gent, Thomas Howlebeame, Jeremy Hubberd, Edward Bleane, William Causbie, William Sanderson, William Collyn, Thomas Whiteheade, George Essex, Rowland Essex, Richard Emerson, Rowland Browne, Robert Bankes, John Banks Master of Arts, William Moulton, Thomas Richmond, Thomas Mayle, Anthony James, John Halden, Edward Halden, Richard Awstene, John Hardingham, Thomas Brigham, William Leaché, Johanne Curde widowe, Henry Leache, Robert Mayle, William Howbeame.

ARTICLE I

<small>Article the First, Mr. Hinde shall enjoy several Inclosures in severalty, in respect of the Manor of Crowlands, Lyles and Moiety of Sames.</small>

<small>Longhill Close, part of Lyles.</small>

First it is agreed, by and between the said parties, for them and every of their heirs and assigns that the said William Hinde, his heirs and assigns shall enjoy inclosed and in severalty, for ever, all his Inclosures in the Fields, Fens, and Parish of Cottenham aforesaid which are now inclosed as they be now inclosed hereafter mentioned; that is to say one Close of Ten Acres, commonly called by the name of Long Hill Close, part of the Manor of Lyles in Cottenham aforesaid, and one Little Close thereunto adjoining, conteyning one Acre, be it either more or less, one end thereof abutting upon a parcel of Long Hill, now being common, towards the northeast, and the other end thereof abutting towards the South West, upon a great Close called Marehill and Tillage. Also the said great Close last before mentioned, called Marehill and Tillage, part of the Manor of Crowlands, in Cottenham aforesaid, one end thereof abutting upon the aforesaid Close of Ten Acres towards the North-east, and in part upon the said Common Ground afore mentioned towards the North-east, and the other end thereof abutting towards the South-west, upon a way called Kings's Cross Way, leading from Cottenham aforesaid to Landbeach.

<small>King's-cross close, part of the Manor of Crowlands.</small>

Also one other Close called King's-cross-close, part of the said Manor of Crowlands, the one end thereof abutting upon King's-cross-way aforesaid towards the North-east, and the other end thereof towards the South-west, abutting upon a Close belonging to

Acres, (be it more or less), one end thereof abutting in part upon a Close belonging to the Manor of Burdlaries, alias Harlstons, towards the South-West, and the other end thereof towards the North-east abutting upon a Close parcell of the said Manor of Lyles, called Horsemore Close.

Also one other Close before mentioned, called Horsemore Close, part of the said Manor of Lyles, containing by estimation Ten Acres, (be it more or less), lying between the Dunstall Field on the North-West, and a Close belonging to the Moiety of the Manor of Sames, late in the tenure of the said John Pepys, deceased, and a close belonging to the Manor of the Rectory of Cottenham aforesaid, on the South-east. Also one other Close, being in a field of Cottenham aforesaid called Foxall Field, late in the Tenure of Thomas Halfhead, lying on the North-east side of a Way that leads from a place called Lambs Cross to Histon, and lying on the South-west side of a Close, now in the tenure of Richard Scott or his Assigns. Also one other Close called Kitsbush Close, part of the said Manor of Crowlands aforesaid lying next the Way called Cambridge Way, leading from Cottenham towards Histon aforesaid, towards the North-west, and next to a Close belonging to the Manor of Burdlaries alias Harlstons, towards the South-east. And it is agreed, as aforesaid, that the same Closes shall lie and be several unto the said William Hinde, his heirs and

Horsemore Close, part of the Manor of Lyles.

Kits'-bush Close, part of Crowlands.

assigns, for ever, to his and their sole, proper use and behoof ; provided always that the Great Inclosure upon Marehill, lying and adjoining unto Crikle Fen, which heretofore was common, and hath been inclosed, and now lieth open and to be enjoyed as common again, shall not be said to be any of the said Inclosed Grounds, but that the said Ground shall be and remain in Common unto all the Inhabitants of the town of Cottenham, their heirs and assigns, for ever having good right of common in the said Fens, wastes and Commonable Grounds in Cottenham aforesaid.

Inclosures on Mare-hill to lie as Common to all the Inhabitants.

ARTICLE II

Christ College to enjoy Sixty Acres of certain Inclosures in respect of the Manor of Harlstons.

And it is agreed, as aforesaid, that it shall be lawful for the Master, Fellows, and Scholars of Christ College in Cambridge and their successors, and every of their Farmers, Tenants, and assigns, to hold and enjoy inclosed and in severalty, for ever, all the inclosures and Grounds inclosed, hereafter mentioned ; (that is to say) One Close containing by estimation Three Score Acres, (more or less), belonging to the Manor of Burdlaries, alias Harlstons, now in the occupation of Francis Brown, gent, or his assigns, lying on the South-east side of Kits'-bush Close aforesaid, and on the North-west side of the Common Drain that lieth between the bounds of Cottenham aforesaid and the said town of Histon before mentioned. Also one other Close belonging to the Manor of Burdlaries alias Harlstons, one end thereof abutting upon a Close late in the occupation of Anthony Green, gent., belonging to the Manor of Lyles, towards the North-east, and lyeth on the South side of the Dunstall Field aforesaid, and on the North-west side of a Close belonging to the Rectory of Cottenham, now in the occupation of the said John Pepys, gent.

ARTICLE III

The Parson to enjoy his Moor

Also, it is agreed, that it may and shall be lawful to and for the Parson and Incumbent of the Rectory and Parsonage of Cottenham end thereof toward the South-west abutting upon a way that leadeth from Cambridge Way to Histon Moor. Also, two other Closes in Alborowe, in the occupation of the said John Pepys, belonging to the Manor of the said Rectory, one end thereof abutting upon the Church Field towards the South-west, and lyeth on the North-west side of a Close, now in the occupation of the executors and Assigns of John Pepys, deceased, being the Freehold of the Heirs, Executors, or Assigns of the said John Pepis.

ARTICLE IV

Also it is agreed that it shall and may be lawful to and for the heirs, executors and assigns of John Pepys, gent., deceased, and their Farmers and assigns, to hold and enjoy in severalty, for ever, the several Inclosures and Grounds inclosed, hereafter mentioned, (that is to say), one Close divided into Five Parts, belonging to the Moiety of the Manor of Sames, late in the tenure of John Pepys, deceased, one end of the said Close abutting in part upon the said Close, called King's-Cross Close, towards the North-East, and in part upon the said Close, now in the tenure of Henry Annys, his assign or assigns, towards the North-East, and lying on the North-west side of Histon Moor and Landbeach Moor. Also two other Closes in Alborowe, now in possession of the Heirs, Executors, or Assigns of John Pepis, deceased, one end of the same Closes abutting upon the Church Field aforesaid towards the South-west and lying the South-west side of a Close belonging to the Manor of the Rectory of Cottenham, now in the occupation of John Pepis, gent.

The heirs of John Pepys, to enjoy certain Inclosures in respect to their Moiety of Sames.

ARTICLE V

Christ College to enjoy one Close, next their close and Land.

Also it is agreed, as asforesaid, that the Master, Fellows, and Scholars of Christ's College in Cambridge, may inclose and hold in severalty, for ever, all that One Acre adjoining to their Close in ferne-Field and the Hempland.

ARTICLE VI

Richard Scott to enjoy certain Grounds.

Also that the said Richard Scott, his Heirs and assigns, may inclose and hold in severalty, for ever, all that One Close at Curds Willows in the said Field, called Dunstall Field; and one broad Land, lying in the Common field of the said town, called Farm Field, abutting upon a way that leadeth from Cottenham aforesaid to Cambridge, towards the South-East; and One Acre lying in the said Foxall Field, abutting upon Stone Ditch towards the South-East; [and] one Broad Land, adjoining to the said Richard Scott's own house; so that he and they shall leave forth a convenient way leading over the said broad land for all kinds of Passages and Carriages, for ever, within twenty feet where a way is now used.

ARTICLE VII

St. John's College to inclose Five Acres at Stone Ditch, or elsewhere.

Also that the Master, Fellows, and Scholars of St. John's College in Cambridge may Inclose and hold in severalty, for ever, all those their Lands which lie against a place called Stone ditch, or any other of their lands in the said Town of Cottenham, so as they exceed not the quantity of Five Acres.

ARTICLE VIII

Pelham's Close to be enjoyed by the Dean and Chapter of Ely.

Also that the close called Pelham's Croft Close shall be enjoyed in severalty by the Dean and Chapter of Ely and their successors and Farmers, without any challenge of any way to be made through the same.

COTTENHAM AND STRETHAM 201

ARTICLE IX

And it is further agreed as aforesaid, in consideration of the said Inclosures to be held and enjoyed, as is aforesaid, that the said Master, Fellows, and Scholars of Christ College in Cambridge, their Farmers and assigns, for and in respect of the Demesnes of the Manor of Burdlaries ; and the Parson of Cottenham aforesaid and his Successors, Farmers, and Assigns, for and in respect of the Demesnes of the Manor of the Parsonage of Cottenham aforesaid ; and the Heirs, Executors, and Assigns of John Pepys, gent, deceased, and their Farmers and Assigns, for and in respect of the Demesnes of the Moiety of the Manor of Sames, shall be hereafter clearly excluded from having any Sheep going or depastured in any of the walks, feedings or places in Cottenham aforesaid other than in their or every of their several Grounds inclosed, any usage or custom heretofore had or used to the contrary, notwithstanding. Except three score Sheep, hereafter mentioned, to be kept by the incumbent of the Parsonage Manor, in manner and form hereafter mentioned.

The Lords excluded from keeping Sheep.

ARTICLE X

Also, it is agreed, as afforesaid, that the said Mr. William Hinde, his Heirs, Farmers and Assignes, in consideration of the said Inclosures by him and them to be held and enjoyed as is aforesaid, shall keep no Sheep within the bounds and limits of Cottenham, aforesaid, without his Pastures inclosed in the Right of the Manors of Lyles and Crowlands, or of his Moiety of the Manor of Sames at any time hereafter, or in the Right that he hath by virtue of a Lease of or in the said manor of Burdlaries, or by any right that Sir Francis Hinde, father of the said William Hinde, heretofore had, or that the said William Hinde, his heirs or assigns, ever had, hath, or may have at any time hereafter to and in the said Manors of Burdlaries, Crowlands, Lyles, and Sames, or any of them, saving always such benefit of Common feeding and pasturing

Sheep with a proviso for Westwick.

of sheep to and for the copyholders of the Manors, and of any of them, as they have heretofore had, to be ordered and used according to the true intent of these presents. Provided always that it shall be lawful for the said William Hinde, his heirs and assigns, to have his and their proper sheep to go or be depastured for and in respect of the Manor of Westwick in the Holme, in time commonable, in and upon Thistly Hill and Little North Fen, unto a place called the Runnels, near the Lands-ends, but not between the Runnels and the Lands-ends, nor elsewhere within the bounds of Cottenham.

What Sheep shall be kept for Westwick; what Sheep go not in the Severals. Also Alborough to be fed as Common.

And, it is agreed, as aforesaid, that there shall be for the Manor of Westwick and the inhabitants there dwelling but one Flock of Sheep kept, wherein both the Sheep of the said William Hinde, his heirs and assigns, and also the Sheep of the said Inhabitants and occupiers of any lands in Westwick in respect of any Common for any Lands in Westwick, shall go and be depastured. And that it shall be lawful for the said inhabitants of or in the Town of Cottenham aforesaid, their heirs and assigns, having Tenements in Cottenham aforesaid whereunto common of or for sheep doth belong, to keep in times commonable their sheep in the said Holme, Thistly Hill, and Little North Fen, and all other places and fields in Cottenham aforesaid except in Grounds which are now several and inclosed, or that hereafter shall be inclosed by virtue of this agreement when they are inclosed, and to erect as many sheep folds as they, or any of them, shall think good, at any time hereafter, within the arable fields of Cottenham, aforesaid.

ARTICLE XI

Also it is agreed, as aforesaid, that all the Meadow Ground in Cottenham, called Alborowe, shall be fed and lie Common for ever, according as is herein mentioned. And, also that one other piece of Ground or Leys, lying between the said field, called Dunstall Field, and the said close, called Kit's Bush Close, shall lie Common for ever. And also, it is agreed, as aforesaid, that the said William

Hinde, his Heirs, Farmers, and Assigns, shall not at any time hereafter feed or keep or cause to be fed or kept upon the Meadow, called Alborowe, or upon any such grounds as are or shall be appointed by virtue of or according to the true meaning of any article herein mentioned, for the pasture of the herds of Milch Kine or Bullocks within the limits and bounds of Cottenham aforesaid, without his Pastures Inclosed, above the number of fifteen milch kine, at any time hereafter, in the right of the seite of the Manor of Crowlands; nor above the number of fifteen milch kine for his seite of the Manor of Lyles, nor for the seite of his moiety of the Manor of Sames, above six milch kine, and those milch kine to be kept and fed at such times and in such places as the milch kine of most part of the inhabitants of Cottenham aforesaid shall be depastured and kept in Cottenham aforesaid and not otherwise.

ARTICLE XII

Also it is agreed, as aforesaid, that neither the said William Hinde, his Heirs nor assigns, nor the Master, Fellows and Scholars of Christ College in Cambridge, nor their successors nor their assigns, nor their nor any of their Tenants or Farmers, shall take any manner of cattle to be depastured and fed as by way of joistment or hiring in or upon any grounds within the bounds and limits of Cottenham aforesaid without their several pastures now inclosed, or which by any Article herein mentioned and be agreed to be inclosed by virtue of this agreement.

No Cattle to be taken in to Joist or Adjistment.

ARTICLE XIII

And it is also agreed, as aforesaid, that the said William Hinde, his Heirs and Assigns, nor any of them, shall not inclose or fence in, to keep in severalty, at any time hereafter, any other grounds, within the bounds or limits of Cottenham than is already inclosed, save only that it shall be lawful for the said William Hinde, his Heirs and Assigns, to inclose twenty acres more than is already

Holme Closes allowed Twenty Acres.

inclosed, whereof the Leys of his own, abutting on the way leading over the Holme-bridge and upon the Holme corner, shall be part, and the rest shall be likewise of land of his own, or of such as he can purchase adjoining to the said Leys.

ARTICLE XIV

No Houses to be built upon the Common, and those already built to be pulled down.

And also it is agreed, as aforesaid, that no Houses, Hovels, Sheds, or other like buildings, shall be made by any person or persons at any time hereafter upon any part of the Common Fens or wastes in Cottenham aforesaid, nor in any grounds, by these presents meant to be had or used as or for Common, except one little cottage or shed, which may be erected hereafter for the keeper of the Fen, by the consent of the greater number of the order-makers hereafter mentioned, and that the houses already builded by Robert Lyon, William Curde, and widow Turner, shall be pulled down before Easter term next, by the Town Officers, or their deputies, which shall have authority there by most of the order-makers hereafter mentioned.

ARTICLE XV

The Inhabitants to use the Commons, which were Ccmmon for sixty years past, to their best benefit.

Also that the said Inhabitants of Cottenham aforesaid, their Heirs and Assigns, shall have all the profit and use of all the Common Fens and waste grounds and places in Cottenham aforesaid, which have been used for Common all the time of the year within this threescore years last past, except such as be herein mentioned to be kept in severalty or inclosed, and to use them to the best commodity of the said inhabitants, for ever, and in and about them to make banks and ditches as the most part of the order-makers hereafter mentioned shall think good, and to do what they or the most part of them will or shall think convenient for the bettering of the said Commons, or any part of them, according to such order as shall be made in such manner as shall be hereafter mentioned; saving always to the said William Hinde, his Heirs

mentioned and the orders hereupon, by, or according to these presents to be made.

And, that the said William Hinde, his Heirs and Assigns, Farmers and Tenants of the said Manors of Crowlands, Lyles, and Moiety of the Manor of Sames, shall, and may keep the number of milch kine, before mentioned, in such manner and form as is before mentioned, according to the true intent and meaning of these presents.

ARTICLE XVI

Also, it is agreed as aforesaid, that whereas the Inhabitants of Cottenham, aforesaid, have made a Bank and a Ditch in Smithy fen from the bars next unto North Fen unto the place called Stone-hill, that they, the said inhabitants, shall have and take, twelve feet of ground there, for the ditch, and fourteen feet for the bank, for ever; and that the said inhabitants, their Heirs, successors and Assigns, shall, from time to time, cast, scour, maintain and keep all the fences and ditches about Smithy Fen, and also Charlode, for ever, and that all the banks and ditches in Cottenham aforesaid, which have been laid forth, made and staked by the said inhabitants, their heirs or assigns, or shall be by such their officers as shall be chosen, as hereafter is mentioned, shall be kept and maintained for ever in good and sufficient reparation, by those persons, their heirs and successors, to whom they be, or shall be severally limited, allotted, and appointed, to be maintained, scoured and kept; upon pain of 16*d.* to be forfeited and lost by those persons, their heirs, successors or assigns, to whom the said reparation shall be limited and appointed, for every pole, not sufficiently repaired.

[margin: Allowances for ditches and banks in Smithy Fen, and what forfeited if not maintained.]

ARTICLE XVII

Lords may plant the banks with wood and have the profit, with the fishing and Charlode to the town.

And also it is agreed that any of the Lords in Cottenham, their heirs and assigns, and the Freeholders and Copyholders in Cottenham aforesaid, their heirs and assigns, may plant and set any kind of Wood or Willows, Oziers, Sallows, or other Wood upon that part or parts of the banks or ditches to him or them limited, to be repaired at his or their pleasures, and likewise that he or they which so shall plant the same, they, their heirs, and assigns, shall or may take the commodity thereof for ever. And the fishing and other profit of those parts of the ditches and banks, to them severally limited, to be repaired, and the same to use at his or their discretion as often as they or any of them shall think good and convenient, without any denial of any person or persons whatsoever, having right to any Estate of Inheritance of or in any Lands or Tenements within the said town, saving that the said Inhabitants of the said Town of Cottenham, their heirs and assigns, shall have the fishing of the said Charlode for ever, to be let by them, their heirs and assigns, to bear the common charges, whereby the said Inhabitants of the said Town shall or may be, in common or together, charged.

ARTICLE XVIII

Officers to levy penalties.

And further it is agreed, as aforesaid, by all the said parties to these presents, for them and every of them, their and every of their heirs and assigns, that the Town Officers that shall be appointed from time to time by the makers of orders, by virtue of this agreement, shall and may levy by way of distress or of distraining of the goods and chattels of any person or persons which shall offend or neglect the performance of any of these orders, whether they be any of the Tenants of the said William Hinde, his heirs or assigns, or of any other, or otherwise which shall be found in any place in the said parish of Cottenham banks and ditches, decayed, until they be sufficiently repaired.

ARTICLE XIX

And also it is agreed, as aforesaid, that Smithy Fen shall continue and remain for ever dowelled and staked according as it now lieth, saving that the said Inhabitants shall have the fourteen roods that Robert Rivers had in Smithy Fen, which was laid by Sir Francis Hinde, Knight, deceased, to a cottage tenement, wherein the said Robert Rivers now dwelleth, in Cottenham aforesaid, belonging to the Crowlands hold ; and that those fourteen roods shall be laid and dispersed into several parcels, one parcel of two roods to every fee, where the said Robert Rivers usually had the same, upon the outside of every fee next the stake or landmark for the parcels of the said fen belonging to the Manor of Burdlaries alias Harlstones, and that the said Inhabitants of Cottenham, their heirs and assigns, shall so take and enjoy the same hereafter for ever, and bestow the profit thereupon arising upon the common charges of the said town. *Robert Rivers; fourteen roods to be for the Town charge for ever.*

ARTICLE XX

Also, it is agreed, as aforesaid, that the said Inhabitants of Cottenham shall have to them, their heirs and assigns, all the wood that is growing or that hereafter shall be growing in the common fens, wastes, and commonable grounds in Cottenham, to bear such the common charges as before mentioned, for ever ; except, that every one, their heirs and assigns, shall or may take such of the said Wood as they or any of them have planted or *The Town to have the Wood growing in the Fens, for public use.*

shall plant, upon any of the said banks in the said Fens as is before mentioned, and except all woods now growing, or that hereafter shall grow, in any of the grounds now inclosed or meant to be kept several or agreed to be inclosed hereafter by [any] of these presents.

ARTICLE XXI

<small>The Inhabitants to have the leavings.</small>

Also it is agreed, as aforesaid, that the said Inhabitants, their heirs and assigns, shall, for the common use and benefit of the inhabitants, their heirs and assigns, of the said township of Cottenham, have for ever the use and profit of one piece of ground in Smithy fen called the Young Man's fen. And of one other piece of ground in the Holme, called the Bull Piece; and also the profits of the parcels of the said Smithy Fen, called the leavings, not set out or divided as is aforesaid ; and also the Fishing in the Abbot's Creeke and in the new ditch in Smithy Fen, saving that yearly after Michaelmas until the feast of the Annunciation of our Lady the Virgin, the said parcel of ground shall be used still in common as the other commons and wastes have been.

ARTICLE XXII

<small>The form, and when the Order Makers are to be chosen and allowed.</small>

Also it is agreed by all the said parties to these presents, for them, their heirs and assigns, that before the feast of the birth of our Lord God, next ensuing the date of these presents twenty customary Tenants or Copyholders of the Manors or Lordships in the Town of Cottenham shall be named and published in the Church of Cottenham by the Lords of the said Manors in Cottenham aforesaid, their Deputies or Farmers, in manner and form following : viz : the said William Hinde, his heirs, farmers or assigns, shall name of or for the Manor of Lyles five Copyhold Tenants of the said Manor. . And, for the Manor of Crowlands, five Copyhold Tenants of the said Manor ; and, for his or their moiety of the Manor of Sames, one Tenant ; and that for the

Manor of Burdlaries alias Harlstones, three Copyhold Tenants of the same Manor, shall be named there by the Master of Christ College in Cambridge, or the Farmers of the said Manor of Burdlaries, or his or their deputy ; and for the Manor belonging to the Rectory, three Copyhold Tenants of the same Manor shall be named by the Parson of Cottenham, for the time being, or his deputy or Farmer. And, there shall be then named by the Dean and Chapter of Ely and their successors, farmers or assigns, for the Manor of Pelhams, two Copyhold tenants of the same Manor ; and that Thomas Alcock, his heirs and assigns or farmers, for his moiety of the Manor of Sames, shall then name one Copyhold tenant of the said Manor ; and upon or in default of such nomination to be made, by any of the said lords, their farmers or assigns, the Copyholders of every the said Manors, so named as is aforesaid, or the greater number of them, shall within one week then next following, nominate and appoint so many Copyholders of every of the said Manors as is aforesaid as shall not be nominated or appointed by the said lords, their farmers, or assigns, as is aforesaid : all which customary tenants so named, or so many of them as shall be so named and will ; the Farmers of the Manor or Rectory of Cottenham ; the Farmers of the Manor of Crowlands, if they will ; and so many of the Freeholders of the same Town inhabiting there as will, shall on the twelfth day of January next coming, and yearly after, on every twelfth day of January, before ten o'clock in the forenoon (not being Sunday, if it shall fall upon the Sunday, then the next day following at the same time) meet in the Chapel in Cottenham aforesaid, sometime used for a school-house, and that they or the greater number of them that do so meet, shall and may make Orders and Bye-Laws, for the feeding, mowing, ditching, fishing, or other convenient usage of all the Fens, Wastes, and Commonable Grounds, in Cottenham aforesaid, and assess Pains and Penalties of or upon the breakers of the same or any of them. And that the said twenty customary tenants, so named as aforesaid, or so many of them as shall be so named to be Order Makers, in manner and form as is herein mentioned, shall so remain and continue for and during their natural lives, or until they shall leave their dwelling and habitation in the said town of Cottenham, and whensoever, any of the said Copyholders, shall die or depart from his said habitation in the said town, then the lord or the owner of the said Manor, for which the said Copyholders so dying or departing as aforesaid was nominated, shall nominate before the feast of the nativity of our Lord God, next ensuing such death or departure, in his place or stead another Copyholder or customary tenant of the same Manor of or for which the party dying or departing was named, in manner and form aforesaid ; and upon default of such nomination, as aforesaid, by any the lords or their deputies, then it shall be lawful for the rest of the said Order makers, or the greater number of them which shall be nominated from time to time, to nominate or appoint so many of the Copyholders for every of the said Manors as shall be wanting of the number or numbers aforesaid to meet and make Orders in manner and form aforesaid ; and the parties so to be nominated to do and execute all and every thing as the parties so first named did or might do according to the true meaning of these presents.

ARTICLE XXIII

How all the Penalties accepted for banks and ditches shall be bestowed. Also, it is further agreed, as aforesaid, that all the sums of Money obtained or levied by reason of any the Pains, Penalties or Forfeitures, forfeited or lost by virtue of this agreement, or by any order hereafter to be made by the said Order-makers, or the greater number of them, in manner and form aforesaid, except for the banks and ditches, shall be divided and paid as follows ; (that is to say), the one half of the said pains, forfeitures and amerciaments, so levied shall be paid to the lord of whom the tenement is holden whereby the person forfeiting any penalty doth claim to have or use any common there ; and, the other half shall be paid, the one half of the last mentioned to the use and profit of the said Inhabitants to bear the common charges of the said town of Cottenham, and the residue they the said officers may retain to the use and profit of the said officers, in consideration for their said pains.

And it is further agreed as is aforesaid, that the Orders and Bye-Laws, and Pains, so made and agreed upon by the said Order-makers, or the greater number of them, being not contrary nor repugnant to the true intent and meaning of the parties to these presents in this book expressed, shall stand and be good and available and be kept until some other Order in that behalf be made by the said Order-makers or the greater number of them at the like time assembled, whether the consents of the lords or owners of the said Manors, or any of them, or of any other tenant or owner of any lands, tenements or hereditaments in Cottenham aforesaid, their or any of their heirs, successors or assigns, be had or not; provided always that the said Orders and Bye-Laws, nor any of them, shall not extend to the rating of the said Inhabitants to any certain number of cattle, except milch kine. And if any rate for milch kine shall be made hereafter, it shall extend to all the inhabitants in general, and not that any one person that hath right of Common for keeping milch kine, according to the true intent of these presents, shall be rated to keep more milch kine than another, saving, that it shall be lawful for the parson of the Rectory of Cottenham to keep eight kine, above the rate, so that he keep not above twenty kine in all, at one time.

[Marginal note: All orders made by the Order Makers, not repugnant, shall be in force till they be repealed by the like authority.]

ARTICLE XXIV

And it is also agreed, as aforesaid, that the said makers of Orders shall within fifteen days after the making of the said Orders cause the same to be put in writing and published in the Parish Church of Cottenham aforesaid; and shall at the same time that they do make Orders, appoint yearly two of the Inhabitants to be Officers for the town for one whole year. And that the said two Officers shall see the said Orders and Bye-Laws, so made and agreed upon, kept and performed, and, as well the said Bailiffs of the said Lords shall or may distrain for and levy the one half of the said penalties,

[Marginal note: Orders to be wrote and published in the Chapel within fifteen days after made.]

forfeitures and amerciaments due to the said lords as is aforesaid, and also that the said Officers shall or may distrain for or levy the other half of the said penalties and forfeitures, which shall be forfeited for the breach of any Article contained in this Composition or Agreement, or of any Orders or Bye-Laws, that shall be made as aforesaid, to be employed as is aforesaid. And it is further agreed, as aforesaid, that as well the said Officers as also the said Bailiffs of the said Lords, for their portion, shall and may distrain the beasts or goods of him that doth refuse or delay to pay the same amerciaments or pains forfeited by him, wheresoever they be found in Cottenham aforesaid, so they be distrained for within one year after they be forfeited, and not otherwise, and impound the same distress or distresses until the money be paid for which they were distrained and sell the same distress if the money be not paid within five days after such distress impounded. And that the said Officers shall make a true and just account of their receipt of all and every the penalties, forfeitures and amerciaments that they shall so receive or levy, unto the Order-makers, or the greater number of them, at the time, place and day of their next meeting for making of Orders, and that the said Officers shall yearly within eight and twenty days, next after their accounts to the said Order-makers made and determined, pay all such sums of money as shall be then remaining in their hands, that is to say, so much as is due to the inhabitants shall be paid by them to the Town Officers, newly chosen, for the next year following, upon pain to forfeit double so much money in the name of a penalty, as shall then remain in their hands unpaid, the last mentioned penalty to be employed to bear the common charges of the said inhabitants.

ARTICLE XXV

No Laws to be made in any of the Lord's Courts.

Also it is agreed, as aforesaid, by and between the said parties to these presents, and every of them, for them their heirs and assigns, do grant and agree to and with either of them their heirs and assigns, that neither the said William Hinde, nor any of his heirs, executors administrators or assigns, nor any other lords, lord or owner of any other Manor in Cottenham aforesaid, or any their jurors, homage or tenants, or suitors of or to any Court or Courts of any of the said Manors in Cottenham aforesaid, shall make or suffer to be made in any Court or Courts of the said Manors or of any of them any Order or Bye-Laws touching or concerning any Order or Article herein mentioned, or touching or concerning any Order or Bye-Law, according to the true meaning of these presents to be made by the said Order-makers, in manner and form aforementioned, nor shall distrain for or levy any fines, but shall, if they will, from time to time ratify and confirm in their courts all or any of the said Orders so made or to be made by the said Order-makers as is aforesaid, and the said lords shall not distrain for nor levy any fines, pains or amerciaments touching anything of or for or concerning the which any pains or amerciaments shall or may be assessed or levied by the true meaning of these presents, other than for such as his or their moieties as is aforesaid.

ARTICLE XXVI

And also it is agreed, as aforesaid, that no person or persons shall use or enjoy any of the Commons or Liberties of Commonage, within the bounds or limits of the said Town or places of Cottenham Commonable aforesaid, for any longer time than his family be or shall be inhabiting or resident in Cottenham aforesaid, and that he keep no house in any other place than in Cottenham aforesaid ; provided always that it shall be lawful for John Russel, gent., and the said Thomas Alcock, gent., during either of their lives, to Common there with all manner of their cattle, in respect of their lands and tenements there, in such sort as the rest of the inhabitants do, or may lawfully common, although that they and their wives be not couchant there, so that their families be resident there ; neither shall any person or persons common or use any feeding or pasture in common but only for one tenement, and that for the tenement whereupon he or his family dwelleth or coucheth;

What persons are to use Commons.

saving that it shall be lawful for the said Mr. William Hinde and his heirs males, not inhabiting in the said town of Cottenham, for his said Manor of Lyles, to have feed for his or their own proper great cattle in such places, and in such sort, and at such time as the said inhabitants, their heirs and assigns, shall keep and feed their great cattle ; provided always that the said William Hinde, his heirs and assigns, shall and may keep the milch kine before mentioned in manner and form as is before set down and ordered. Provided also, that if at any time hereafter the said Order-makers shall rate the inhabitants to any certain number for milch kine, that then the said William Hinde, his heirs and assigns, shall be rated and stand to keep as the other inhabitants do for his and their Manors of Lyles and Crowlands, and not otherwise, any thing in these presents to the contrary notwithstanding. Provided also, that it shall be lawful for the Parson of Cottenham aforesaid and his successors, keeping and performing the Covenants and Articles hereafter mentioned on his part and behalf to be performed, to have the feeding of his own proper great cattle and three score sheep, in the said Commons of Cottenham, not couching in the said town, and that at such time or times and in such places as the inhabitants shall feed their own cattle, so long as he doth keep the said Articles and covenants on his behalf, the which sheep and cattle shall be for the maintaining of the hospitality and housekeeping of the said Parson in the said parsonage of the said town and not elsewhere ; and the said Parson of Cottenham doth for him and his successors and assigns grant and agree to and with all the other parties to these presents, and every of them, their heirs and assigns, that in consideration of this grant of Commonage and of his said Inclosures that he, the said parson of Cottenham, nor his successors nor assigns, shall not demand or take hereafter any tithes which have not heretofore been usually paid, within three score years now last past, before any inclosures were made by the said Sir Francis Hinde, knight, or his assigns, within the bounds of Cottenham ; provided, that if any arable land in the common fields of Cottenham aforesaid, shall

ARTICLE XXVII

Also, it is agreed as aforesaid, that no person or persons shall put any kind of cattle into any part of the Common belonging to the said town which be not his own proper cattle, except such as by these presents are mentioned to be excepted, and also except such cattle as any person inhabiting in Cottenham aforesaid, with the allowance of the said Orders-makers or the greater number of them, shall have to draw in his cart or plough, and kine to milk for the relief of his house, and they to go in such places as the other inhabitants' milch kine and working cattle do go.

What Cattle to be put on the Common.

ARTICLE XXVIII

Also, it is agreed as aforesaid, that all the ground between Chittering Hill and the Lot ditch next Topymoor shall be laid several and kept from all manner of cattle, yearly hereafter for ever, from the first day of March until the four and twentieth day of June, and so long after as the greater part of the Order-makers shall think meet and convenient; and, that the same ground, yearly upon the morrow after Midsummer day, or at such time as the greater part of the Order-makers shall think meet, shall be by the Town officers or their deputies parted, divided, and allotted, evenly and indifferently, into lots and parts amongst all the said lords and inhabitants in Cottenham aforesaid having right of Common in the said town of Cottenham, to the end that every of them may mow and convert into hay or stover all their and every of their parts so to them assigned and allotted. And, that Bullocks-Harst, Dellfen, Alborowe, and all other grounds between the Close at King's-Cross-Way and Crykle Fen bank, and the ground aforesaid adjoining to Marehill and Crykle Fen, which was heretofore Common and lately inclosed and now laid Common again, shall

Dividing Lots and Weanling Calves.

be kept several from all manner of cattle from the twentieth day of February until the first day of May, yearly, for ever hereafter, except so much ground as is between the said King's Cross Close and the clay pits, to be used for the weaning of Calves and to be several as aforesaid ; and, that after the first day of May until the latter end of harvest no manner of cattle shall be fed or depastured in the said grounds and places before mentioned, except milch kine or such kine kept to be milch the next year following, and bulls, as shall be allowed by the said Order-makers or the greater number of them, except Weanling Calves in the grounds before excepted for calves; and, that the ground called Michelleye and all the ground lying between Crykle Fen bank and the Lots ditch in Topymoor, shall be yearly laid several and kept from all manner of cattle from the twentieth day of February until the first day of May, and from thence until the first day of November, no jeest cattle shall be depastured there except oxen which do work in the plough or cart, and burlings under the age of one year, and sick bullocks. And, no sheep shall be depastured in any of the said last mentioned grounds, but only from one month before the feast of the nativity of our Lord God, yearly, unto the twentieth day of February and no longer, upon the pain of Sixpence to be forfeited for every sheep, by the owner thereof, which shall feed or depasture in any of the said last mentioned grounds, contrary to this Article.

ARTICLE XXIX

When, and why and by whom, the keepers of the fen, are to be chosen and appointed.

And, it is agreed as aforesaid, that yearly upon the Sunday before Candlemas day, after Evening prayer being ended, or within twenty days next before the said Sunday, two Men, or more shall be chosen or hired by the greater number of Inhabitants, being present in the Church of Cottenham aforesaid, having right of Common in the said Town and Fens, to keep the said grounds and places from cattle for and during all the times that they are to be laid and kept several in such manner and form as is before mentioned, which keepers or their deputies shall not suffer any cattle to go or feed in any of the said grounds or places, otherwise than is appointed by this Article or shall be appointed hereafter by the said Order-makers or by the greater number of them. And then also in like manner two other persons or more shall be chosen as aforesaid to impound all such cattle as they find feeding in any of the said grounds or places, contrary to any Article contained in these presents or contrary to any Order hereafter to be made by the said Order-makers or the greater number of them. And the cattle so impounded shall from time to time be redeemed out of the pound at the costs and charges of the said parties so as aforesaid chosen and hired to be the said keepers. And if in default of the said keepers or their said deputies the owners of the said cattle shall at their own charges redeem their own cattle so impounded out of the pound, then they may abate so much of the said keepers' wages as shall be paid for redeeming of the said cattle. And that every person shall yearly pay for his said lot or part, which he hath of or in the said ground lying between Chitteringhill and the Lott ditch next Topymoor, four-pence, and for every milch cow, which shall be kept or put before any of the said herdsmen of either of the milch herds, between the first day of May, and the four and twentieth day of June, one penny. The which sums of fourpence and one penny shall be employed and paid towards the payment of the said keepers' wages; and that every person that shall not pay all the said money to such persons as shall be appointed to collect the same within ten days next after the same shall be demanded, shall lose his lot aforesaid for that year, the which lot shall be sold by the Town Officers abovementioned for the time being and the money thereof coming shall be employed toward the bearing of the common charges of the Town, and also towards the payment of the said keepers' wages. And if there shall not be hired any keepers as aforesaid by the Inhabitants in manner and form specified in this Article, then the said Town Officers or their deputies shall and may impound all such cattle as they shall find going and feeding in and upon any part or parcel of the said ground, contrary to this Agreement or to any order hereafter to be made by the said Order-makers, or the greater number of them. And the said cattle so impounded there to detain and keep until every owner thereof do pay for the first time that his cattle shall be so impounded two pence, and for the second time within the same year, three pence, and for the third time within the same year, four pence. And if he or they shall have this warning three times and therein be taken offending in like manner afterwards, with his cattle in the same year, then to pay Sixpence for every Pounding, so often as they shall be taken unto the said Officers or Impounders.

ARTICLE XXX

For Cow-way.

Also it is agreed, that the way called Cow-way, now used, leading from a place called Wronglane's End unto the Cow Pasture within the limits of Cottenham aforesaid, shall continue for ever to be from time to time used as a Way only, as well by all and every the parties to these presents, their heirs and assigns, and all other the Inhabitants of Cottenham aforesaid which do and shall consent and shall continue their consent and agreement to this present Composition, and by none other, for the drift of their kine and other cattle, and also for their passages and carriages whatsoever necessary for their several uses. And, that the said William Hinde, his heirs and assigns, shall before the feast of the Annunciation of our Lady, next ensuing the date of these presents, upon reasonable request thereof made, convey unto any person or persons and their heirs, upon whose lands the said Way lieth, so much other land in quantity, not holden of the Queen Majesty her Heirs or Successors by Knight Service in chief, as whereof the said persons do or shall lose the profit by reason of the said Way.

ARTICLE XXXII

Also, that Smithy Fen shall be yearly, from the feast of St. Michael the Archangel, kept from Sheep until the twentieth day of February, hereafter for ever.

What time Sheep to be kept out of Smithy Fen.

ARTICLE XXXIII

Also, that no person or persons having right of Common in Cottenham aforesaid shall suffer by way of Coloring, the Cattle of any person or persons in Cottenham, neither the cattle which he shall have jointly or in common with any person or persons, to be depastured or fed in his right or name in any part of the Commons of the said town of Cottenham, except all such joint owners or owner in Common of Cattle as have Common in the said Town and be dwelling there, upon pain to forfeit and lose for every beast so depastured and fed, contrary to this Article, thirteen shillings and fourpence, and, the said money to be paid to the said Town Officers and to be divided, distributed, and accounted for, as is aforesaid.

For Coloring of Cattle.

ARTICLE XXXIV

Also, that no Swine shall be suffered but only by way of drift to go and feed in Smithy Fen, Bullocks Harst, Mitchelleye, nor from the Stone Bridge to the Becks, Delffen, Alborowe, in the

For Swine, where they shall go.

ground between King's-Cross Close and Crykle Fen Bank, and from thence to the Lot ditch in Topymoor nor in the Lots, at any time hereafter, upon pain that the owner, knowing thereof, shall lose for every swine for every time going and feeding contrary to this Article, four-pence, to be divided, levied, and distributed and accounted for as aforesaid.

ARTICLE XXXV

or Bye-
erds.

Also it is agreed, as aforesaid, that yearly from Candlemas until the first day of November, no person or persons shall keep any Bye-Herds of great Cattle, or put any bullocks to be depastured in any part of the Commonable Grounds or Fens belonging unto the said town of Cottenham but before the Town Herdman, upon pain of twelve pence for every offence, to be levied of the offenders goods and divided, distributed, and accounted for as aforesaid, except in Little North Fen and Great North Fen; and except Working Cattle, sick Bullocks, Burlings under the age of one year, Horses, Mares and Geldings, in manner and form as in this Article is agreed, and not otherwise.

ARTICLE XXXVI

irections
or choosing
ield Reeves
nd Fen
fficers.

Also it is agreed, as aforesaid, that those persons which by the true meaning of these presents shall be appointed to make Orders and Bye-Laws, or the greater part of them, shall at such time as they do meet, appoint and choose two men of the inhabitants to be Fieldreeves, which Fieldreeves shall see such Orders and Bye-Laws kept and performed as shall be made and agreed upon by the said Order-makers or the greater number of them, for the water furrowing and gripping of the fields. And shall likewise at the same time appoint and choose two men, being of the said Inhabitants, to be Town Officers, which Town Officers or their deputies shall see all the Articles and orders now made and hereafter to be made, performed and kept by virtue of this agreement; and that the said

Officers or their deputies shall collect and gather the aforesaid keepers' wages; and shall also divide into Lots all the ground mentioned in these presents to be divided and allotted to that purpose, before the fifteenth day of July, yearly. The which Officers shall have each of them for their pains taken about those things some outcast or leaving of the said ground, so that either of their parts by good estimation be not above the value of twenty shillings. And that the said officers shall have power and authority to levy and distrain and take all the penalties, pains and forfeitures for the breach of all and every Article, Order and Bye-Law, made or hereafter to be made by virtue of this agreement, to be divided as aforesaid. And the Fieldreeves shall have the like authority for any Order and Bye-Law made for the Fields, and the money thereof coming to divide, distribute and account for as aforesaid. And if any person or persons, so chosen by the Order-makers as is aforesaid to be the Town Officers or Fieldreeves, do refuse and neglect to execute the same, every such offender shall forfeit three pounds, six shillings, and eight pence, to be levied by distress and to be divided, distributed and accounted for as aforesaid.

ARTICLE XXXVII

Also it is agreed, as aforesaid, that the said William Hinde, his heirs and assigns, shall not molest or trouble any of the said Inhabitants, their heirs and assigns, for any Pales, Walls, Hedges, or other fences standing before their Houses towards the Street in the said Town at this time, and shall suffer them and all such like Fences hereafter as shall be set up, to continue and remain and be maintained for ever; so that they which shall be hereafter made shall not stand further into the Street than without the compass of the outmost part of the eaves' drop of the house.

For Pales and Walls.

ARTICLE XXXVIII

<small>For Suits commenced against any Officer.</small>

Also it is agreed, as aforesaid, that if any Suits shall happen to be commenced against any of the said Officers for any thing to be done by them or any of them, by or concerning their office and this agreement, the same Suit or Suits shall be maintained and borne, the one half by the parties above named, their heirs and assigns, and the other half by the said William Hinde, his heirs and assigns.

ARTICLE XXXIX

<small>For those who willingly break this Agreement.</small>

Also it is agreed, as aforesaid, that if any person or persons which now hath or hereafter shall have any Right, Interest or title of Common within the bounds of Cottenham shall willingly break this agreement, or interrupt the same or any part thereof, then the said William Hinde, his heirs or assigns, shall bear or sustain the one half of the charges which shall be spent in the Law about the same, and the party above named, their heirs and assigns, shall bear the other half thereof, until the cause shall be by Law determined, and if any recovery or eviction hereafter had or made against any of the parties above named, their heirs or assigns, of any thing, benefit or commodity, contained in this agreement, by any act or acts heretofore done by the said Sir Francis Hinde, Knight, or by any claiming by, under or from him, or done or hereafter to be done by the said William Hinde, his heirs or assigns, or any claiming by, from, or under him, for any his Lands or Leases, wherein he had right, title or interest, or shall hereafter, that then the said William Hinde, his heirs or assigns, shall make sufficient recompence for the same, and shall then also yield unto the said parties and every of them, their heirs and assigns, such damages, charges and costs, as they or any of them shall sustain by reason of the loss for not having such profits and commodities as they ought to have had by virtue of this agreement.

ARTICLE XL

Also it is further agreed, as aforesaid, by and between the said parties, their heirs and assigns, that such of the above named parties, their heirs or assigns which shall not consent, agree, and continue their consent unto this agreement, and shall not subscribe their names to these presents at such times as they shall be required, shall receive no benefit by any Article or thing contained herein, until he or they do consent and subscribe their names or marks unto the Articles of this agreement, any thing to the contrary notwithstanding.

For them who do not consent to this agreement to subscribe

ARTICLE XLI

Also it is agreed, as aforesaid, that all the charges of passing and perfecting of these Articles of Agreement, and of all other assurances concerning the same which shall be reasonably devised by Council learned in the Law of the said William Hinde, his heirs and assigns, and of the parties abovesaid, their heirs and assigns, shall be borne indifferently by the said William Hinde, his heirs and assigns, and the said parties, their heirs and assigns. And that ten pounds expended and laid out by George Pepys, gent., and also all other charges heretofore spent sithence the feast of Easter in the seven and thirtieth year of her Majesty's reign, in the behalf of the said Inhabitants, about the controversy of the Inclosures made by the said Sir Francis Hinde, Knight, or touching the Common, or any part of them, shall be borne indifferently by the said parties, their heirs and assigns, by any assessment heretofore agreed upon by divers of the said parties, which is for every tenement forty shillings, if it will serve, if not, to be paid by the money due, or hereafter to be due, unto the Inhabitants to bear the common charges of the Town of Cottenham aforesaid.

For the charges of passing this Book.

ARTICLE XLII

For Droves and Drifts.

Also it is agreed, as aforesaid, that the said William Hinde, his heirs and assigns, shall suffer the Town Officers and all other parties to these presents, their heirs and assigns, at any time hereafter, to put the Droves and Drifts of Cattle, which shall be at any time hereafter driven forth off the common fens or wastes, into the usual Drove yard of the said William Hinde, and that the said officers and other parties, their heirs or assigns, shall have authority to hold the said cattle, so driven into the said drove yard, until such time as they shall think good to deliver the cattle, so by them put in.

ARTICLE XLIII

Mr. Hinde to make his Drifts.

Also it is agreed, as aforesaid, that it shall be lawful to and for the said William Hinde, his heirs and assigns, to make his or their Drift of Cattle out of the Fens and Commons of Cottenham aforesaid yearly upon the feast day of Saint Michael the archangel, for the taking up of Strays, as heretofore have been used. Provided that if any decay shall happen to be in the Lyles Farm yard, by reason of the Inhabitants impounding of their said cattle, that the same shall be repaired at the costs and charges of the Inhabitants of the said Town of Cottenham.

ARTICLE XLIV

To consent to Ratify to bring this Decree to an Agreement.

Also it is agreed, as aforesaid, that the said William Hinde, his heirs and assigns, and all other parties to these presents, their heirs and assigns, shall, as much as in them lieth, procure and assent to have all the premises Ratified and concluded by decree in Chancery by Act of Parliament, or both, or otherwise, assured howsoever, as the learned Counsel of the said William Hinde, his heirs or assigns, and of the said Inhabitants shall devise. In consideration of all which premises before contained by these presents,

assigns, for every of their several Lordships, Messuages, Tenements, Freeholds, Copyholds or Leaseholds, respectively, thirty shillings apiece, of lawful money of England, as parcell of the forty shillings levy aforesaid, towards the payment of the three hundred pounds of like lawful money of England, at or in the Church Porch of Cottenham aforesaid, upon the five and twentieth day of March, which shall be in the year of our Lord God one thousand five hundred and ninety eight; which three hundred pounds is granted unto him the said William Hinde in consideration of this present agreement. And the said above named John Russel, Thomas Jackson the elder, George Pepys the elder, Robert Banks, Thomas Jackson the younger, Thomas Humfrey, and John Brigham, the elder, being the seven men, receivers of the rents of the Lands, given towards the common charges of the said Town of Cottenham, do further covenant, and grant to and with the said William Hinde, his heirs and assigns, by these presents, that they the said John Russel, Thomas Jackson the elder, George Pepys the elder, Robert Banks, Thomas Jackson the younger, Thomas Humfrey, and John Brigham the elder, or some of them, will pay or cause to be paid at the Church Porch aforesaid, one and fifty pounds of lawful money of England, towards the payment of the residue of the said aforementioned sum of three hundred Pounds, upon the first day of November, which shall be in the year of our Lord God one thousand five hundred and ninety eight, until which said day it is provided by these presents, the said seven men or some of them, shall receive and take towards the payment of the said fifty one pounds all the rents and commodities that shall or may be levied or made of the aforesaid parcels, which are before by these presents granted by the said William Hinde, to the said inhabitants their heirs and assigns, to bear common charges, any thing herein before mentioned to the contrary notwithstanding. Provided always that if all the rents and commodities that shall be made of the premises, before granted by these presents to bear common charges, and of all other lands and tenements whereof they are appointed to receive the rents, will not before the said day amount to the sum of fifty one pounds, over and above all other charges and expences which shall be by them laid out for the said Township, that then the said seven men shall still receive and take the rents and commodities which shall or may thenceforth be levied or made of the aforesaid parcels, until they have received sufficient into their hands to discharge all the said fifty one pounds, and every part and parcel thereof.

ARTICLE XLV

To pay or give security for the three hundred pounds.

Also, it is agreed, that the said parties to these presents, their heirs and assigns and every of them, shall at or before the eight and twentieth day of May next ensuing the day and year first above written, give security by their several bonds to the said William Hinde, his executors or assigns, for the true payment of their said parts and portions, at the day and place by these presents limited and appointed, to be paid by them respectively, which is thirty shillings for every tenement, with interest for the forbearing of the same after the rate of ten pound in the hundredth for one whole year; provided that if the said parties to these presents, their heirs, successors and assigns, excepting such parties, their heirs, executors or assigns, as be or hereafter shall be farmers or servants unto the said William Hinde, his heirs or assigns, shall not give security by their several bonds to the said William Hinde, [his] executors or assigns, at or before the said eight and twentieth day of May, for the true payment of their said parts and portions, by these

keep in severalty until they and every of them, their heirs or assigns, or some other parties for them, have either paid their parts and portions, with interest for the forbearing thereof as is aforesaid, or give security for the true payment thereof unto the said William Hinde, his heirs or assigns; and also for such costs and charges as the said William Hinde, his heirs or assigns shall expend in and about the fencing of the said inclosure. Provided further, that if the said John Russel, George Pepys the elder, Thomas Jackson the elder, Robert Banks, Thomas Jackson the younger, Thomas Humfrey and John Brigham the elder, or some of them, shall not by their bonds jointly give security unto the said William Hinde, his heirs and assigns, at or before the said eight and twentieth day of May, for the true payment of fifty one pounds at in or upon the feast of All Saints, which shall be in the year of our Lord God one thousand five hundred and ninety eight, at the place agreed upon by these presents, that then it shall be lawful for the said William Hinde, his heirs or assigns, to enter into the said Inclosures, and the same to hold and keep in severalty until they or some of them, or their succesors, have given security for the payment thereof as aforesaid. Provided also that none of the said parties to these presents, their heirs executors, administrators or successors, or any one of them, shall be charged or sued by virtue of any Article in these presents contained, for or by reason of the breach or non-performance of any of the said Covenants or Articles, contained in these presents, other than for or by reason of the breach or non-performance done or committed by himself, or those whose estate he hath, which so shall be sued, his heirs, executors, administrators, or successors; excepting the heirs, executors or

ARTICLE XLVI

ing's College Tenants to enjoy the Common.

Also it is agreed, as aforesaid, that all and every the Farmers and Tenants of the Provost and Scholars of King's College in Cambridge, for the time being, of those two several messuages or tenements in Cottenham wherein Thomas Holbeam and William Holbeam do severally inhabit shall or may for ever hereafter take and use the benefit of the Commons in Cottenham aforesaid, in such manner as the other Inhabitants of the said Town shall or may, according to the true intent and meaning of these presents, notwithstanding that the said Messuages or Tenements were of late newly erected and built.

ARTICLE XLVII

ow any mistake is to e rectified.

And also, whereas it was agreed in one Article herein concluded, that if any question, ambiguity or doubt should be moved upon any matter, clause, or sentence, or word, which should not be agreed upon by the Learned Counsel of the aforesaid parties, that the same shall be referred unto the Right Honorable the Lord North, treasurer of her Majesty's Household, and one of her majesties privy counsel to be decided for all parties. Now, to testify that the said Articles are concluded and agreed upon, by the agreement of the Council of both parties, the said Lord North hath hereunto pleased to set his hand ; Roger Goade, Provost of Kings ; William Hinde ; Umfrey Tindall ; Thomas Nevill ; Edmund Barwell, Master of Christs ; John Russell ; Richard Scott ; George Pepys, the elder ; Thomas Jackeson, the elder ; Thomas Jackeson, the younger ; William Lovell ; Robert Banks ; William Treeve ; Francis Brown ; Thomas Humphrie ; John Brigham, the elder ; John Denson ; John Brigham, the younger ; John Ewsden, the elder ; John Bull, the younger ; Elizabeth Banks ; John Philipe ;

Cropwell ; John Halden ; John Tayler ; Edward Norman ; Robert Philipp ; William Saunderson ; Edward Mayle ; William Houlbeam ; Thomas Houlbeam ; Thomas Smyth ; Thomas Ryvers, the younger ; John Haddow, the younger ; Rowland Browne ; Rowland Essex ; William Causby ; William Walker ; Thomas Brigham ; John Essex, the elder ; Richard Norman ; Richard Briggs ; Thomas Haddow ; William Fordham ; William Emerson ; Thomas Awsten · William Leach ; Johan Curde ; Henry Leache ; William Philipp ; John Glover ; Thomas Badcock ; Elizabeth Norman ; Robert Norman ; Richard Emerson ; John Roger ; Robert Wimple ; Thomas Roger ; Thomas Pepys, the younger ; John Haddow, the younger ; Thomas Wimple ; Walter Reeve ; Thomas Vale ; Richard Bridgeman ; Richard Towneson ; Elizabeth Cambridge ; Richard Mayze ; Richard Caverly ; Margaret Brown ; John Mayze ; Thomas Gibson ; Robert Pepys de Norff[olk] ; Thomas Pepys, the elder ; the Master of Saint John's College, in Cambridge ; Robert Rivers ; Anthony Green ; Richard Clayton ; Thomas Watts ; Richard Whitinge ; Edward Haldyn ; William Moulton ; Henry Gylate ; Thomas Barnes ; Edward Rymer ; Robert Mayle ; John Norman ; Henry Langham ; John Warryn ; John Reade ; John Essex, the younger ; Robert Barnard ; Anthony James, and Thomas Richmond.

ORDERS MADE

AND AGREED VPON THE TWELFE DAY OF JANUARY IN THE YEERE OF OUR LORD 1639. FOR AND CONCERNINGE THE BEST BENEFIT AND CONVENIENT VSUAGE OF ALL THE COMONABLE GROUNDS IN AND ABOUT THE BOUNDES OF COTTENHAM.

<small>1. Swine forbidden to feede in the Lowfenns.</small> Imprimis, it is ordered that no Inhabitant in this Towne shal put or cause to be put any swine in or vpon any parte of the **Arrable** fields or comonable grounds, except they be so ringed that they roote not, vpon paine to forfeit for every swine so put contrarie to this Order, iiij. *d*.

Neither shal any swine vnringed be suffered to continue in any parte of the said Comons at any time after a dayes warninge given by the Bellman vpon the like paine for every swine, iiij. *d*.

And further that no persons shal put any swine to staie and feede in any parte of the Lowfenns nor in Great Northfen to continue therein at no time of the yeere, vpon paine to forfeit for every swine so taken, xij. *d*.

<small>2. Y^e number of swine.</small> It is ordered that no person haveinge right of Comon shal not put or cause to be put into any of the said commons aboue the number of ten swine, vpon paine to forfeit for every swine aboue the said number, v. *s*.

<small>3. No swine to goe upon Chitteringe.</small> And likewise that no swine shalbe suffered to goe vpon Chitteringe hill at any time upon the paine of vi. *d*. for every swine; and also if any swine shall goe by escape into any part of the cow-pasture without the priuitie of the owners of them.

<small>4. The penaltie for swine taken in ye Cowpasture.</small> Then the sayd owners shal vpon warninge given by the Officer or Officers or any other person, within one day after, driue them out of such forbidden grounds vpon paine of such default for every swine so taken, vj. *d*.

It is ordered that if any persons shal cutt or pull downe, breake or carrie awaye any Oziers, Willowes or other sort of woode as hedges, gates stakes Railes, posts, barres, hardles, stonnes or any other thinge or thinges that are sett layinge or beinge in or vpon any parte of the commons of this Towne or any waie belonginge to this Towne without the priuitie and leaue of the Officers or one of them, then the partye or partyes so offendinge shal forfeit for every time so offendinge, x. s. 5. A penaltie on those that conueigh away any of the Towne goods.

It is Ordered that before the xijth daye of Aprill next comminge every commoner haveinge right of common in this Towne shal, with a stake marked with his or their vsuall brande, wherewith he brandeth his Geast bullocks[1] or sheepe, marke out his parte or Layer[2] of all his bankes, vpon paine of default or neglect thereof to forfeit vj. s. viij. d. to the towne officers for every layer not so staked or marked, and the penaltie to be bestowed as all other penalties for the good of the Towne. 6. The Order for stakeing and markeing of their bankes.

And if it be prooved any person to have pulled vp or carried awaye any of the sayd stakes, he shal paie to the owner of the sayd stake so pulled or digged vp fiue shillinges. And the Officers shal give notice thereof to the owner of the sayd Stakes, and the owner thereof shal marke and stake it againe within three weekes after such notice given to him or them, vpon the like paine of fiue shillinges.

---

[1] Bullocks, a term which includes any cattle of full age, on agistment. See order 21, below.

[2] The portion of banks, or ditches laid out for each commoner to keep in order. Article XVI.

7. For setting of their Netts and Fishing.

It is Ordered that no person vseinge fishinge shal neither lay nor sett any engine or nett within the fenn side of the bankes to take any fish nor within ten poles of any Lakes ende or in or vpon any gull or Breach that shal or may happen vpon any mannes bankes Common place or stoppinge in or about the bounds of Cottenham, except they first hire them of the Towne Officers, vpon paine for every time so offending ten shillinges and the penall losse of their nett or engine so sett.

And that no person shal sett any nett in any Loade or Lake narrower then the full bredth of the same Loade or Lake where they shall sett, vpon paine of two shillings to be likewise forfeited as aforesayd.

8. Against those that make hauoke and spoile the bankes and Cresses.

It is Ordered that if any persons shal cutt or pull vp or putt downe any parte of the fenn bankes, Stoppinges or Cresses in or about any part of the commons without the consent of the said Officers or the greater parte of the Ordermakers agreeing thereto, the partye so offendinge as afforesayd shalbe pained for every such default ten shillings. And if any servant offend as aforesayd, the Maister of the said Servant shal paie the said penaltie for him, ffor the ^{Wch} the sayd Maister may deteine somuch of the servants wages.

9. For proprietie or branding of cattle both Cottenham and Westwicke.

It is ordered that no persons haveinge right of common in this Towne shall put or cause to be put any sort of great Cattle or Sheepe (Except milch Kyen) into any parte of the Commons after ye twentyeth day of Aprill next vntill they be branded wth his or their vsuall brand for Sheepe or Bullocks, and so to keepe them continually, vpon paine for every beast and Sheepe not so branded as aforesaid, vj. s. viij. d.

And likewise that the Inhabitants of Westwicke shal marke and brand all their cattell in such sort as ye Inhabitants of Cottenham are enjoyned, in manner and forme before specified, before they shalbe put into any of the sayd commons, vpon the like paine of vj. s. viij. d. for every beaste.

10. And all Comoners to bring

It is Ordered that every Comoner in this Towne and Westwicke shal before Mayday next bring a Coppie of his Brande to y^e

xx. s. for every beast or Sheepe so taken, if it be probably founde against him or them within one yeere after such offence comitted. And likewise the owner or owners of such Cattle shalbe pained for every such beast xx. s.

It is Ordered that if any person leaue open any Raile or barre or gate whereby any Cattle may goe into forbidden grounds that every person that shal make such default shalbe pained for every such default comitted iij. s. iiij. d. Whereof xij. d. shalbe giuen to him or them that shal take such offenders W^{ch} sayd penalties shalbe leuied of the same persons Maister or parents of such as shal so offend. And the Maister may deteine somuch of the servants wages.

_{12. The forfeiture for leaueing open any Raile barre or gate.}

It is Ordered that if any person haue any vnruly cattle W^{ch} will not be kept out of forbidden groundes by reasonable meanes, the owner or owners of such cattle shal vpon warninge given them remoue fetter or otherwise so order them as that they may be ruled and kept out of such forbidden grounds vpon paine for every such Beaste or default, xij. d.

_{13. For ordering of vnruly cattel.}

It is Ordered that no Jades or other Cattle be suffered to goe or be depastured in any parte of the Cowpasture (Except milch kine) vntill S^{ct} Michael the Archangell next. And also that every person Sonne or deputie shall driue or cause to be driuen all their Jades and other cattle (Except before excepted) beyond barreditch into Michelleye, except the feunes be so drowned or overflowen by waters that the sayd Cattle may not there abide vpon paine for every such default, xij. d.

_{14. Jades excluded from feeding in the Cowpasture vntill St Michael.}

234 COMMON RIGHTS AT

15. Against driueing of cattle through Smitheyfen.

And it is Ordered that no persons shall driue or cause to be driuen any sort of Cattle through Smitheyfen vnto any of the other grounds or feedinges next adjoyninge vpon it from the xxv day of March vntill ye first day of August, vpon paine to forfeit fiue shillings for every time so offendinge.

16. Against driueing of Cattle thorow the Cowpasture.

It is further Ordered that such persons as haue Pastures in Alborough Closes, Longhill Denny, or haveinge any other severall grounds adjacent and layinge vpon the Cowpasture, shal not driue nor cause to be driuen any sort of Cattle through the Cowpasture not aboue twice in the weeke to and from their sayd pastures, from the twentieth day of ffebruary next vntill ye first day of May ensueinge, vpon paine for every time so offendinge contrarie to this Order to forfeit fiue shillinges. And that the Officers or any of them or any other persons that shal finde such default done by any other persons shal take of them ye penalties as aforesayd.

17. Sechal and ye ground beneath Micheleye to be kept from Geast Bullocks.

It is Ordered that no sort of Geast cattle shal either feede or be depastured in the fen called Sechall nor beneath Michaelleye or any parte thereof on this side the new ditch vntill the first day of August next comminge, vpon the paine or penaltie of fiue shillinges for every Geast bullocke that feedeth there before the daye prescribed by this Order.

Item, it is concluded and agreed that no Jades shal goe into the Cowpasture, nor any Jades shal be put into Dunstall field nor into the Halme field[1] vntill S^{et} Michael the Archangell next, vpon paine to forfeit xij. d. for every beast taken contrarie to this Order.

18. Against drift Cattle and other drie Cattle of the Butchers.

Item, wee Order that no Comoner or Inhabitant, nor any other persons in this Towne haveinge any dealinge in buyinge of Cattle and vseinge droveinge, shal put any of their drifte Cattle to feede or be depastured vpon the sayd commons or any other parte of them, vpon paine to forfeit for every such offence xx. s. And it is further Ordered that no Inhabitant in this Towne vseinge Butcherie shall put any sort of drye cattle wch they or any of them shal happen to prouide for their dealeinge in their trade vpon any parte

[1] The field which was in stubble, according to the regular rotation. The term has no relation to the Holm meadow mentioned below.

of the Cowpasture, vnder the penaltie of xij. *d.* to be forfeited for every daye so offendinge.

It is Ordered that no Sheepe shalbe fedd or depastured in the Lowfenns called Sechall Chairefen and Chitteringe hill and the Lotts from the xxth day of March vntill such time as the Sheepe doe vsually goe in the Cowpasture. *19. They must not put any drie Cattle into the Cowpasture.*

And that no Sheepe be depastured vpon Bullocks harst vntill the xxth day of ffebruary, vpon paine for every Sheepe so goeinge, iiij. *d.* It is Ordered that no bullockes shalbe fedd and depastured in Smitheyfen, or in any parte of the Comonable grounds or fields, from S^{ct} Thomas day next vntill the xxv day of March followinge vpon paine for every beast so goeinge, iij. *s.* iiij. *d.* It is Ordered that no cattle shalbe fedd or depastured in any parte of the Cowpasture from the xxth day of ffebruary next vntill the first day of Maye followinge. Nor any Geaste bullocks to feede betweene the Newditche and Michaeley [*gap*] from the xxth day of ffebruary next ensueinge vntil Michaelmas, vpon paine for every beast taken there to forfeit, xij. *d.* *20. Sheep shal not goe in the Lowfen vntill convenient time that they goe into the Cowpasture*

It is Ordered that no person or persons shall put, folde or depasture, or cause to be put folded or depastured, any manner of cattle whatsoeuer in or vpon any parte of the Halme field vntill one weeke after Harvest be ended, vpon paine for every beast there founde before the day prescribed, iiij. *d.* *21. The Halme Fielde is reserued from Cattle for a weeke after Haruest be ended.*

It is Ordered and agreed that it shalbe lawfull for any person that hath right of common to depasture and feede any kinde of Cattle on northfenside and little Northfen. As also in the fallow field and common plate of ground betweene the closes at any time of the yeere, with free libertie nothwithstandinge any order herein mencioned and formerly made concerninge bye heards.[1] Prouided also, by vertue of this Order, that it shal not be lawfull for any Commoner to put any of their milch Bullocks[2] nor any sort of their geast bullockes whatsoeuer into Greatnorthfen from this instant xij day of January vntill the xxvj day of Aprill

---

[1] Any herd kept apart from the main herd; see above, order 14.
[2] See above, order 6, note

next comminge vpon paine to forfeit for every beast so taken, xij. d.

It is Ordered that no person or persons shal digge any earth in Northfen to carrie to any of their Landes, or otherwise to their vse in any sort, nor in the leames nor in any other grounds or places profitable and where cattle feede, vpon paine of iij. s. iiij. d. for every Loade taken from any such places contrarie to this Order.

<small>22. The Holme ditch to be scoured.</small>

Item, wee Order that all the ditch separateinge the Holme Meadow from the Arrable fields and extendinge vnto the Holme close shalbe well and sufficiently ditched and scoured accordinge to the discrecion of the fieldreeues and by the paines and charges of the owners and fermors of those Lands therevpon abuttinge, before the xxiiijth day of June next comminge in this present yere, vpon paine of default or neglect thereof to forfeit xij. d. for every halfe acres bredth.

And further that ye ffieldreeues or Officers, or some of them, shal make or cause to be made a barre gate at the entrance into the Holme in convenient time to preserue the sayd meadow from the feedinge of Cattle.

<small>23. The number of milch keine and for keeping of Bulls.</small>

It is Ordered that no Comoner shal keepe aboue the number of xij milche keine vpon the Cowpasture, and for ye sayd number of twelue keine, he shal keepe a sufficient Bull in the heard with them vntill Michaelmas followinge.

And likewise that no comoner shal keepe aboue the number of nine Milch Keine vpon the sayd Cowpasture (Except he keepe a Bull as aforesaid), vpon paine for every Cow aboue the sayd number of twelue, and nine allowed as aforesaid, ten shillinges.

<small>24. No comoner to haue or keepe any of their number of Milch keine seclusive y and aparte from the Milch heard.</small>

It is Ordered that no Commoner or owner shal haue any Milch Keine to feede a parte and seuerly by themselues in the fen called Sechell nor beneath Michaelleye, nor in any parte of the Lowfenns, but that their number of xij milch keine, and all vnder ^{Wch} they esteeme for the benefit of milch keine shal goe in the Milch heard, and that in such manner as is accustomed and in the former Order mencioned and specified, vpon paine to forfeit fiue shillings for every milch Cowe that shalbe kept against this Order.

before Harvest be ended, but onely vpon his own Baulkes forrends or furrowes, vpon paine to forfeit for every beast so goeing and feedinge, v. s.

It is ordered that the Heardsmen and Shepherds shal not take to keepe any cattle of any other person or persons whatsoeuer but onely those of the Inhabitants of this Towne. And further that if the said heardsmen doe know of any such person or persons W^{ch} doe take to keepe and cullur[1] the cattle of any stranger contrarie to this Order vpon any certaine intelligence of such Cattle so retained, the sayd Heardsmen and Shepherds shal giue notice thereof presently to the Towne Officers or to one of them, vpon paine that ye Heardsmen and Shepherds that doe contrarie to this Order shal forfeit x. s. for every beast. And if any person or persons being a Commoner and so offendinge, shal be pained for every such offence x. s. and shal loose the benefitt of their common for a yeere and a halfe, after such offence done and justly prooved against him or them.

27. Against Heardsmen and Shepherds that take in strangers Cattle.

It is Ordered, condiscended and agreed by all and the greater number of the Ordermakers, that all the ground in the Vndertakers peece,[2] W^{ch} is contained within the compass of the new ditch and

28. The Undertakers peece to be kept seuerall

---

[1] For an owner of common right to colour cattle was to pass off as his own cattle which really belonged to a person who had no common right; see Preface p. 181.

[2] The Undertakers Piece or Adventurers Land in the lot book of the Bedford Local Commissioners. This had been set out, but from a variety of causes had not been entered upon by the Adventurers.

238   COMMON RIGHTS AT

for a time and equally parted among the Commoners. Chitteringe Hill. next it, shalbe kept seuerall from all manner of cattle from the first day of March next comminge vnto the xth day of July immediately after, vpon paine to paye for every beast feedinge there against this Order, xij. d.

And that the Officers by them chosen this yeere, with the helpe and assistance of the Ordermakers or some of them, shal meete vpon the xth daye of June next immediatly after to conferre about ye due disposeinge, orderinge, measureinge and impartinge of the same peece of ground indifferently and equally to euery of the Tennements that hath right of comon in this Towne in such sort as is conveniable by their discrecion.

29. No thistles to be mow^{e}n, vnless ye Officers giue leaue. And it is ordered and agreed that no persons shal ✶utt any thistles growinge vpon any parte of the Commons vnless they first obtaine leaue of the towne Officers, vpon paine to forfeit fiue shillinges for every daye.

30. The Order for diseased cattle that shal chance to be taken feeding vpon the Commons. It is Ordered that no persons shal put or cause or be put any horse or mare haueinge the maungie or scabbe, or haueinge farcie or any infectious disease vpon any parte of the Comons or vnsowen fields, vpon paine to forfeit for euery day that any such diseased Cattle shal goe, or feed vpon the aforesaid grounndes iij s. iiij d. to be leuied by the Towne Officers or by one of them or their deputyes or by any other persons that will vpon the owners of such horses.

31. To preuent ye infection of diseased cattle. And further that no Inhabitant shal put forth to feede vpon any parte of the Commons any sicke bullocks of the Gargit vntill they be so whole that they dropp not, vpon paine for every beast so put xij. d. a day.

It is ordered that all diggers of Claye or gravill, shal fill and leuill vp their pitts as neere as they can, vpon paine to forfeit for every pitt not so filled as is required, xij d.

32. The order for preserueing of the bed of slaite between the closes. And wee find it convenient and hereby do giuc warninge that no man shal digge or open any ground for claye or gravill any neerer the vsuall road waie then ye outside of the pitts that hath bein formerly opened for claye and gravill, from Cowaies ende to Longhill [*gap*], vpon paine to forfeit xij. d. for every loade digged

their pitts as plain and as even as the Loosmyre will aford, and that before the xxiiij daye of June next comminge, vpon paine to pay for every pitt not so filled and leuelled vp as is here directed, five shillinges.

It is Ordered that no willowes shalbe cutt vntill they be six or seuen yeares growth accordinge to ye discretion of the Officers, vnlesse it be vpon extremitie to make vp suddaine breaches or gulles, vpon paine to paye for every tree if they shall cut them contrarie to this Order to forfeit, xij. d.   33. Willowes to be preserued from cutting.

It is Ordered that if any Inhabitant sendinge his servant Sonne or deputye to Comon daye worke or other businesse, that hereafter shalbe appointed to be done by the Officers, and when the sayd Officers shal finde ye said servant Sonne or deputie to be stubbourn or negligent to worke Or els refuse to doe all such businesse or layer as shalbe to them assigned and appointed by the said Officers, then the partye so offendinge shalbe sent home and the Parent or Maister of such an offender shalbe pained for every such offence, xij. d.   34. Against such as are negligent in theIr comon dayes works and a penaltie on them.

It is Ordered that every Comoner in this Towne shal doe all such dayes workes layers or partes as shalbe thought needfull to be done hereafter, and at such times and in such places as the sayd Officers shal appoint, vpon paine for every pole not done to the approbation and likement of the Officers to forfeit, ij. s. And for euery day that they shalbe called with a Carte, either to sende a Carte or ij. s. And for every daye for a man to come the first or second day or send, vj. d., vpon paine to forfeit for every day behinde after two dayes warninge xij. d. And for every Cart   35. An Order to enjoyne those wch keepe teame and cart vnto such workes as in the order is expressed.

that is found behinde after the two dayes warninge given, ij. s. vj. d.

And in like manner wee doe Order compell and enjoyne every Commoner that receiueth the benefitt of keepinge the number of ten Bullocks in the Lowfenns[1] in such regard shal vpon every such daye, and so often as shalbe founde requisite, either sende a Carte or two shillinges, or els to forfeit the penaltie of ij. s. vj. d. if such default be, and in such sorte as the residue in the former Order are pained.

<small>36. For makeing ye fen Bankes, and in what manner they are to be amended.</small>

It is Ordered that every owner of Tennements and every ffermor for terme of yeeres shal, within ten dayes after warninge given them by the Bell, make and finish all their bankes in the fenns now layed or that shalbe indifferently layed and diuided vnto any of them by the said Officers in manner and forme followinge viz. they shal make euery of their sayd bankes foure foote hie and five foote broade on the toppe, and they shal digge all ye Earth that they shal vse in makeinge and mendinge their bankes Betweene the River and the outcaste of their bankes, So that they come no neerer the banke then the middle of the olde ditch, if there be roome ynnough besids to make the banke; and if any person digge neerer than is here limitted, He shall fill and land vp all such digged places with Earth to be taken betweene the River and the banke as the River and ditches will giue leaue.

<small>37. The penaltie to be imposed on such persons as doe make default in ye amending of their bankes.</small>

And if any person be found wantinge in maintaininge of his Bankes in manner and forme aforesaid, then the partye so offending shal paie to the towne Officers within six dayes after the sayd ten dayes so much as they shal laye out and so much more to the proper vse of the sayd Officers. And if the sayd Officers do not accordinge to this Article, Then the ffenreeues or stewards of any Lordship or any Tenant shal and may distraine the Officers and Offenders for such like penalties as the sayd Officers should haue distrained others, and shal doe in all pointes touchinge the bankes accordingly.

---

[1] This was a privilege which was not included in the recognised common right, but had to be arranged for with the Order makers and paid for.

or pitt of six foote broad and the length of one turffe in depth vpon paine for every person that diggeth contrarie to any pointe of this Order to forfeit, x. s.

It is Ordered that no persons whatsoeuer shal digge any Turves vpon the olde Layers being it is provided for them to digge vpon the new Layers W^{ch} shalbe allotted to ech Comoner this present yeere after such sort and manner as is before recyted vpon paine to forfeit for every thousand digged against this Order x. s.

It is Ordered that every Comoner and Inhabitant shall scoure and ditch all the ditches of their lands ends wheresoeuer abuttinge or layeing by any of the Towne commons or any parte of them or any other Towne therevnto adjoyninge, as also all other ditches or gripes W^{ch} may serue for the better draineinge of the arrable fields belonging to this Towne in such manner and forme as shalbe appointed by the ffield Recues. And all such ditches shalbe ditched and scoured and so maintained in such manner before mencioned in all points from this xijth day of January now instant vntill the eleuen day of January next ensueinge. *39. Lands ends to be ditched for ye better draining of ye fields.*

And the ditches in the fallow field shalbe made in the same sort within fiue dayes after warninge given them, vpon payn to forfeit to the ffield Recues for every default twice so much as the field Reeues shal laye forth and dispend in and aboute the sayd ditches. *40. Further duties of the Fieldreeues.*

And it is hereby further ordered, condiscended and agreed that the sayd ffield recues shal doe or cause to be done all the rest of the ditches aforesayd wch are not so done within fiue dayes after the time appointed, and shall distraine the offenders for all such offences, wch said penalties shal remaine to the proper vse and benefit of the feelde Reeues. And if the ffieldreeues shal make default herein, then the Towne Officers shall haue full power to doe and execute therein and shal see the worke performed and shal take the penalties forfeited as aforesayd.

<small>41. Penaltie on those wch doe offend against the Composition or that repugne any of these Orders.</small>

It is ordered that if any person offend against the Composition or against any Artycle therein contained, Or against any Order made by the Order makers, Then the Towne Offycers or their Deputyes or servants or any other person, being a Comoner within three dayes after they shall haue knowledge given them by an Inhabitant W^ch will justifie and warrant their knowledge to be true, Or of their owne knowledge doe know of any such persons so offendinge, Shal and may distraine the offender or offenders and leuie the penalties that they haue forfeited. But if the Officers neglect to doe as aforesaid, Then the Officers shal forfeit to him or them that gaue such notice so much as the Offenders should haue forfeited, wch forfeiture the partye or partyes that gaue such knowledge shal and may distraine the Officers and leuie so much of their goods.

<small>42. Cattle feeding contrarie to the Composition to be impounded by the deputyes Fenreeus hawards.</small>

And further it is Ordered that the Officers or their deputyes, ffen Reeues, Hawards or any other person whatsoeuer dwellinge in this Towne, shal and may impound any Cattle wheresoeuer goeinge or feedinge contrarie to any Artycle in the Composition or any Order now made and agreed vpon. As also any Cattle goeinge in Smitheyfenne contrarie to the vsuall custome, so that the fences be sufficiently made and maintained.

It is Ordered that the Officers shal cause to be made double fallinge Gates[1] at the waies and places where they haue bein vsed, viz. at the entrance into Michelleye and Toppymore, and also at the Lakes ende, and so to keepe them at the charges of the Towne.

[1] A pair of gates shutting in the middle between the two posts.

to be stollen, and shall make a noate of them in writeinge betweene them of every particular, W^ch noate, together with the barres and other Engines shalbe deliuered to the next chosen Officers vpon their entrance into their Office vpon paine for every barre, post and Raile or other Engine ij. s. vj. d, ffor the wch the nexte chosen Officers shal distraine them, Or els make the sayd gates or other Engines so missing by their not distraininge good at their owne proper costs and charges. *45. Officers to preserue the Town goods and Implements.*

Item, it is agreed that whatsoeuer person, being a Cottager or otherwise haveinge right of Common and hath no Cattle feedinge vpon the Comous in this or their right of Commonage, Shall not be conjoined or charged to do any Layers, as any other Comoners and owners of Cattle are by Equitie enjoyned. Provided that all such Layers and partes wherevnto they shalbe conduced and required shalbe done by the charge and expence of the owners of such Tennements. *46. For assoilement of any Comoner being a Tennant onely and keepeth no cattle.*

It is Ordered that no man shal lay nor cause to be layd any Compose or dunghill vpon the Cowwaie nor vpon any other place about the fennes or fields whereby to annoy the hiewaies, vpon paine for every loade so layed, iiij. d. *47. Against those that annoy the hie waies dunghills.*

If is Ordered that no person or Heardsmen belonging to this Towne shall receiue to keepe or take in charge any Cattle of the Inhabitants of Westwicke, vpon paine for every beast so kept, iij. s. iiij. d. *48. The herdsmen forbidden to take in any cattle of Westwicke.*

It is Ordered that every person whatsoeuer haueinge any Cattle that shal happen to dye in the limmits and boundes of Cottenham, shal take such order for the burieinge of the carkases of all such Cattle so dyeinge, presently vpon the takinge off of the hide. And if the heardsmen or any other person shal so burie such carkase before the owner haue notice thereof, Then the owner of every such beaste shal paie and giue vnto such Heardsmen or other person iiij. *d.*

49. The owners to pay for burieing of their Cattle that happen to die.

Provided that every beast be buried foure foote deepe in the ground and be covered ouer about ij. foote thicknes of earth at the leaste. And if any owner doe refuse to paie the sayd iiij. *d.* for buryinge such carkase, he shal forfeit xij. *d.* to be leuied by the Towne Officers.

50. The Officers to leuie the penalties forfeited and to be accomptable for them.

It is Ordered that the Towne Officers or other deputyes or one of them shall leuie every paine, sume of money, forfeiture or penaltie as aforesayd and shall make a true and just account of them to the Ordermakers W^ch shalbe assembled in the Scholehouse vpon the xij. daye of January next comminge before ten of the cloke in the forenoone of the same daye.

51. Orders to be published.

It is Ordered that these Orders shalbe faire written and published within xv. dayes after the makeinge of them at the charges of the Towne by the discretion of the Offycers, and them to remaine in the hands of the then chosen Officers for the time beinge.

And it is further Ordered that the Towne Officers shal, on Sunday next before the xij. day of January next comminge, Reade or cause to be reade the Names of all the Ordermakers W^ch are to meete together and to be present at the makeinge of the Orders.

52. Officers nominated and chosen for this yeer 1640 by whole consent of the Ordermakers.

It is Ordered and hereby condiscended and agreed by all or the greater number of the Ordermakers that Thomas Lovell and John Wright shalbe defended to determinate and execute the place of Towne Officers to see the Artycles in the Composition duely performed and these Orders here sett downe, obserued and kept:

And if the said Officers shal make default herein, or of the makeinge of their true Accounts of all their Receipts and disburcements in writeinge wholly and joyntly togeather, and the same to

EXTRACT

FROM THE DECISION OF DR. EDEN, VICAR GENERAL OF THE BISHOP OF ELY IN THE CASE BETWEEN THE EXECUTORS OF DR. MAW RECTOR OF COTTENHAM AND WALTER MALE IN REGARD TO SUBSTRACTION OF TITHE.

Pronuntiamus Eundemque Walterum Male anno domini 1622 mensibusque in eodem concurrentibus, necnon anno domini 1623 mensibusque in eodem concurrentibus, necnon anno domini 1624 mensibus eodem concurrentibus et eorum annorum quolibet annuatim habuisse et possedisse infra parochiam de Cottenham predicta finesque limites ac loca decimalia eiusdem has res decimales et iure ecclesiastica que sequuntur in schedula proximo sequenti ad valorem etiam siue valores annuatim et quolibet annorum predictorum se extendentes et extendisse iuxta confessionem prefati Walteri Male in hac parte iudicialiter factam pronuntiamus, decernimus et declaramus vizt

The first schedule.

Imprimis 70 loads or Carryes of hey every such load or carrye worth viij. s.
Item 9 Calues euery Calf worth 9s.
Item 50 Lambes every Lamb worth 4s.
Item 60 fleces of woolle euery fleece of woolle worth 1s. 4d.
Item for oblacions at Easter for himselfe or his wife 2d.
Item tenn Bushells of Aples one Bushell of Peares, one Bushell of damsins and other plomes euery such bushell of Apples one with another worth xij. d. every busshell of damsins and other plomes worth iiij. d., fortie Piggs euery pigge worth xij. d.

Imprimis 70 loads or carryes of hay euery such load or cary of hay worth viij. s.
Item 12 Calues euery Calfe worth 9s.
Item 50 Lambes euery Lamb worth 4s.
Item 60 fleeces of Woole euery fleece worth j. s. 4d.
Item oblacions at Easter for himselfe or his wife 0s. ij. d.
Item tenn Bushells of Apples, one bushelle of Peares one Bushell of damsins and other plumes euery such Bushell of Apples one with another worth xij. d. euery Bushell of damsins and other plomes worth iiij. d.
Item 40 piggs euery pigge worth xij. d.

Eundem igitur Walterum Male in summa xix. ti. xij. s. ij. d. pro decimis et iuribus Eccleciasticis libellatis ac ad prefatam schedulam xix. ti. xij. s. ij. d. iuxta propriam ipsius confessionem vero calculo siue raciocinio rite adhibito se extendentes, videlicet.

	ti.	s.	d.	
Imprimis for tyth hay	2	16	0	Anno domini 1622
Item for tyth Calues	0 ..	8	1	
Item for tyth lambs	1 ..	0	0	
Item for tyth woolle	0 ..	8	0	
Item for oblacions for him selfe and his wife	0 ..	0	2	
Item for tyth Apples	0 ..	1	0	
Item for tyth Peares	0 ..	0	1 ob.	
Item tyth plomes	0 ..	0 ..	0 q.	
Item for Tith piggs	0 ..	4 ..	0	

Anno domini 1623	Imprimis for tyth hay	2 .. 16 .. 0
	Item for tyth Calues	0 .. 8 .. 1
	Item for tyth lambes	1 .. 0 .. 0
	Item for tyth woolle	0 .. 8 .. 0
	Item for oblacions for himselfe and his wife	0 .. 0 .. 2
	Item for tyth Apples	0 .. 1 .. 0
	Item for tyth Peares	0 .. 0 .. 1 *ob*
	Item for tyth plomes	0 .. 0 .. 0 *q*.
	Item for tyth pigges	0 .. 4 .. 0
Anno domini 1624	Imprimis for tyth hay	2 .. 16 .. 0
	Item for tyth Calues	0 .. 8 .. 1
	Item for tyth lambes	1 .. 0 .. 0
	Item for tyth woole	0 .. 8 .. 0
	Item for oblacions for himselfe and his wife	0 .. 0 .. 2
	Item for tyth Apples	0 .. 1 .. 0
	Item for tyth Peares	0 .. 0 .. 1 *ob*.
	Item for tyth plomes	0 .. 0 .. 0 *q*.
	Item for tyth Piggs	0 .. 4 .. 0
Anno domini 1625	Imprimis for tyth hay	2 .. 16 .. 0
	Item for tyth Calues	0 .. 10 .. 8
	Item for tyth lambs	1 .. 0 .. 0
	Item for tyth woolle	0 .. 8 .. 0
	Item for oblacions for himselfe and his wife	0 .. 0 .. 2
	Item for tyth Apples	0 .. 1 .. 0
	Item for tyth Peares	0 .. 0 .. 1 *ob*.
	Item for tyth Plumes	0 .. 0 .. 0 *q*.
	Item for tyth piggs	0 .. 4 .. 0

Unacum expensis legitimis exparte prefatorum Leonardi Maw Thome Burwell et Nicholai Maw factis et faciendis eisdemque seu parti siue cum parte principali predicto, videlicet, prefatis summa xix. *li.* xij. *s.* ij. *d.* soluenda etiam condemnando condemnamus per

AN ACCOUNT
OF THE TITHING OF CATTLE,[1] &c.

Cows, &c.   For every Milch-Cow Two Pence instead of the Tithe Milk, and for a Heifer of the first Calf, Three Half-pence.

Calves.   For Calves, if they have any, Six or under, and sell them, the Tenth Penny is due; if they wean them, pay a Half-penny apiece: but if they have Seven or above, under Ten, a Tithe Calf. And then the Parson is to give back Half-pence apiece for so many as wants of Ten: if just Ten, a Tithe Calf; the last of Ten to be the Tithe Calf, or of Seven Eight or Nine. If it chance that a Man kill a Calf in his house, then to pay for the Tithe thereof a Penny, to be reckoned and made even at Easter, without driving any of them to another Year.

Foals.   For Foals, if Seven a Tithe Foal (the Owner to choose Two and the Parson to take his out of the rest at Allhallowtide) allowing to the Owner a Penny apiece for so many as there are short of Ten: and if they have under Seven, and sell all or any of them before Easter following, then to pay for so many as shall be sold the Tenth Shilling. But if they wean them and keep them another Year, a Penny for every Foal; and not drive them to another year.

Lambs & Sheep.   For Lambs, they Tithe them at Shear-Day, the Owner to take two and the Parson the next, and so on for as many as there be, if but Seven he is to give back for what is wanting of Ten, half-pence a piece to the Owner. If a Man has under Seven, and wean them, half-pence apiece; but if they are sold before Shear-Day, the Tenth Penny: if they are sold coupled Ewe and Lamb, before Shear-Day, the Parson to take his Lamb when they are to be had away, and for the Wool Ten Pence the Score. And if any be bought in before Candlemas, and are kept till Shear-Day, then the

---

[1] Compare Article xxvi. This schedule of customary tithe at Cottenham occurs in the printed copy of the Articles of Agreement, but not in any of the written copies.

COMMON RIGHTS

Parson is to have his full Tithe. But if after Candlemas, and are sold before Shear-Day, for so many Months as they go, Fourpence a Score. If Sheep be under a Month's feeding, no Tithe is due: but if above a Month, Tithe is due, as above mentioned. If any one remove his Sheep and depasture them in another Parish, what Tithe is due in that Place where they are kept is to be abated out of the Tithe at home.

Tithe-Gozlings, at Seven, Eight, Nine or Ten, and for Chickens a Penny is paid per annum. GOZLINGS.

For Communicants, every one at Easter Two-pence Oblations Married or Single, unless it be a Single Man or Woman born in Town and then they are to pay but a Penny. COMMUNICANTS.

For Tithe Pigs, if there be seven of a Litter, the Parson is to have One, allowing (as for the Calves) half-pence a piece; if under Seven the Owner must pay half-pence apiece; every Litter to be tithed by itself. PIGS.

For Eggs, every Family five Eggs, if they have any hens; if no Hens a Penny is to be paid. EGGS.

For Pidgeons the Tenth is to be paid; as also for Fruit. PIDGEONS.

Of Hemp the Tenth Sheaf. HEMP.

Of Honey the Tenth Part. HONEY.

No Tithe of Wood was ever paid in the memory of Man, but instead, and for Pasturage on the Common, there is a Penny paid called anciently a Plow-Penny. WOOD.

No Tithe of Hay and Fodder in Smithy-Fen is or hath been paid in Kind, within the Memory of Man: but there is certain Parcels of the Ground before-mentioned, yearly laid out for the Parson, amounting to the number of Forty Acres, instead of the Tithe of the said Fen; which is likewise exempted therefrom by Virtue of the Composition in the twenty-six Articles. All the antient Inclosures do pay Tithe of Hay in Kind, when they happen to be mown; but divers late Inclosures are exempted by the Composition, made between the Lords, the Parson and the Tenants; because the Parson hath allotted (instead thereof, and of a Sheep-Walk, and of such other Tithes as have not been usually paid within this HAY.

Parish of Cottenham) an Inclosure of Seventy Acres, besides an ample Improvement to the Parsonage of One Hundred Marks yearly at least in other things and Profits, on account of the said Composition.

MARRIAGE.   For Marriage, Fifteen Pence is due to the Parson, and to the Clerk Four Pence.

CHRIST-
NINGS.   For Christning and Churching Eight Pence : if the Child live till the Woman be Churched ; but if it die before, only Two Pence.

BURIALS.   For Burials, Mortuaries are paid.

ERS OF THE MANOR.

And it is alsoe by this Courte ordered and decreede that every Copiholder of a yard land Copihold held of the said Mannor of Streatham his heiars and assignes shall yearelie well and sufficientlie plowe, in wheate seede one acre of land once over onelie for the said Sir Myles Sandis, his heires and assignes lords of the said Mannor of Streatham, And in barlie seed one other acre of land once over onelie, and accordinge to that proporcion for every half yard land to plowe half an acre in wheat scede once over onelie, and halfe an acre in Barlie seede once over onelie, and accordinge to a greater or lesse proporcion of Copihold landes which haue byn parte of the yard or half yard lands more or lesse plowinge, They the said Sir Miles Sandis, his heires and assignes, lordes of the said mannor makinge vnto the said Tenantes the vsuall allowances due for the said workes. And the Tenantes of the said Copihold howses or Tenementes which haue byn accustomed for theire said howses or Tenementes to doe certaine workes called pownd Reapes they, theire heires and assignes, shall for ever doe the said workes and in suche manner and sorte as the same haue vsuallie of late byn done the Lordes of the said mannor makinge vnto them the vsuall allowances due for the same, and noe other. And that the said Sir Miles Sandis his heires and assignes Lordes of the said Mannor of Streatham shall haue the foldage in his and theire fold within the said Mannor onelie of such Cottagers sheepe as haue vsuallie folded the same in Lords folde.

Copieholders to plough yeerly for the Lord:

Pound Reapes to bee done by the Tennants to the Lord.

Foldeage of Cottagers sheep in the Lords folde.

the Lordes Folde and of soe many onelie of the sheepe of such Cottagers as are And ought to be kept by them in the Right of theire Cottages onelie. And that not any other Freehold or Copihold Tenant of the said Mannor, nor any other Owner or Inhabitant within the said Mannor shalbe from henceforth Compellable to fold his sheepe in the Lordes fold, but that it shalbe for ever heereafter lawful to the said Freehold and Copihold Tenantes, and other Owners and Inhabitantes within the said mannor, and to every of them, theire and every of theire heires and assignes, to fold such sheepe as they or any of them maie lawfullie keepe in the Fieldes and Commons of Streatham aforesaid vpon theire or any of theire landes at theire seuerall wills and pleasures, without the Interrupcion of the said Sir Miles Sandis his heires and assignes. And it is alsoe by this Courte nowe ordered and decreede that all

Coppiholders, Tennants and Cottagers quietlie to enjoy their holdes.

the Copihold Tenantes and Cottagers of the said Mannor of Streatham theire heires and assignes shall against the said Sir Miles Sandis, his heires and assignes Lordes of the said Mannor of Streatham, for ever heereafter severallie haue hold, and enioy quietlie and without his or theire interrupcion all the land meadowe pasture and marish nowe in the seuerall occupacion of them or any of them or of theire seuerall assignes as parcell or now reckened, accompted, reputed or occupied as parte or parcell of the said seuerall Copiholdes or Cottages yet vnder and subiecte vnto the aunciente forfeytures, Conditions, Customes, Dueties and services other then such as are heereafter heerein decreed to be discharged or dispenced withall. And that the said Sir Miles Sandis, his heires and assignes Lordes of the said Mannor of Stretham, shall for ever heereafter be barred vnder colour of demeasne landes to demaund against the said Copihold Tenantes or Cottagers or against Theire heires or assignes anie of the landes, pasture, meadowe, or marishe now by them or any of them, or by theire or any of theire assignes vsed as parcell of the said Copiholdes, or Cottages aforesaid. And that the said Sir Miles Sandis, his heires and assignes Lordes of the said Mannor of Streatham, shalbe from henceforth debarred from all manner of Claime and demaund

red from the demaunding or having anie greater Fine vpon or for the admission of any Copiholder or Cottager within the said mannor to any such Copihold or Cottage, or to any the landes, meadowe, or Marishe therevnto nowe appertaininge or belonginge, or heereafter to be apertaininge or belonginge otherwise then onelie proportionablie after the rate of one yeares value of the Lordes old and vsuall rent of the said Copihold or Cottage, and the landes meadowe and Marishe therevnto nowe belonginge, or heereafter to be appertayninge, whervnto admission is to be made or given, excepting onelie the next Fines due or to be due for or vpon the next admission vnto the Copihold landes, tenementes and hereditamentes alreadie Surrendred or discended, or agreed vpon before the fifteenth daie of May last paste to be heereafter surrendred. And alsoe by this Courte it is ordred and decreede that it shalbe lawfull for the Copiholders and Cottagers of the said Mannor of Streatham, theire and every of theire heires and assignes, to fell and sell theire woodes and Timber growinge vpon anie of theire Copiholdes or Cottagholdes at all times, without demaundinge anye licence therefore of the said Sir Miles Sandis, his heires and assignes lordes of the said Mannor, and without incurringe anie daunger of forfeyture therefore, or for anie other wast Committed or to be Committed by the said Copiholders or Cottagers, theire or anie of theire heires or assignes, vpon theire said Copiholdes or Cottages, except the wilfull pullinge downe of theire Copihold bowses or Tenementes and not reedifienge the same within three yeares next after suche pullinge downe, and except alsoe the wilfull

Fine Certaine onelie, due to the Lord.

Power giuen to Coppiholders to sell the trees groweing on their Coppiholds.

Coppiholders to reedifietheir Copiholdes.

permitting theire Copiholde howses or Tenementes to decay, and to continue in decay vnrepayred by the space of three yeares after notice or warning given by the Lord of the said Mannor for the time beinge or his Bayliffe to the Copihold Tenant or Cottager of the same howses or Tenementes wilfullie permitted to continue in decay, for the repayringe or reedifienge the same. And that it shall be lawfull for all or anie the said Copiholders, and Cottagers Tenantes of the said Mannor, theire and every of theire heires and assignes, from time to time and att all times heereafter, at his and theire pleasures, to demise his or theire sayd Copiholdes and Cottages, or anie parte thereof for the tearme of one and twenty yeares or vnder vnto such persons as the said Copiholder or Cottager shall thinke fitt without incurringe any forfeyture therefore, soe that the said Copiholder soe demisinge his said Copihold or Cottage, or anye parte thereof, at the Courte of the said Mannor of Streatham next followinge the said demise, or within one yeare next after such demise, doe paie or cause to be paid vnto the Lord of the said Mannor for the time beinge or to his Bayliffe proportionablie after the rate of one yeares value onelie of the lordes old and vsuall rent of the said Copihold or Cottage soe demised, or wheareof anie parte or parcell shalbe soe demised, for and in the name of a Fine.

Lawfullness for Coppiholders to lett their Coppiholds.

» » ‑

And that if the said Sir Miles Sandis his heires or assignes shall at anie time heereafter acquire purchase or haue anie landes, Tenementes or hereditamentes in Stretham and Thetford aforesaid, nowe held occupied or enioyd by anie the Tenantes, Owners Inhabitantes or Comoners aforesaid, that then he the said Sir Miles Sandis his heires and assignes shall in regard thereof haue such like interest lottes, partes, Commons, benefittes, and comodities onely and noe other nor otherwise in the said Fennes called Thetford Hall Fenne and Grvnty Fenne, and in the said sixteene hundred acres to be assigned as aforesaid, then as the Owner or Owners of the same enioyd, or rightlie might haue enioyd, by the Orders and Bylawes within the said mannor of Stretham, And that

Sir Miles to common for purchased houses as other inhabitants and not otherwise.

Sir Miles tyed to the Orders and bylawes of Stretham as well as others.

other the Tenantes, Owners and occupiers in Stretham and Thet- 1. Stint.
ford aforesaid, Vnlesse the same be altred by a generall assent and 2. Order.
consent of the said Sir Miles Sandis, his heires and assignes, and of 4. Gouerne.
all the Tenantes, Owners, Inhabitantes and Comoners aforesaid. 5. Seuer.
And this Courte doth alsoe order and decree that the said Sir Miles Consent for
Sandis, his heires and assignes, at all and every time and tymes alteration
heereafter maie lawfullie and quietlye without the lett, trowble, most not bee
disturbance or deniall of the said nowe Complainantes or other the of a major
Tenantes, Owners, Inhabitantes, and Comoners aforesaid or of any part onelie
of them, or of the heires or assignes of them or of any of them, but generall.
fence, ditche, and in severall inclose all the arrable landes, meadowes, Sir Miles his
and landes endes of him the said Sir Miles Sandis his heires or power to
assignes lyinge in the Fields of Stretham, or asmuch thereof as shall enclose his
seeme good vnto him or them, in which arrable landes, meadowes, arable.
and landes endes, and in everye parte thereof soe inclosed, the said
nowe Complainantes and other the Tenantes, Owners, Inhabitantes
and Comoners aforesayd, and the heires and assignes of them and
of every of them, are to be barred and excluded of and from all
manner of Comonages and depasturinge sheepe or cattle; and
immediatelie vpon the incloasure of anie parte thereof as aforesaid,
the said Sir Miles Sandis his heires and assignes are for ever to be Uppon en-
barred and excluded from Keepinge anye cattle whatsoever as closure of his
Lordes of the said Mannor of Stretham within anie the Comon Sir Miles is
arable fieldes or Common waies or Comon meadowes adioyning to to lose sheep
the Comon Arrable Feildes of Streatham aforesaid not inclosed. common.

An acre to be allowed in leiw of the house and ground where now Jer. Townsend liues as e man. March 22. 1637	And that yt shalbe lawfull for the said Sir Miles Sandis his heires and assignes to erecte and hold one Cottage or Cote to be at the newe intended Ferry, not takinge therefore above one acre of grownd, allowinge for the same one other acre of like land and of like condicion in some other place, and likewise allowinge to the Tenantes, Owners Inhabitantes and Comoners in Streatham and Thetford aforesaid such freedome and priveledge of the Newe intended Ferry
Prieledg of ferriage.	for the price of the ferriage of themselues, theire families, servantes and cattle over the River from the one side of the newe intended Ferry vnto the other side thereof, as they haue heertofore enioyd at the old Ferrye. And this Courte doth alsoe order and decree
Sir Miles and his heyres for ever excluded from all the proffit of the 1600 acre as Lords.	that the said Sir Miles Sandis his heires and assignes shall, with asmuch speed as convenientlie may be, assigne, measure, and sett ont the sayd sixteene hundred acres heerby before allotted vuto the said Nowe Complainantes and other the Tenantes, Owners, Comoners and Inhabitantes of Streatham and Thetford aforesaid, and from and after the sayd measure and assignement that he the said Sir Myles Sandis, his heires and assignes as Lordes of the said Mannor of Stretham, (except in Cases provided as aforesaid) shalbe vtterlye barred and secluded for ever from takinge of anie Commonage or other profitt whatsoever by feedinge, mowynge, ditchinge, agistinge or improvinge in or out of the said sixteene hundred acres and in or out of the said Thetford Hay Fenne alias Thetforde Hall Fenne, and in or out of the after pasture of the aforesaid seuerall meadowes of Ellford and the aforesaid several meadowes or marishes in Hole Fenne (except before excepted).

* *

Sir Miles to haue noe stroake or claime in anie after subdiuision.	And yt is alsoe ordered and decreed by this Courte, at the desire of the nowe Complainantes by theire said Bill, and with the assent of the Nowe defendant within the said Towne in his said answeare, that if the now Complainantes and the Tenantes, Owners, Comoners and Inhabitantes of both the said Townes of Streatham and Thetford shall heereafter sue vnto this Courte for an equall subdevision of the said sixteene hundred acres to be made betweene every of

COTTENHAM AND STRETHAM 259

them, that then he the said Sir Miles Sandish, [h]is heires and assignes Lordes of the said Mannor of Streatham, shall yeald his and theire assent thervnto, and that in the meane time vntill such subdivision shalbe, that parcell of the said sixteene hundred acres called Hole Fenne Lazer and Chaire Fenne plaines shalbe yearelie preserved to be Mowen and devided amongst the Tenantes, Owners and Comoners of both the said Townes of Streatham and Thetforde, accordinge to the Custome heertofore vsed; and that soe muche of the said sixteene hundred acres as lyeth betweene Barlake and Snowte ditche shalbe fedd onelie with the Milche Kine and weanelinge Calues of the Tenantes, Owners, Comoners and Inhabitantes within the said Towne of Streatham, from the Feast of S^{ct} Mathias the Apostle in every yeare vntill all the harvest of the sayd Towne of Streatham be fullie ended; and that parcell of the said sixteene hundred acres called Stallocke and soe much of the said Fenne called Haie Fenne as shall be comprised within the said sixteene hundred acres yearelie from the Feast daie of the Annunciacion of the blessed Virgin Marie vntill the full end likewise of the said harvest shalbe fedd onelie with theire Workinge horses, and that noe sheepe shalbe fedd or kept upon the sayd growndes in anie yeare betweene the said Feast Daie [of the Annunciacion of the blessed Virgin Marie and the feast day][1] of S^{ct} Andrewe the Apostle. And lastlie it is ordered and decreed by this Courte that the greater parte of the Comoners of each of the said two Townes of Streatham and Thetford respectivelie shall and maie from time to time have power and authoritie, without the assent or intermedlinge of the said Sir Miles Sandis his heires or assignes Lordes of the said Mannor, to make Orders and Bylawes for and towching the feedinge of such Fenne growndes as are in or by this order and decree severallie allotted to each of the said Townes. And that to and for the keepinge and performinge of such orders and Bylawes soe to be made, not onelie the makers of and assenters vnto the said Orders and Bylawes, but alsoe all the other Comoners of both the Townes are tyed and bound by the decree of this honourable Courte.

The Cow-pasture for Milche kine weaneling calues.

Horse common.

Power giuen to make Bylawes.

[1] These words omitted, but supplied from the certified copy.

Fanshawe

Termino : Pascae Jacobj 11°

A COPPIE OF AN AFFOEDAUIT
MADE BEEFORE THE BARONS OF THE EXCHEQUER.[1]

Cant.

Memorandum quod Mich : Flud de Stretham clerke et Tho: Frankham de Thetford infra Insulam Eliensem in comitatu Cantebrigie venerunt coram Baronibus Scaccarij xxv^{to} die Maij hoc termino in proprijs personis et sacrum suum præstitere corporale in his Anglicanis verbis sequentibus viz :

That whereas within the Commons and common Fenn grounds of Stretham and Thetford aforesaid the Commoners and Inhabitants of each towne respectiuelie haue had libertie, and of right ought to haue libertie, of feeding and depastureing their workeing horses and workeing mares. Now these deponents say that by reason of libertie giuen to the greater part of either towne abouesaid respectiuelie by an order or decree made in this Courte, in Trinitie terme Anno 5° Jacobj, giueing power to make bylawes, the commoners and inhabitants of Stretham and Thetford aforesaid are debarred of their aunceient libertie by a bylawe made by the greater part whereby the Commoners of Stretham are not allowed to keep a sufficient and competent number of workeing horses or workeing mares there. And the Commoners and inhabitants of Thetford aforesaid haueing libertie to feed as aforesaid are, by a bylaw latelie made, vtterlie debarred and excluded from keeping anie manner of workeing horses or workeing mares vppon those commons, where by auncient custome and by right they ought to bee kept, whereby the arable lands of Thetford aforesaid especiallie lie vntilled and the corne now groweing within the sayd feilds not like to bee preserued in due time at haruest for want of workeing horses and workeing mares for the necessarie vses of the commoners of each towne aforesaid. Soe, &c.

Præstitere sacramentum suum 25 die Maij 1609.   Geo : SNYGG,

[1] Originally written "to bee made beefore a master of Chancerie," and altered as above.

AND WORKEING MARES BY VERTUE OF A COMMISSION TO VS AND OTHERS DIRECTED OUT OF HIS MAIESTIES COURT OF EXCHEQUER FOR THAT PURPOSE.[1]

First it is ordered by the sayd Commisioners that the sayd inhabitants within the towne of Stretham or the precincts thereof haueing anie auncient commonable messuage or Tenement shall and may, by right of his or hir sayd messuage or Tenement, yearlie depasture in the sayd Commons fiue working horses or mares with their foales, soe they bee of his or hir owne proper goods and at such times of the yeer onelie as hee or shee of right beefore this order might haue done, for the bringing home of fother and turffs for his or hir provision. _{5. workeing horses for euerie auncient commonable house.}

Item, it shalbee lawfull for anie of the said inhabitants, haueing an auncient Commonable messuage or tenement as is aforesaid wherewith hee or shee vseth in tillage within the Mannor of Stretham to the number of fifteen acres or vnder, to depasture one _{6. horses for 15 acres.}

---

[1] No doubt this Commission was the result of the complaint made by Michael Fludd and Thomas Frankham, 25 May 1609, as to the insufficient number of working horses allowed to be fed on the Commons. See p. 260.

workeing horse or mare with hir foale aboue the number of fiue in the Commons aforesaid of his or hir owne proper goods and in manner aforsaid, and that by right of his or hir said messuage or tenement. And for him or hir that vseth in tillage as aforesaid to the number of 30 acres, to depasture two workeing horses or mares with their foales aboue the sayd number of fiue in the Commons aforesaid of his or hir owne proper goods and in manner aforesaid by right of his or hir said messuage or tenement. And for him or hir that vseth in tillage as aforesaid to the number of 45 acres, to depasture three workeing horses or mares with their foales of his or hir owne proper goods aboue the said number of 5 in the commons aforesaid and in manner aforesaid by right of his of hir said messuage or Tenement. And for him or hir that vseth in tillage as is aforesaid to the number of 60 acres, to depasture fower workeing horses or mares with their foales of his or hir owne proper goods aboue the said number of fiue in the Commons aforesaid and in manner aforesaid by right of his or hir said messuage or tenement.

7. for 30 acres.

8. for 45 acres.

9. for 60 acres.

Parson to keep 3 horses or mares more than anie man.

Item, it shalbee lawfull for the Parson of Stretham for............ in regard of getting in his harvest within the Mannor............ to haue and depasture yeerlie in the said Commons............ aboue the rates aforesaid three horses or mares with their foales of his owne proper goods and in manner aforesaid, by vertue of his Parsonage house being a Commonable house.

Lastelie, that noe man shall presume to exceed the rates afore set downe or disturbe anie Comoner in keepiug accordeing to the rates aforesaid vntill it shalbee otherwise ordered in his Maiesties Court of Exchequer.

MILES SANDYS.   R. COX.   JAMES TAYLOR.

ORDERS SET DOWNE

THE 28 OF JUNE 1609 BY SIR MILES SANDYS, SIR RICH. COX, KNIGHTS, AND JAMES TAYLOR DOCTOR OF DIUINITIE FOR THE INHABITANTES OF THETFORD WITHIN THE ILE OF ELIE AND COUNTIE OF CAMBRIDG, CONCERNING THE VSEAGE OF THEIR COMMON IN GOLDESMORE VNDE UIDED WITH THEIR WORKEING HORSES AND WORKEING MARES BY VERTUE OF A COMMISSION TO VS AND OTHERS DIRECTED OUT OF HIS MAIESTIES COURT OF EXCHEQUER FOR THAT PURPOSE.

For Thetford Goldsmore.

First it is ordered by the said Commissioners that euerie inhabitant within Thetford or the precincts thereof, haueing anie auncient Commonable messuage or tenement, shall and may, by right of his or hir messuage or tenement, yeerlie depasture in their said Commons three workeing horses or workeing mares with their foales, soe they bee of his or hir owne proper goods and at such time of the yeer onelie as hee or shee of right in former times beefore this order might haue done, for the bringing home of fother and turff for his or hir owne prouision. *3. horses,*

Item, &c. [This section is similar to the corresponding section of the rules made for Stretham, except that there is no reference to any holding of more than 45 acres, " which number noe commoner doth now exceed."] *4. for 15 acres. 5. for aboue 15 acres. 6. for 45 acres.*

Item, it shalbee lawfull for the Lord of Thetford or his fermor by right of his **mannor** house, beeing an auncient commonable messuage, to depasture two **workeing** horses or mares with their foales *The Lord to keep 5.*

18

in the commons aforesaid and in manner aforesaid aboue the said number of three, in regard hee hath euer of olde been allowed a greater proportion both of moweing and feedeing within the Commons then other commonable houses.

Lastelie noe man shall presume to exceed the rates afore sett downe, beeing verie sufficient for all sortes, they haueing beesides verie good entercommons to put in their workeing horses and mares, nor to disturbe anie commoners in keeping accordeing to the rates aforesaid vntill it shalbee otherwise ordered in his Maiesties Court of Exchequer.

MYLES SANDYS.   R. COX.   JAMES TAYLOR.

AFORESAID THE DAY AND YEER ABOUEWRITTEN.

1. Imprimis wee finde Thomas Egnie faultie in that hee hath not scoured his drayne, and therefore wee doe payne him to amend it by the 10th of May next comeing in, iij. s. iiij. d.

2. Item, there standeth a wall uppon the common where Richard Sheirbrooke dwelleth, and wee doe enjoyne him to put it downe by the 10th of May nexte, in payne of 5s.

3. Item, wee finde that the chimney where widow Salmon dwells is in default, and wee doe payne hir to amend it by the 15th of May next, in payne of 20s.

4. Item, wee finde that Francis Barker hath cast up a ditch from clay lakes end vnto Elford which is a great annoyance to our Heard, and wee doe enjoyne him to throw it or cast it in agayne by the 12th of May next comeing, in payne of 5*li*.

5. Item, wee order and appoynt that noe man woman or childe shall sett anie nett or netts in anie of our common lakes or ditches after sunn bee downe halfe an howre, in payne for euerie default soe proued, iij. s. iiij. d.

6. Item, wee find that John Ramsies chimnie is in default and wee doe payne him to amend it within 10 dayes in the summ of 10s.

7. Item, wee finde Richard Sheirbrooke dwelleth vppon a ground

encroached vppon the common and therefore wee payne him to amend it within 14 dayes in 40s.

8. Item, we finde Christopher Isacson hath taken in to his house one Robert Webb and wee payne him to auoyd him by Whitsontide next comeing or to put in securitie to discharge the towne, to the constables and churchwardens for the time beeing, in x. *li.*

9. Item, wee finde George Wells is taken into the towne by Wm. Piggott and wee payne him to auoyde him by Whitsontide next or to put in securitie to discharge the towne, to the constables and churchewardens for the time beeing, in payne of 10*li.*

10. Item, wee agree that euerie man shall make his part sufficientlie in the pound wall yeerlie and euerie yeer within 4 dayes warning giuen by the constables or fennreeues vppon payne to forfeit for euerie such default, iij. *s.* iiij. *d.*

11. Item, wee agree that euerie man shall make his Particular part on the East side of Bar-lake from tyme to tyme within 3 dayes after warning giuen by the fenreeues vppon payne to forfeit for euerie default, iij. *s.* iiij. *d.*

OF SCOTLAND THE 47th
ANNO DOMINI 1614.

1. Imprimis wee order and appoynt that whereas diuers idle euill disposed persons vnder pretence and colour of glayning doe often times in time of Haruest yeerlie take and carrie away much of the corne and grayne of diuers of the inhabitants of Stretham, by meanes whereof the true owners and occupiers of the aforesaid lands haue not sufficient libertie to suffer their corne beeing reaped, mowed, and shocked in the feilds to haue that wythering and season of the yeare that were requisite. For remedie whereof wee appoynt that at noe time or times heerafter it shalbee lawfull for anie person or persons whatsoeuer within the parish of Stretham aforesaid to gleane, perceaue and take anie corne or grayne in and vppon anie part or parcell of the arable or corne feildes beelonging to the mannor of Stretham aforesaid. Nor shall cause or procure anie person or persons whatsoever directlie or indirectlie to gleane, perceaue and take anie corne or grayne in or vppon anie part or parcell of the said arable or corne feildes vntill the Harvest there bee fullie ended, vppon payne to forfeit for euerie such particular default and for euerie time soe gleaneing or offendeing, the somm of fiue shillings, to bee forfeited and leuied by way of distress of such offenders or such persons who shall procure, abett, or giue entertaynment or harbor to anie such person or persons whatsoeuer so gleaning as is aforesaid.

Gleaneing.

None to gleane till after haruest.

Poena 5s.

2. Item, wee order and appoynt that notwithstandeing this order aforesayd it shall and may bee lawfull to and for anie man, woman or childe, beiug vnder the age of 16 yeeres and aboue the age of 60 yeeres, or beeing otherwise sicklie and not able to worke a dayes worke in tyme of Harvest, soe to be adjudged by the Parson and churchewardens for the time beeing, and not haueing vseing or occupieing anie part or parcell of a commonable messuage as aforesaid, to gleane lawfullie anie such scattered corne or grayne as shalbee left by the owner or owners thereof then and after that all the grayne (the gleanings and scatterings onelie excepted) shalbee carried away and not beefore. Soe that such gleaner or gleaners doe not gleane within the bredth of 3 lands of anie corne standeing or lying vncarried, vppon the payne aforesaid to bee forfeited and leauied of the persons aforesaid.

<small>None to gleane but vnder 16 or aboue 60 yeers of age.</small>

<small>Poena 5s.</small>

3. Item, wee order and appoynt that it shall not bee lawfull for anie owner farmor or occupier of anie lands within the feilds or limitts aforesaid to suffer or permitt anie person or persons to gleane or gather vppon his or anie of their lands, soe occupied as aforesaid, contrarie to the true intent and meaneing of anie of the orders aforesaid, anie corne or grayne whatsoeuer, vppon payne to forfeit and pay for euerie suche default the summ of fiue shillings, to bee leauied of the offendors goods by way of distress as aforesayd.

<small>Noe owner to suffer gleaners on his land.</small>

<small>Poena 5s.</small>

4. Item, wee order and appoynt that it shall not bee lawfull for anie person or persons whatsoeuer to gather or glayne anie scattered corne or grayne in and vppon anie part or parcell of the arable or corne feilds beelonging to the Mannor of Stretham aforesayd beefore the houres of 8 of the clock in the aforenoone daylie and euerie day in time of harvest yeerlie, nor after the howres of six of the clock in the afternoone daylie and euerie day yeerlie, vppon payne to forfeit and pay for euerie such particular default, the summ of fiue shillings of lawfull monie of England, to bee leauied and taken by way of distress out of all or anie the offenders goods : Or otherwise to bee leauied or taken by way of distress out of all or anie the goods or chattels of anie person or

<small>Not to gleane beefore 8 in the morning after 6 at night.</small>

<small>Poena 5s.</small>

England to be leauied and taken by way of distress out of all or anie of the offendor or offendors goods or chattells or to be leauied and taken out of all or anie the goods or chattels by way of distress as aforesaid of anie person or persons who shall procure suffer abett, giue harbour or entertaynment to anie such gleanor, or gleanors as aforesayd.

6. Item, wee order and appoynt that it shall and may bee lawfull for the Parson of Stretham for the tyme beeing, or his sufficient deputie or deputies, or for anie owner, farmor or occupiers of anie arable lands within the fields and lymitts of Stretham aforesaid to collect, leauie and take all or any the summ or sommes of monie by way of distress as aforesaid and being payable as aforesaid. <small>Either Parson or owner may distreine and the one moietie to the Lord the other to the Distreiner.</small>

And to render and giue vp the moyetie and one halfe thereof onelie to the Lord of the mannor of Stretham aforesaid or to his bayliff for the time beeing within six dayes next after anie such some or somes of monie shalbee had and recouered as aforesaid.

And the other halfe or moyetie thereof all charges and expences of the law if anie shall happen beeing first deducted to take and convert to his or their owne proper and priuate vse or vses anie thing in this order notwithstanding.

7. Item, wee order and appoynt that its hall not bee lawfull for anie person or persons haueing or which shall haue anie Pease or <small>None to giue leaue to gather Pease</small>

270   COMMON RIGHTS AT

<small>without sendeing one of his house with them.</small>
Beanes groweing in anie of the feilds of Stretham aforesaid to procure, suffer or giue leaue to anie person or persons whatsoeuer to take or gather anie pease or beanes in or vppon anie of his or their land or lands within the feilds aforesaid. Except that euerie such person or persons, soe haueing Pease or beanes groweing as aforesaid, shall first procure and send one of his owne familie to bee continuallie present with such person or persons to whom hee shall giue or graunt such leaue to gather as aforesaid soe long <small>Poena 5s.</small> as anie such person shalbee gathering, vppon payne to forfeit and pay for euerie time soe offendeing the summ of fiue shillings, to bee leauied by way of distress as aforesaid and to bee collected as aforesaid.

<small>None to gather Pease without a Deputie.</small>
8. Item, wee doe order and appoynt that if anie person or persons whatsoeuer shall at anie time heerafter take or gather anie pease or beanes in or vppon anie land or lands of anie person or persons within the feilds and limitts aforesaid and not haueing his or their sufficient deputie or deputies beeing one of his owne familie soe present as formerlie is appoynted, then euerie such person or persons soe offendeing and all and euerie other person or persons who shall procure, abett, giue harbour or entertayn- <small>Poena 5s.</small> ment to anie such offendor as aforesaid shall forfeit and pay for euerie such particular default and for euerie time soe offendeing, the summ of fiue shillings, to bee forfeited and leauied by way of distress as aforesaid and to bee collected as aforesaid.

<small>Parson or owner to take away gleanes.</small>
9. Item, wee order and appoynt that if anie person or persons whatsoeuer shall at anie time heerafter gleane, perceaue and take anie corne or grayne whatsoeuer within the limits of Stretham aforesaid contrarie to anie of the orders heerin mentioned, then it shall and may bee lawfull for the Parson of Stretham or his deputie or anie owner, farmour or occupier of anie arable lands beeing within the limits of Stretham aforesaid to take away all such gleaned corne which shalbee soe gleaned or vehementlie sus- pected and adjudged to bee soe gathered or gleaned contrarie to anie of the orders aforesaid, and the same soe taken away to scatter abroade to anie of the shocks next adjoyneing of that

occupie, vse, or enjoye the aforesaid Loade called wortt loade shall likewise clense, rook, haff and scowre the same from side to side at the full breadth and soe keep it continuallie from time to time and at all times heerafter, vppon like payne to forfeit and pay the summ of fiue pounds as aforesaid of good and lawfull monie of England.

11. Item, wee finde that there hath been heertofore auncientlie a load or drayne from the new coate now called Barkers coate which leadeth through the cowpasture and horsepasture and soe in to Hay fenn and from thence into the lake called long lake beeing within the 100 acres which vsuallie hath been heertofore clensed and cast by the inhabitants of Stretham vnto long lake, aforesayd and therefore wee order and appoynt that the sayd loade or drayne leadeing from Barkers coate as aforesaid to the lake called long lake shalbee by the inhabitants of Stretham aforesaid scowred, haffed, clensed and cast in such bredth as it shalbee sett out and thought fitt to bee done by the constables of Stretham aforesaid, accordeing to the custome of the mannor aforesaid, beefore the last day of Julie next comeing, vppon payne to forfeit and pay the summ of fiue pounds. Soe that Sir Miles Sandys knight will make the like drayne thorough the 100 acres. *Long-lake.*

12. Item, it is ordered by the said Jurie that if anie person or persons inhabiting within the towne and limitts of Stretham shall refuse or neglect to doe such worke and works for the scowring and clenseing of the aforesaid draynes, beeing sett out

and thought fitt to bee done by the constables as is aforesaid, as hee or they ought to doe, and beeing therevnto warned by the constables aforesaid accordeing to the custome of the said Mannor, that then euerie person soe offendeing shall forfeit and pay for euerie pole and soe after the rate of a greater or lesser proportion soe sett out for him to doe and not perfited and sufficientlie done accordeing to the appoyntment and likeing of the constables aforesaid by or beefore a certayne day which the constables shall then limitt and appoynt, the summ of tenn shillings of good and lawfull monie of England.

13. And for that the neglecting or refuseing of the scowreing clenseing or ditching of anie part of the aforesaid drayne may bee verie prejudiciall and hurtful to diuers of the inhabitants aforesaid who shall well and sufficientlie scowre and clense their parts, accordeing as it shalbee by the said constables aforesayd appoynted; Therefore wee order and appoynt that it shall and may bee lawfull for the constables for the time beeing to collect and gather by way of distress the aforesaid summ of 10s. of euery person or persons who shall soe neglect or refuse to doe and perfitt his or their part or parts, accordeing to the day and manner thereof, as it ought to haue been done, and the monie soe collected and gathered or soe much thereof onelie as shalbee fitt and necessarie to bee imployed in and about the aforesaid business shalbee by the constables aforesaid vsed and imployed in the makeing or mending such places neglected as aforesaid. And the ouerplus thereof to their own proper vse or vses.

14. Item, wee finde that a lake called thorough lake, beeing an aunciert drayne or Sewer, is not sufficientlie scowred and clensed. And wee order and appoynt John Coateman the elder now owner thereof shall clense, rook, haff, and scowre the same from side to side at the full bredth thereof, as it vsuallie hath been done or ought to haue been done, beefore the last day of May next comeing And soe keep it clensed, rooked, haffed and scowred vppon the payne to forfeit and pay the summ of fiue pounds of good and lawfull monie of England. And that euerie other person

publique warning giuen by them, or otherwise by priuate warning pasture
ouer night, anie common dayes workes for the keeping, mayn- Cow pasture finable.
tayning, or amendeing of all or anie the aforesaid Banks or for the
new makeing of any banks within anie other part of the cowpasture
or horsepasture aforesaid ; Or shall otherwise lay out and appoynt
the same to bee done by lotts and parts, Then euerie such person or
persons soe refuseing or neglecting to doe his or their part or parts,
soe sett out and thought fitt to bee done by the constables aforesaid
accordeing to the custome of the mannor aforesaid, shall forfeit
and pay for euerie pole and soe after the rate of a greater or lesser
proportion soe sett out for him or them to doe and not perfited
and sufficientlie done accordeing to the appoyntment and likeings
of the constables aforesaid, the summ of 10*s*. of good and lawfull Poena 10*s*.
monie of England, to bee leauied and taken by the constables of
the goods of such offendors and to bee employed as formerlie is
appoynted. And that euerie person or persons who shall refuse or
neglect to doe his or their common dayes worke or workes, beeing
thereunto warned as aforesaid, or shall not procure or send a
sufficient person in his roome or stead from time to tyme and at
all times heerafter soe to bee adjudged by the constables for the
time beeing, then euerie such person or persons soe offending
shall forfeitt and pay for euerie such particular default and for
euerie such particular day or time soe neglected or omitted, the

274 COMMON RIGHTS

Poena ij. s. somm of ij. s. to bee taken and leauied out of the offendors goods by the constables aforesaid by way of distress and to bee imployed by them as formerlie is appoynted.

None to throwe downe anie banck made. 16. Item, wee doe order and appoynt that if anie person or persons whatsoeuer shall at anie time heerafter cutt, breake, throw downe, waste or destroye anie Hill or Banck now made or which shalbee heerafter at anie time made for the preservation of anie of the commons aforesaid except it bee by the appoyntment of the constables and churchewardens of Stretham aforesayd for the time beeing then euerie such offendor shall forfeit and pay for euerie *Poena* 10*li.* such particular......... the summ of tenn pounds of good and lawfull monie of England ; Or if anie person or persons shall sett his nett or netts in anie such breache, gapp, or gull, shalbee adjudged and reputed his fact and thereuppon shall forfeit and pay the summ of 40*s*. of like monie of England.

Noe cattle to bee put into the feilds till 6 days after haruest ended. 17. Item, wee order that noe person or persons shall put into anie of our corne feilds anie cattle within six dayes after Harvest bee done.

Owners of gees to pay iiij. d. a foot marke for gees goeing on horse or cowpasture. 18. Item, wee agree that the owner of euerie marke or flock of geese of one foot-marke shall pay vnto the fennreeues the somm of fower pence for euerie default, goeing vppon the horsepasture or cowpasture.

[Here follows a list of 26 names of those who signed these orders.]

THE HONOURABLE CORT OF HIS MAJESTIES EXCHECKURE AS FOLLOWETH THE FOWRE AND TWENTY DAYE OF FEBRUARY 1622.

1. Imprimis it is ordered and agreed by the consent of the greater part of the Inhabytants aforesayd that it shall not bee lawfull for any freehowlder or coppyhowlder or inhabytant Inhabyting or occupying any ancient communable messadge or tennent to haue euse or inioye the feed common of any more communable howses then one, vpon which one he and his famylie shall for the most part bee coutching and abyding, vppon the payne to forfeit and pay for euerye such beast, cow, or calfe, horsse or mare soe kept contrarye to this order and bylaw in lue of anye suche double common for euerye particular default, the summ of tenn shillings of good English monie. *To common for one one-lie commoning house and that to bee couchant on.* *Poena 10s.*

2. It is ordered and agreed by consent of the greatest part as aforesayd that it shall not bee lawfull for anie commoner aforesaid to ioyne with anie other to make vp or keep anye part of the stint of milche kine, workeing horses, or workeing mares except the sayd Cottage or tenement have heertofore or shall heerafter descend to anye coheyres, vppon payne to forfeit and pay for euerye such particular default the summ of **tenn** shillings. *None to joyne with other to make vp full stock vnless coheires.*

Prouided allwayes that if, notwithstandeing this order and bylaw, two seuerall persons shall and will keep cattle vppon the cowpasture or horsepasture aforesayde whose goods shalbee seuerallie distinguished and knowne to either of them for that one commonable house onelye wherein the sayd two parties shall cohabit and dwell, that then it shall and may bee lawfull to and for the ouerseers of these orders, or their lawfull deputies, to impound the Cattel of all and euerye such double Commoner soe offendeing and to take for euerie beast soe kept contrarie to this order and bylaw for euerye particular default of euerye offender or offenders whose goods shalbee soe impounded as aforesayd, the summ of x. s. of good and lawfull English monie.

Poena 10s.

Cowpasture. 6 cowes 2 weanelings. 3. Item, it is ordered and agreed vpon by the consent of greatest part of the Inhabitants aforesaid that it shall and may bee lawfull to and for all and euerie the freehoulders, coppiholders, and Commoners inhabiteing and dwelling within the towne of Stretham aforesaid to keep (accordeinglie as is formerlie set downe) or depasture within the heardwalke of Stretham six milche kine and two weaneling calues onelie and noe more : Prouided alwaies that if anie commoner aforesaid shall and will keep and depasture vppon the said heardwalke a sufficient bull which shalbee valued at the summ of fortie shillings at the least, then euerie such commoner soe keepeing such a sufficient Bull as is aforesaid shall keep one cow the more aboue the number of six formerlie proescribed And what commoner soeuer aforesaid shall exceed anie of these rates respectiuelie formerlie sett downe for euerie particular beast soe kept contrarie to this Order and bylaw, shall forfeit and pay the summ of tenn shillings of good English monie.

7 cow's with a bull.

Poena 10s.

Horsepasture. 8 workeing horses mares with their foales vnder 9 moneths old. 4. Item, it is likewise ordered and agreed that it shall and may bee lawfull for euerie commoner as is aforesaid to keep and depasture within the horsepasture in Stretham aforesaid called Stallock Hay Fenn, and the green, the number of 8 workeing Horses or workeing mares with their sucking foales soe as the said sucking foales bee vnder the age of nine monethes olde and noe greater number and of noe greater Age vppon payne to forfeit

or guile for the space or terme of 6 monethes at the least and soe ^{to bee kept} 6 monethes.
shall keep them, vppon payne to forfeit and pay for euerie such
particular cow, horse or mare soe had or hired and not kept to the
full number of the time of six monethes as is aforesaid, the summ ^{Poena 10s.}
of tenn shillings of good English monie.

    6. Item, it is ordered and agreed that it shall not bee lawful for ^{A prouiso or exception to} anie commoner aforesaid to keep and depasture anie weaneling ^{the third} calfe vppon the cowpasture aforesaid which hath been or shalbee ^{Article for weanelings.} calued beefore the feast of St. Michael yeerlie, to bee kept the
summer followeing vppon the heardpasture aforesaid in the name
of a weaneling calfe vppon payne to forfeit and pay for euerie
suche particular calfe, soe kept contrarie to this Order and bylaw ^{Poena 5s.}
the summ of fiue shillings of good English monie.

    7. Item, it is ordered and agreed that it shall not bee lawfull for ^{A prouiso or exception to} anie commoner aforesaid to keep and depasture vppon the horse- ^{the fourth} pasture anie horse or mare vnder the age of two yeeres olde ^{Article.}
except the same horse or mare bee a common and vsual workeing
beast or shalbee adjudged to bee fitt soe to bee for stature by the
ouerseers of theise bylawes, vppon paine to forfeit and pay for
euerie suche particular horse or mare soe kept contrarie to this ^{Poena 10s.}
order and bylaw the summ of x. s. of good english monie.

    8. Item, it is ordered and agreed by the consent cf the greater ^{None to common but} part of commoners aforesayd that it shall not bee lawfull for anie ^{residents.}
person or persons whatsoeuer to keep or depasture within anie
part or parcell of the sixteen hundred acres prescribed and sett

downe by the honourable court of his Majesties exchequer to the commoners and inhabitants of Stretham and Thetford onelie anie milche kyne, weanling calues, workeing horses or workeing mares, or anie other cattle of what qualitie or sorte soeuer the same bee or heerafter shalbee for anie commonable messuage or tenement within the bounds and lymitts of Stretham aforesayd, except euerye person aforesayd, or at least the wife, children, or familie of euery such person or persons so commoning as aforesayd, shall continuallie bee resideing, abydeing, inhabiteing and dwelling in and vppon euerie such commonable messuadge or tenement. vppon payne to forfeit and pay for euerie such particular default and for euerie such particular beast soe kept contrarie to this order and bylaw the summ of x. s. of good english monie.

Poena 10s.

Joysteing forbidden.

9. Item it is ordered and agreed by the conseut of the greater part as aforesaid that it shall not bee lawfull for anie commoner whatsoeuer to colour or take to joyste anie beast whatsoeuer vppon payne to forfeit for euerie such particular beaste soe coloured and taken to joyst as is aforesayd the some of 40s. of good English monie. Prouided allwayes that if anie person or persons whatsoeuer beeing formerlie tolerated and allowed to hier his stynt of milche kyne and workeing horses for the space of six moneths as is aforesaid and shall not haue, vse, occupie, and enjoy all and euerie such beaste and beastes soe had, hyred, and obtayned by the whole terme and tyme of six moneths aforesayd, then euerie such beast, soe had hyred and beeing not kept by the space of six moneths aforesayd, shalbee adjudged to bee a coloured beast, and then euerie person who did keep such beast shall pay as is aforesayd the summ of 40s. of good english monie.

Poena 40s.

A second prouiso against the 5th article.

Poena 40s.

Agaynst infectious cattle.

10. Item, it is ordered and agreed by the consent of the greater part as aforesayd that it shall not bee lawfull for anie commoner, or commoners whatsoeuer to depasture and put to feed within the bounds and lymits of the cowpasture or horsepasture of Stretham aforesayd anie Horse, Mare, cow, or other beaste whatsoeuer which shall anie way bee infectious but shall within one daies warning giuen by the ouerseers of these bylawes or the fenreeues for the

time beeing remoue and put away euerie such infectious beast, vppon payne to forfeit and pay for euerie such infectious beast soe kept and not remoued from off the commons aforesayd the summ of tenn shillings of lawfull English monie. *Poena* 10s.

11. It is ordered and agreed by consent as is aforesayd that it shall not bee lawfull for anie person or persons whatsoeuer to cutt, crop, or mow anie edich¹ or edgrowth, in anie common fenns of Stretham aforesayd at anie tyme in the yeer after it is or shalbee once mowen for that yeer, vppon payne to forfeit and pay for euerie such howres worke, and soe after the rate of a greater or lesser proportion of time the some of fiue shillings of good English monie. *Fodder to bee but once mowen in eache yeer.* *Poena* 5s.

12. It is ordered and agreed by the consent of the greater part as aforesayd that it shall not bee lawfull for anie person or persons whatsoeuer to brink cart, or carrie anie Hay, stouer, or fodder out of anie of those grounds called Feedall fenn, charfen Hills, or willow fen into or thorough anie of those our commons called Howle fenn and charr fenn playne, or into anie partes or members of the sayd fenns for anie stranger or strangers whatsoeuer, not beeing a commoner in Stretham aforesaid, vppon payne to forfeit and pay for euerie such loade or carriage soe carted or carried as is aforesayd the summ of fiue shillings of good english monie. *Noe fodder to bee carted or carried for strangers.* *Poena* 5s.

13. Item, it is ordered and agreed by the consent of the greater part as is aforesayd that it shall not bee lawfull for anie person or persons whatsoeuer or anie their assignes to cutt or digg anie Hassocks, fireing or turberie within anie part of anie of the common fenns of Stretham aforesayd called Lazer, charfenn playne and Howle fenn, vppon payne to forfeit and pay for euerie such howres worke and soe after the rate of a greater or lesser proportion of time the summ of v. s. of good English monie. *Noe fireing to bee cutt and taken out of the common fenns.* *Poena* 5s.

14. Item, it is ordered and agreed by the consent of the greater part as aforesaid that euerie person or person whatsoeuer haueing anie part or partes in the partition ditch called Barlake, which is beetween the [cow-]pasture and horsepasture of Stretham afore- *Euerie man to scowre his part in Barlake ditch.*

¹ This term applies strictly to the growth on the stubble, (or haulm), field, but is here used of aftermath generally.

said, shall yeerlie and euerie yeer from time to time and at all times needfull and convenient ditche, scowre, clense and sufficientlie keep his or their such part or partes in the said partition ditch called Barlake after two daies warning giuen to him or them by the ouerseers of these orders, or anie one of the fenn reeues for the time beeing, vppon payne to forfeit and pay for euerie suche faultie part or partes not sufficientlie kept and scoured as is aforesaid the summ of three shillings fouer pence of good English monie.

<small>Poena 3s. [stc.]</small>

<small>Prouiso.</small>
Prouided allwayes, that if after such warning giuen as aforesaid anie part or partes shall continue and remayne vndone or not sufficientlie scoured as is aforesaid, then wee order and agree that it shall and may bee lawfull to and for the ouerseers of these orders or anie one of them to procure, hyer and gett anie man whatsoeuer to scowre, ditch, and amend the same and to pay the same labourer or labourers for such their worke and workes out of the aforesaid forfeited summ or somes of iij. s. iiij. d. as is aforesaid.

<small>ebarring of orse from owpasture: ows from orse-asture.</small>
15. Item, it is ordered and agreed by consent of the greater part as aforesaid that it shall not bee lawfull for anie commoner or commoners or anie other person or persons whatsoeuer to depasture and put to feed within anie the bounds and lymits of the cowpasture aforesaid anie workeing horses, workeing mares, or suckling foales or to depasture and put to feed within anie the boundes and lymits of the horsepasture aforesaid anie milche kine or weaneling calues, except the same shalbee soe agreed vppon by consent of the greater part of the commoners and inhabitants of Stretham aforesaid, vppon payne to forfeit and pay for euerie such particular beast respectiuelie soe kept and depastured contrarie to this order and buylaw the summ of fiue shillings of good english monie.

<small>oena 5s.</small>

<small>gaynst y-heards.</small>
16. Item, it is ordered and agreed by the consent of the greater part as aforesaid that it shall not bee lawfull for anie commoner or commoners whatsoeuer, or other person whatsoeuer, to despasture and put to feed within anie the bounds and lymits of the cow-

COTTENHAM AND STRETHAM 281

pasture of Stretham aforesaid anie by-heard, or heards, bee the number thereof great or small, but shall suffer and permitt the common heardman of Stretham aforesaid to driue and bring home euerie such beast and beasts among his whole heard without interruption or contradiction, vppon payne to forfeit and pay for euerie such particular beast and for euerie particular time soe kept contrarie to this order and bylaw the summ of iij. s. iiij. d. of good English monie. *Poena 3s. 4d*

17. Item, it is ordered and agreed by the consent of the greater part as is aforesaid that it shall not bee lawfull for anie commoner or commoners, or anie other person or persons whatsoeuer, to put back and leaue beehinde anie milche cowe after the whole Heard for the moste part is come home to the end to depasture and feed the same within anie the bounds and lymits of the cowpasture of Stretham aforesaid, except the same milche cow shalbee soe lame that it cannot well come home or shall haue newlie calued, and soe for the first night onelie, vppon payne to forfeit and pay for euerie such particular beast and for euerie time soe kept back or left beehinde wilfullie contrarie to this order and bylaw the sum of iij. s. iiij. d. of good English monie. *Agaynst leaueing of cowes all night in the cowpasture.* *Prouiso.* *Poena 3s. 4d.*

18. It is ordered and agreed by the consent of the greater part as aforesaid that it shall not bee lawfull for anie commoner or commoners or other person or persons whatsoeuer to cutt, digg, delue, or thrust thorough or make anie breache, gapp, or gull, in anie part of anie banke or fence made by consent for the keeping of anie the commons aforesaid from inundations and ouerfloweings of the waters, except the same shalbee thought fitt and appointed to bee done by the constables of Stretham for the time beeing, together with the consent of the ouerseers of these orders and bylaws for the time beeing, vppon payne to forfeit and pay for euerie such particular default and for euerie suche particular breache or gull for euerie particular time the same shalbee done contrarie to this order and bylaw the summ of 10s. of good english monie. *Agaynst makeing anie gaps or gulls in anie banck.* *Poena 10s.*

Prouided allwayes, that if anie person or persons soe offendeing *Prouiso.*

282

shall not haue goods and chattells sufficient goeing vppon anie the commons aforesaid which shall and wilbee able to answer the penaltie aforesaid, it shall and may bee lawfull to and for the ouerseers of theise orders and bylawes, or anie one of them for the time beeing, to take and seize into his or their hands and custodies as damniage phesant all and euerie the nett and netts of euerie person or persons soe offendeing as is aforesaid.

<small>Noe net to bee set in anie breache.</small>

19. Item, it is ordered and agreed by consent of the greater part as aforesaid that it shall not bee lawfull for anie commoner or commoners or anie other person or persons whatsoeuer to sett, or sett downe anie manner of nett or engine whatsoeuer in anie breache, gapp, or gull, beeing made contrarie to the order aforesaid at the riseing and ouerfloweing of the waters vppon payne to forfeit and pay for euerie such particular nett or engine soe sett or caused to bee sett in anie such particular gapp, or gull the summ of 40s. of good English monie.

<small>Poena 40.</small>

<small>Prouiso.</small>

Prouided allwayes, that if anie person or persons whatsoeuer shall put or sett downe anie manner of nett or engyne whatsoeuer in anie breache, gapp or gull beeing made contrarie to the order before-mentioned at the ebbing and falling of the water then euerie such person or persons haueing formerlie sett his or their netts as aforesaid shall within 3 dayes next after the water is for that season at the lowest amend and embank the same breache, and breaches, agayne vppon payne to forfeit for euerie such particular default the summ of 10s. of good English monie.

<small>Poena 10s.</small>

<small>... dispose of the ...... of charfen hills willow fenn.</small>

20. Item, it is ordered and agreed by consent of the greater part as aforesaid that it shall and may bee lawfull to and for the ouerseers of these orders and bylawes yeerlie and euerie yeer from time to time, and at all times heerafter, to alien, sell, and dispose of all and euerie the proffitts and commodities of .   all the fodder and stouer which now is or which heerafter shall and arise in anie the towne parts of the fenns called char fenn hills, and willow fenn att their best likeings and discretions, And the monie thereof comming or soe much thereof as shalbee requisite to bee by them or anie of them disbursed and layed out

for the answering of anie sute or sutes, action or actions brought or commenced agaynst them or anie of them toucheing and concerning the keeping or breakeing anie of these said orders and bylawes.

Prouided allwaies, that if it shall happen that noe suite or suites, action or actions shalbee commenced or brought agaynst anie of them beefore the Feast of St. Andrew yeerlie, then the ouerseers of these orders haueing receiued monie for the aforesaid fodder grounds shall then yeeld vpp and giue a true and sufficient account of all such monies soe receiued and not by them imployed and layd out accordeing to the discretion of the said ouerseers in anie part of the 16 hundred acres aforesaid. *Prouiso.*

21. Item, it is ordered and agreed by consent of the greater part as aforesaid that if anie inhabitant within our towne of Stretham aforesaid, or anie other person or persons whatsoeuer lyable to these or to anie one of these our orders and bylawes, shall willinglie and wilfullie violate and breake them or anie one of them whereby the ouerseers of these orders and bylawes shalbee stirred and moued either to take as distress for the satisfying of anie penaltie heerin conteyned, or to commence anie sute or sutes, or defend anie action or actions toucheing the keeping and obseruing of all or anie these our orders and buylawes, that then it shall and may bee lawfull to and for the sayd ouerseers or anie two of them for the time beeing, from tyme to tyme and at all times needfull, not haueing formerlie receiued sufficient monie and not by them layd out, to make, leauie, and collect such reasonable rate and rates, summ and summes of monie by taxing and assessing euerie such workeing beast and euerie such milche cow which then shall depasture and feed within the bounds and lymitts of Stretham aforesaid or which shall haue fedd in anie part of the summer beefore the said sute or suites shalbee commenced as aforesaid; which rate or taxation if anie inhabitant or anie other whatsoeuer lyable to these or anie of these our orders and bylawes shall refuse and neglect to pay his or their part or partes from time to time and at all times soe assessed, then euerie such partie and parties *Ouerseers power in towne causes toucheing these orders.*

soe neglecteing to pay the same by the space of sixe daies next after request made by the ouerseers of the sayd orders or anie one of them shall forfeit and pay for euerie such neglect and default ouer and aboue his taxation the summ of 10s. of good english monie.

Poena 10s.

22. Item, it is ordered and agreed by the consent of the greater part as aforesaid that it shall and may bee lawfull to and for the ouerseers of the sayd orders or anie two of them, from tyme to tyme and att all times heerafter dureing the time of their sayd office, to haue perceaue and take all and euerie such penall summs of monie, penalties and forfeitures as are heerin expressed and sett downe, and for default of payment thereof to implead, impownd, driue or distreyne euerie partie or parties or the goods and chattells of euerie partie and parties soe offendeing. And out of such monie or monies soe or anie other way receiued, to make, builde and erect such sluces, draynes, water courses and waterings on anie of the aforesayd proemises as they or anie two of them shall think meet and convenient for the drayneing and letting out or for the letting in or keeping in or keeping out of anie waters in anie place or places in and about anie of the cowpasture or horsepasture of Stretham aforesaid.

Ouerseers power in necessarie publique works.

23. Item, it is ordered and agreed by consent of the greater part aforesaid that it shall and may bee lawfull to and for the fennreeues for the time beeing to bee alwayes assistant and coadjutors to the sayd ouerseers, and at the appoyntment of the ouerseers aforesaid and not otherwise, and in default there bee noe ouerseers; the fennreeues from time to tyme to driue and impound all or anie the goods and chattells of euerie person or persons offendeing and breakeing these or anie of these our orders and bylawes which are or ought to bee obserued, performed, fulfilled and kept.

Fenreeues the ouerseers assistants.

24. Item, it is ordered and agreed by the consent of the greater part as aforesayd that all and euerie the orders and bylawes which shall at anie time euer heerafter bee made toucheing the stinteing, ordering, or directing of the 16 hundred acres of common allotted to the towne of Stretham and Thetford respectiuelie shall for

The time of laying out the fenns.

continue in full force and vertue. And wee doe further order and agree, by consent as aforesaid, that all and euerie these our orders and bylawes shall remayne and continue in force vntill the daies formerlie sett downe and soe forward from time to time and att all times heerafter vntill the same or anie one of them bee reuersed, altered, renued or continued at the said appoynted dayes, and not otherwise, by consent of the greatest part of the inhabitants of Stretham aforesaid.

25. Item, wee doe appoint Francis Frances, Michael Fludd clarke, John Bentlie to bee and remayne ouerseers for these and euerie one of these our orders and bylawes to see that the same bee fullie perfourmed, fullfilled and kept ; And wee doe order and appoynt that they and euerie of them shall continue in their sayd office vntill shrouetide next and noe longer, except the greater part of the inhabitants together, with their owne consents, shall think fitt and convenient to continue them or anie one of them in their said office anie longer time. *Ouerseers of these bylawes.*

26. Item, it is ordered and agreed by the consent of the greater part aforesaid that it shall not bee lawfull for anie person or persons whatsoeuer to keep or put to feed anie manner of swyne hoggs vppon anie part of the cowpasture or horsepasture or anie part of the green parcell of the horsepasture aforesaid vntill the harvest of Stretham bee fullie ended, vppon payne to forfeitt and pay for euerie such particular swyne as aforesaid, and for euerie particular default the summ of two pence of good English monie. *None to keep swine vppon either Cowpasture or Horsepasture. Poena 2d.*

Prouiso.

Prouided allwayes, that notwithstandeing this last order aforesaid it shall and may bee lawfull to and for euerie commoner aforesaid to putt his hoggs and swyne aforesaid at all tymes in the green onelie, beeing lawfullie ringed, soe as none of the aforesaid hoggs beeing soe putt vppon the green as aforesaid shall depasture and feed vppon anie the commons aforesaid, except beefore excepted, vnder the payne and penaltie of the summ of ij. *d.* of good english monie for euerie particular default.

Hee that keeps noe weaneling calfe may keep one cow more than his stint.

27. Item, wee order and appoynt that what soeuer commoner aforesaid shall forbeare to depasture and feed anie weaneling calues within the heardpasture or horsepasture aforesayd shall for the time of such forbearance depasture and keep within the common one cow the more.

Undersetters to keep one cow onlye vppon the commons but not without leaue.

28. Item, wee doe order and appoynt that it shall not bee lawfull for anie inhabitant inhabiteing and dwelling in anie new erected cottage, beeing no auncient commonable house, to depasture and put to feed within anie commons aforesaid more then one milche cow, and whosoeuer shalbee permitted to keep anie such cow shall not presume soe to doe except hee or shee shall first haue leaue giuen him or hir in open churche vppon some Sabboth day after euening prayer by the greater part of the commoners there then present.

Ouerseers of these bylawes.

29. Item, wee doe nominate and appoynt Richard Langford, Thomas Cheuill, Wm. Townson, Richard Bent, John Bent, Edward Hayward and Robert Flintoft to bee and remayne ouerseers for theise orders and bylawes; and wee doe heerby giue to them or anie two of them free libertie and authoritie to receiue and take all such penalties and forfeitures as are heerin agreed vppon for the breache of them or anie of them; and further wee order that if the aforesaid ouerseers shall neglect or refuse to impound anie cattle, geese,

Neglect of the ouerseers to bee supplied by anie inhabitant.

hoggs or sheep which shall depasture or feed vppon anie the commons aforesaid, that then it shalbee and may bee lawfull to and for anie the auncient commoners aforesaid to driue and impound anie beast or cattle soe kept contrarie to these orders and

A COPPIE OF AN ARTICLE
FOR A LIBELL FOR THE TITHE OF HERBAGE OF STEERS, DRIE COWS AND HEIFERS, AND HORSES AND MARES NOT KEPT FOR TILLAGE; DRAWN BY R. C.

That W.B. had in the moneth libellate within the parish libellate &c. viz. in a peece or parcell of marish ground beeing seuerall, conteineing [1]   acres called [1]   , the said W.B. had kept, fed and fatted fortie steers, drie heifers, &c. which were not bred nor weaned within the parish libellate, nor euer vsed, imploied or maineteined for the plough or the payle within the parish libellate, whereof or of the fall of them neuer anie proffit came to the churche to the parish (sic), but they were brought in by the said W.B. when they were leane to bee fed and fatted for the butcher, and were there kept, fed and depastured in the yeers libellate vntill they were fatted and then solde them to diuers butchers and others for farr greater summs of monie than was paid for them when they were leane ; and by such feeding and fatting of those steers and heifers within the parish aforesaid the said W.B. gained in euerie steer xl. s. and euerie heifer 40s. the herbage, pasturage and feeding of euerie such beast beeing worth iij. s. iiij. d. euerie week and the tithe thereof due accordeinglie &c.

[1] Left blank in the MS.

milked and taken from the cowe or cowes, without anie diminution or alteration of anie part thereof, and without anie fraud or deceipt therein whatsoeuer.

That E.H. in the yeer attestate did not sett forth, deuide and pay the whole milke of all his cowes euerie 9th night and 10th morneing accordeing to the custome, but did keep back a part of the best of that milke and added water and other vnwholesome things to that milke hee had sett forth, thereby to deceiue the parson &c.

That if anie time hee did deuide and sett forth the tithe milke trulie and justlie accordeing to the custome, yet E.H. did after the same was soe sett forth take back the same soe sett forth and did employe the same to his owne vse or otherwise soe dispose thereof as it beecame of noe vse or value to the parson.

That if &c. quod non fatetur &c. yet the same was soe sett forth at such unreasonable times and at such places, distant a mile or 2 from the parsonage, and immediatelie taken away agayne beefore the parson could come to receiue it, of purpose to let slip or hinder the parson thereof and of purpose to defraud and deceiue the parson.[1]

[1] This paragraph has been cancelled in the MS.

Adjistment, (joistment), 178, 178n, 203, 278.
Adventurers' Land, 237n.
Alborough, (Alborowe,) 199, 202, 203, 215, 219.
Alcock, Thomas, 209, 213.
Aldrith, Calsey, 179.
Annys, Henry, 197, 199.
Arable Land, 257, 260, 269.
Articles of Agreement, 186, 222, 223, 224, 225-229.
Atkins, Richard, of Cutwell, 179.
Bailiffs, 211, 212, 255, 256.
Banks, Robert, 225, 227.
—, 179, 180, 183, 205, 206, 207, 208, 210, 231, 232, 240, 273. 274.
Barkers Coate, 271.
Barker, Francis, 265.
Barlake, 259, 266, 279, 280.
Barley, 258.
Barnes, Mr., 187.
Barnwell Abbey, 175.
Barreditch, 233.
Bars, *see* rails.
Batisford, John, 184.
Baulks, 237.
Beans, cultivation of, 270.
Becks, The, 219.
Bedford, dukes of, 176.
Bell, warning given by, 240.
Bellman, The, 230

Bent, John, 286.
—, Richard, 286.
Bentlie, John, 285.
Blean, Edward, 225.
Branding, of Cattle, 232, 233.
Breaches, see Gullies.
Bridges, 179, 219.
Brigham, John, 225, 227.
Broad Land, 200.
Brown, Francis, 198.
Bull, John, 225.
Bulls, 236, 276.
Bullock's Harst, 215, 219.
Bull Piece, the, 208.
Burdlaries (*alias* Harlstone) Manor of, 197, 198, 201, 207, 209.
Burlings, 216, 220.
Burwell, Thomas, 248.
Bye-Herds, 220, 235, 280, 281.
Bye-Laws, *see* Orders,
Bynge, Henry, 184.
Cambridge, 175.
—, Christs' College, 178, 194, 198, 200, 201, 203, 209.
—, King's College, 195, 228.
—, St. John's College, 195, 200, 178, 189.
— Way, 197, 199.
Carts, 239, 240.
Cass, Mrs., 181.
Casting, 271.

Cattle, 173, 185, 195, 211, 213, 214, 215, 216, 217, 218, 219, 220, 232, 233, 234, 235, 236, 237, 238, 240, 242, 243, 244, 246, 247-250, 274, 276, 277, 278, 280-282, 286.
— , disease amongst, 238.
— , droves and drifts of, 224, 243.
Charfen Hills, 279.
Charlode, 205, 206.
Chesterton, 175.
Chevill, Thomas.
Childerley, 175.
Chimneys, 265.
Chittering Hill, 215, 217, 230, 235, 238.
Christening, 252.
Christs' College, *see* Cambridge.
Churching, 252.
Close, Alborough, 234.
    , Curds Willows, 200.
    , Eastland, 197.
    , the Holme, 236.
    , Horsemore, 197.
    , King's Cross, 196, 197, 199, 220.
    , Little, in Cottenham, 196.
    , Long Hill, in Cottenham, 196, 227.
— , Marehill and Tillage, 196, 198.
— , Pelham's Croft, 200.
— , Kits' Bush, 197, 198, 202.
Clarke, John, 187.
Clay Lakes End, 265.
Clay pits, 216, 238, 239.
Coateman, John, 272.
Coke, Edward, 178.
Coloring, of Cattle, 219, 237, 237n, 278.
Commoning house, 275.
Common Land, 173, 174, 174n, 179, 198, 202, 204, 207, 209, 211, 213, 214, 215, 219, 220, 223, 228, 230, 232, 237, 238, 241.
— , (in Stretham), 260, 277.
Constables, 266, 271, 272, 273, 274.

Copyhold Tenants, 253, 254, 255, 256, 275, 276.
Cottage, 204.
Cottenham, 194, 196, 197, 200, 202, 203, 204, 205, 206, 207, 208, 210, 211, 212, 213, 214, 215, 218, and *passim*.
— , chapel in, 209, 211.
— , Church of, 208, 211, 216, 225.
· , Common in, 198, 209, 213, 214, 215, 219, 224.
· , Manor of, 197, 199, 201, 208, 209, 213.
· , parson of, 209, 214.
· , Rectory of, 180, 195, 197, 198, 199, 211.
· , School in, 209, 244.
Cotton, Sir John, 185.
Courts, of the lord of the Manor, 212.
Cow Pasture, the 218, 230, 232, 234, 235, 236, 271, 273, 274, 276, 277, 278, 279, 280, 281, 284.
Cowaies end, 238.
Cow-way, 218, 243.
Cox, Sir Richard, 261, 263.
Creeks: the Abbots' Creek, 208.
Cresses, 232.
Crofts, 241.
Crowlands, Manor of, 177, 194, 196, 197, 203, 205, 207, 209, 214, 208.
Crykle Fen Bank, 215, 216, 220.
Curde, William, 204.
Dairy farming, 173.
Damage phesant, 282.
Dellfen, 215, 219.
Ditches, 205, 206, 207, 210, 234, 236, 237, 240, 241, 242, 265, 279, 280.
Drainage, 176, 182, 182n. 204, 241.
Drains, 198, 219, 265, 271, 272, 284.
Drifts, of Cattle, 224, 234.
Droveyard, 224.
Edgrowth, 279, 279n.
Eden, Dr., vicar general of the Bishop of Ely, 246, 249.

INDEX

Egg, rent, 185.
Egnie, Thomas, 265.
Elford, 258, 265.
Ely, Bishop of, 177, 185.
—, Bishop of, *see* Felton.
—, Cathedral of, 195.
—, Dean and Chapter of, 178, 200, 209.
—, Isle of, the, 175, 263, 265.
England, King of, James I, 267.
Epworth, 176n.
Farmers of the Manors, 208, 209.
Felton, Nicholas, Bishop of Ely, 191.
Felton, Nicholas, Rector of Stretham, 191.
Fences, 205.
Fen, keepers of the, 204, 216, 217, 218.
Fens, 179, 196, 204, 279, 284.
—, Michaelleye, (Michelleye, Michaeley) 179, 216, 219, 232, 234, 235, 236, 242.
—, Topham, 179, 180.
—, Denney, 179.
—, Hole Fen Lazer, 259.
—, Stallock Hay fen, 276.
—, Feedall Fen, 279.
—, Willow Fen, 279, 282.
—, Awbrose, 179, 180.
—, Sechall, 179, 234, 236.
—, Sechall Chairefen, 179.
—, Chittering, 179, 180.
—, Common, 179.
—, Cuttes, 180.
—, Willow, 180.
—, Thetford Hall Fen, 256, 258.
—, Grunty Fen, 256.
—, Hole·Fen, 258, 279.
—, Charr Fen Plain, 279.
—, Lazar Fen, 279.
—, Smithey, 179, 205, 207, 208, 219, 234, 235, 242, 251.
—, Chare, 179, 180, 259, 282.
—, Hay Fen, 259, 261, 271.
—, North Fen, 205.

Fens, North Fen, Great, 220.
—, — — Little, 202, 220.
—, Young Man's Fen, 208.
—, Crikle, 198.
—, Stretham, 184.
Fen Reeves, 182, 185, 240, 242, 268, 274, 284.
Ferriage, privilege of, 258.
Ferry house, the, 258.
Fields, 196, 202, 257, 268, 269, 274.
—, Church Field, 199.
—, the Common Field, 200.
—, Dunstall, 197, 198, 200, 202, 219, 234.
—, The Fallow Field, 235, 241.
—, Farm Field, 200.
Fields, Ferne-Field.
—, Foxall, 197, 200.
Field, the Halme Field, 235.
Field Reeves, 220, 221, 236, 241, 242, 245.
Fines, 205, 206, 207, 210, 211, 212, 213, 216, 217, 218, 219, 220, 221, 222, *and* 230-252, 256.
Fireing, 279.
Fishing, 206, 208, 209, 232.
Flintoft, Robert, 286.
Floods, 233.
Flood, Michael, of Stretham, 260, 285.
Foals, 250.
Foot-mark, 274.
Forrends, 237.
Fowls, 251.
Fowl, liberty granted to, 205.
Frances, Francis. 285.
Frankham, Thomas, 260.
French, Mr., rector.
French, Robina, 181.
Fruit, 246, 247, 248.
Furrowes, 237.
Gates, 179, 231, 233, 236, 243.
—, double falling, 242, 242n.
Geast cattle, the, 231, 234, 235.
Geese, 251, 274.

INDEX

Geldings, 220.
Gleaning, 267, 268, 269, 270.
Goldsmore, common in, 263.
Govern, to, 257.
Gravel pit, 238.
Green, Anthony, 198.
— , the, 280, 286.
Gullies, 232, 282.
Haddenham, 176, 177.
Haffing, 271, 272, 273.
Halfhead, Thomas, 197.
Harlstone, *see* Burdlaries.
Harvest, 231, 235, 260, 262, 267, 268, 274, 285.
Hassocks, 279.
Hawards, 242, 243.
Hawk, liberty granted to, 205.
Hay, 246, 247, 248, 251, 279.
Hayhow, W., 187.
Hayward, Edward, 286.
Heardman, the common, 281.
Hedges, 231.
Heifers, 288.
Hemp, 251.
Hempland, 200.
Herdman, Town, 220, 237.
Herd-pasture, the, 277, 286.
Herd-walk, the, 276.
Heriots, 184, 185, 255.
Hildersham, 175.
Hinde, Sir Francis, 177, 178, 201, 207, 214, 222, 223.
Hinde, William, of Maddingley, 178, 179, 180, 187, 188, 194, 196, 197, 201, 202, 203, 204, 205, 206, 208, 212, 214, 218, 219, 221, 222, 223, 224, 225, 226, 227.
Histon, 197, 198.
— , Moor, 199.
Hobson, Thomas, 180.
— , Katherine, 180.
Holbeam, Thomas, 228.
— , William, 228.
Holm, 202, 208, 234, 236.
Holme-Bridge, the, 204.

Holmes' Corner, the, 204.
Holme Meadow, 236.
Honey, 251.
Horsepasture, 271, 273, 274, 276, 277, 278, 279, 280, 284, 285, 286.
Horses, 220, 233, 238, 259, 260, 261, 261n, 262, 263, 275, 276, 277, 278, 288.
Houses, 180, 204, 258, 275.
Hovels, 204.
Humfrey, Thomas, 225, 227.
Hunt, liberty granted to, 205.
Hurdles, 231.
Impounding, 217, 218, 224.
Inclosures, 174, 185, 189, 196, 197, 198, 199, 201, 202, 203, 214, 223, 227, 251, 252.
Inn, the *Bull*, 176.
Isacson, Christopher, 266.
Ivatt, William, 245.
Jackson, Thomas, 225, 227.
— , Thomas, the younger, 225, 227.
Jades, 233, 234.
James I, *see* England, king of.
Jenyns, Soames, 182.
Joistment, *see* Adjustment.
Kings' Cross Way, 196, 215, 216.
Lakes, 232, 265.
　　Long Lake, 271.
　　, Thoroughout Lake, 272, 273.
Lakes Ende, 242.
Lambs' Cross, 197.
Landbeach, 196.
　　, Fen Side, 219.
　　, Moor, 199.
Lands-ends, the, 202.
Langford, Robert, 286.
Layer, 231, 231n, 243.
Leavings, the, 208.
Leys, 202, 204.
Loade, 232.
Longhill, 238.
— Denny, 234.
Loosmyre, 239.
Lot Ditch, the, 215, 216, 217, 220.

INDEX

Lots, 215, 220, 221, 235.
Lovell, Thomas, 244.
Lowfenns, the, 230, 235, 236, 240.
Lyles Farm yard, 224.
——, Manor of, 177, 194, 196, 197, 203, 205, 208, 214.
Lyon, Robert, 204.
Male, Walter, 180, 186, 246, 247.
Manby, Dr. Richard, rector, 181.
Marehill, 215.
Marriage, 252.
Marsh land, in Stretham, 254, 255, 288.
Maw, Leonard, 181, 248.
——, Dr., rector of Cottenham, 246.
——, Nicholas, 248.
Masters, Rev. Robert, 185.
Meadow ground, 202, 203, 236.
Measures, of land, 207, 232, 239, 241, 272, 273.
Milch kine, 203.
Milk, tithe, 289.
Moorecloses, 239.
Mortuaries, 252.
Mowing, 209, 215, 238, 264, 267, 279.
Nets, 282.
Newditche, 235.
North, Lord, 178, 180, 186, 188, 228.
Northfenside, 231, 235.
Nye, Mr., 182.
Oblations, 246, 247, 248, 251.
Officers, Town, 204, 206, 212, 217, 219, 220, 221, 224, 232, 233, 237, 238, 240, 242, *and passim*.
Orders, 211, 212, 213, 220, 221, 257.
Order Makers, the, 183, 204, 208, 209, 210, 211, 212, 213, 214, 215, 216, 217, 218, 220, 221, 232, 237, 238, 241, 242, 244, 245.
Outlaw's Cot, 179.
Oziers, 206, 231.

Page, Anthony, 185.
Pales, 221.
Peas, cultivation of, 269, 270.
Pelhams, Manor of, 209.
Penalties, *see* Fines.
Pepys, George, 178, 187, 188, 223, 225, 227.
——, John, 197, 198, 199, 201.
Peterborough, bishop of, 178.
Phillip, John, 245.
Pigeons, 251.
Piggott, William, 266.
Ploughing, 184, 215, 216, 253.
Plow-Penny, the, 251.
Pound, the, *see* Impounding.
Pound Reaps, 253.
Pound wall, the, 266.
Rails, 231, 233, 243.
Ramsies, John, 265.
Reaping, 267.
Rents, *see* Securities.
Rents, hen, 185.
Rivers, Robert, 207.
Rivers, the Cam, 173, 176.
——, the Ouse, 173, 176, 180.
——, the Nene, 176.
Roads, 200, 218, 238, 243.
Robbins' Lode, 179.
Roods, *see* measures.
Rooking, 271, 272, 273.
Robinson, Richard, 187.
Runnels, the, 202.
Russel, John, 213, 225, 227.
Russells, the, *see* Bedford, dukes of.
Sallows, 206.
Salman, widow, 265.
Sames, in Cottenham, Manor of, 177, 194, 197, 199, 201, 203, 205, 208.
Sandis, Sir Miles, 184, 253, 254, 255, 256, 257, 258, 259, 263, 271.
Securities, for rents, 224, 225, 226.
Severals, the, 202.
Severalty, farming in, 174.

INDEX

Scott, Richard, 197, 200.
Sheds, 204.
Sheep, 216, 219, 231, 232, 233, 235, 246, 247, 248, 250, 251, 253, 254, 257, 286.
Sheep-cot, 175.
Sheep-farming, 174, 177.
Sheep-Walk, a, 251.
Sheirbrooke, Richard, 265.
Shepherds, 237.
Shocking, of Corn, 267, 270.
Slate, bed of, 238, 239.
Sluices, 284.
Smith, Thomas, 225.
Snowte Ditch, 259.
Soham, 176.
Sparke, Dr., rector, 182.
Stakes, 207, 231.
Stallocke, 259, 261.
Standly, Peter, 185.
Steers, herbage of, 288.
Steward, Mark, 185.
Stint, to, 257.
Stone Ditch, 200.
Stone-hill, 205.
Stoppinges, 232.
Stretham, Church, 286.
———, Common, 265, 266.
Streetham, Fen Reeves, 182n.
Stretham, the Green in, 276.
———, rector of, 262, 269, 270.
Streets, in towns, 221.
Swine, 219, 220, 230, 246, 247, 248, 251, 285, 286.
Taylor, James, 261, 263, 264.
Teame, 239.
Telnie, Robert, 189.
Tenants, copyhold, 208, 209, 210, *and passim*.
Tenements, 202, 206, 207, 210, 211, 213, 223, 226, 227, 228, 238, 240, 241, 243, 253, 255, 256, 257.
Thetford, 182, 184, 255, 256.
Thetford, Chapelry of, 189.
Thetford Manor House, 263.
Thistles, on Common, 238.
Thistly Hill, 202.
Tillage, 173, 177, 180, 181, 184, 189, 262, 288.
Tithes, 180, 182, 184, 189, 214, 215, 246-252, 288, 289.
Topymoor, 215, 216, 217, 220, 242.
Townsend, Jer., ferryman, 258.
Townson, William, 280.
Trades : Butchery, 234.
Turner, the widow, 204.
Turves, 241.
Tyndall, Francis, 184, 185.
Undertakers, the, 182.
Undertakers' Piece, 237.
Walls, 265.
Ward, Dr., rector, 182.
Waterbeach, 176, 185, 185n.
Webb, Robert, 266.
Weir Pool, 179, 180.
Wells, George, 266.
Westwicke, 232, 243.
Westwick, Manor of, 202.
Wheat, 253.
Willingham, 176, 182n, 184, 185, 186.
Willows, 206, 231, 239.
Wisbeach Barton, 190.
Wood, 206, 207, 208, 251, 255.
Wool, 246, 247, 248, 250.
Woolfes pasture, 179.
Wright, John, 244.
Wronglane's End, 218.
Wyles, Mr., of Denney Abbey, 187.